THE LAST MAN TO LIVE THE REAL AMERICAN DREAM

POSTSCRIPT

RANDY ROSSI

Nightengale Press
A Nightengale Media LLC Company

THE LAST MAN TO LIVE THE REAL AMERICAN DREAM POSTSCRIPT

For information about Nightengale Press please
visit our website at www.nightengalepublishing.com.
Email: publisher@nightengalepress.com
Library of Congress Cataloging-in-Publication Data

Rossi, Randy,

THE LAST MAN TO LIVE THE REAL AMERICAN DREAM POSTSCRIPT/Randy Rossi

ISBN 13: 978-1935993-57-5
Non-Fiction/Memoir

First Published by Nightengale Press in the USA

January 2014

10 9 8 7 6 5 4 3 2 1

Printed in the USA and the UK

INTRODUCTION

This is a true story about the American dream and the incredible things that can be accomplished by someone living that dream to its fullest. It is a story about going from rags to riches, and from working down on the farm to working with the White House and Pentagon. It is about experiencing the extremes of wielding executive power impacting hundreds of millions of dollars and hundreds of people on the one hand, to simply being part of the food chain when attacked by bears near the Arctic Circle on the other.

It is the story of the son of an immigrant—a product of the American melting pot—starting at the bottom, learning state-of-the-art business processes, and leading a wonderful group of people to achieve world-class business honors and being named one of the ten best manufacturing companies in North America. It is a story of excitement, danger, and the wilderness from the Arctic to the Rockies, from the desert to the swamps of Savannah, and on top of and under blue water all around the world. And it is the story of some very special and beautiful people as well as murderers, thieves, and creeps.

I had the privilege and honor of living that American dream. Born to an Italian immigrant from the big city and a beautiful DAR (Daughter of the American Revolution) mother from the farm, I got to live in and experience multiple cultures and environments that I don't think kids get to experience anymore. The experiences are very real and span the full spectrum of life.

I have shoveled pig manure on the farm and I have flown

on private jets and sailed on hundred-foot private yachts. My wife and I have gone from collecting bottle deposits in order to pay for a meal of macaroni and cheese to living the good life and retiring early. I have gone from a night-shift laborer at a foundry to a group president responsible for hundreds of millions of dollars in sales and hundreds of people. I have slept in a Doge's palace in Venice and under a rock in the Arctic Circle to keep from freezing to death. And I have hunted, sailed, dived, toured, and done business in a large part of the world which has allowed me to experience extremes in life that most people would not believe are possible.

This book is a celebration of those contrasts in life and what living the American dream to its fullest can mean. Yet it outlines a growing concern that others will not have the chance to experience the breadth of what used to be the great American dream and being a "traditional" man. There is something for everybody in this book whether you like the excitement of sailing in hurricane-force winds or you want to hear about world-class business practices. No doubt this book will anger some people as its title might suggest because this is a story about what the American dream and being a man used to be all about. In today's stifling culture of political correctness, "metro male," and cultural diversity, that rich and colorful world is rapidly disappearing and fading into one of beige and grey. It is up to those of us who have had the privilege of living life to the fullest to remind everybody how rich life can and should be.

That is the goal of this book.

Postscript Introduction:

For those people who read the first edition of my book, you know that I have benefitted from a wide range of extreme experiences in life around the world that most people will never get to have. That is what motivated me to write my book. But the next five years since then have dramatically added to those extreme experiences, especially when I was a elected to be a local politician. I saw firsthand, the tragedy of the decline our current political system and watched the destructive path our magnificent country is taking. The last chapter in my new "Postscript" may be the most important words I have ever written, as I share the perspectives of people I talked to in Prague and Budapest who suffered under the tyranny of the Nazi's and the Soviet Union, along with my time in politics as I watched our country suffer. My goal is to share my extreme life experiences with the reader in the hope of providing a "wake up call." I believe we can turn this country around and ignite "The Great American Renaissance" if we simply learn from the successes and mistakes of the past and reestablish our great American traditional values.

CONTENTS

For my wife Evelyn who saved my life
and made me the man that I have become.

"If you would not be forgotten as soon as you are dead,
either write something worth reading
or do something worth writing." —Benjamin Franklin.

I hope that I have accomplished both!

Chapter One

The Miracle of the American Melting Pot

In the old world, I could not exist. My father and mother would never have been able to meet, let alone get married. Two strong cultures would have forbidden it. After all, my father was an Italian immigrant living in Chicago and my mother a DAR from the farm. From the Italian tradition, dad would have been expected to marry a good Italian girl who was Catholic and would follow the rigid Italian lifestyle. Born in Bologna to a strong-willed World War I hero who had to leave Italy or be killed by Mussolini, there was no doubt about what was expected of him. After all, my grandfather was named Augusto (after Emperor Augustus) and he named my father Rome to make it clear that our Italian heritage was front and center.

So the idea that my dad would end up marrying a Protestant Daughter of the American Revolution was unthinkable. My mom was a beautiful farm girl from very rural southern Illinois. The nearest town had a population of six hundred. We are talking the boonies where there was no electricity or running water in the house until my mom was in her late teens.

Yet these two brave people fell in love and broke tradition and cultural barriers to get married. In time they would achieve great things and raise three kids who they would send to college. I was oblivious to the pressures that they faced and the risks that they took for much of my childhood. It all seemed normal to me. That is the miracle of the great American melting pot and the fact that my parents were determined to make it normal.

My first inkling of what they went through came at age sixteen. I came home a few minutes after curfew and my father read me the riot act (he was right). Playfully, I told him to "calm down, he was acting like an old-time wop." I was shocked when he punched me in the nose because he had never been violent with me in the past. He immediately apologized and explained that all through his life he had to fight prejudice against his Italian immigration background. He and his friends had been called wops, dagos, grease balls, and every other offensive name all of their lives. And there was simply only one acceptable option open to a man when that happened, and that was to stand up and fight. And therefore his reaction to my calling him a wop was instinctive, automatic, involuntary, and the result of decades of conditioning. Yet until then, I did not even know that those conditions existed.

After that event, my dad started to explain a little of the prejudice that was common against Italians in those days. He talked about how when his dad came to the US, he fought every day against prejudice. Augusto came to the US alone and with nothing. He had to flee Italy when he was told that Mussolini and his black shirts were going to kill him. Augusto was an official in the Italian railroad union and I suspect that he was a communist (the family does not talk about that) since Bologna was and remains a very left-wing city today. He left Italy immediately, leaving his family with the knowledge that they would probably not be harmed in his absence.

Arriving in America with nothing, he went from a powerful war hero and union official in Italy to a laborer and carpenter with nothing. The favorite family story is about the day that Augusto was arrested and charged with assault and battery. Augusto stood about five foot five inches, but he was one tough son of a bitch. He served in the Italian Alpine Corps fighting against the Austrians in the First World War. He was shot three times (my brother saw the wounds) and was the only survivor in his unit after a poison gas attack. He spent six months in a hospital to recover. That is tough and determined!

The assault and battery incident was the result of a Swede who worked with Augusto as a carpenter, constantly insulting Augusto's Italian heritage. One day when they were both working on a roof, the Swede just went too far and Augusto beat the crap out of him and then threw him off the roof just to make sure that there was no confusion about how upset he was. Augusto was arrested and hauled to court.

So when the judge walked in to the court, there stood Augusto at five foot five and the Swede at over six feet. The obvious question was "why in the world would the short guy take on the giant?" When the judge heard that the Swede consistently insulted Augusto's heritage and that Augusto beat the crap out of him in response, he immediately dismissed the charges. Augusto was suddenly a hero and justice was done. I would like to think that the judge was Italian or Irish and knew something about prejudice.

My dad then explained the kind of prejudice that he

and his friends experienced every day as he grew up. But the way he explained it, it was no big deal. You just had to stand strong, stand together, and never, ever give in. Remember, we are talking about guys named Augusto, Rome, and Rocky (childhood friend of my dad). You were born to be tough. I remember being with my dad when he was sixty and he felt that someone had insulted him (no words, just a look!) in the parking lot of a Seven Eleven. I was a VP of a large firm and I thought that I was going to have to go to jail defending my five foot, six inch tall dad who was going to take on two hoods who looked at him wrong. I just did not understand at the time, but I was able to get my dad to calm down and there was no battle that day.

It is one thing to hear about prejudice and quite another to live it. I simply could not understand the intensity of his feelings having never experienced the prejudice that he had. It was not until I experienced that prejudice first hand that I understood how he felt.

I was on a wild boar hunt in the swamps near Savannah, Georgia. We went to the swamp shack of some locals who someone in our hunting party knew. Picture the movie *Deliverance*! The shack at the edge of a dismal swamp was falling apart. Spanish moss was draped over every tree in the swamp and cast a dark foreboding shadow over the shack. We very carefully walked onto the porch to get to the door since every other board on the porch floor was missing. Opening the door, we first saw a small portable TV sitting inside the broken-out picture tube of what was a large console TV. Very classy! Trash, squalor, filth, and loaded guns were everywhere and we were introduced to two men who seemed to us to be nothing more than sorry-looking, drunken, redneck jerks. I felt like I had walked into hell and I was glad that I was wearing my sheath knife.

Prejudice and hate talk started right away after the introductions. Our drunken hosts started bragging about killing uppity "niggers" (sorry, it feels creepy even writing that word) and throwing their bodies in the swamp. Disgusting talk, and my friend and I wanted to leave. We perceived that these individuals were bad news and that their prejudice was wrong. But it was not personal yet. I just felt disgust and revulsion.

Then it got very, very personal when our hosts learned that my friend and I were Italian. Suddenly I heard things that I never personally heard before. Suddenly *we* were dagos, wops, and grease balls. *We* were papists (I am not; I was an Episcopalian at the time, and besides, who even uses that term in this century?). They talked about how all Italian women are whores and how they liked to fuck young little Italian girls (sorry, their words, and they were trying to be as insulting as they could be). It got very ugly and both parties were about to explode.

Now rationally, this should have not bothered my friend Drew and I. After all, he and I were college graduates and at the time, we were VPs making six-figure incomes. Given our perceptions that these two jerks were bad news, we should not have cared what they thought. But that is not the way it works. My friend and I looked at each other and the loaded guns around the room. The message was clear to each of us. We both knew which gun we were going for, and which guy we would kill. They were drunk and we were stone-cold sober. I unsecured my sheath knife so that I could get to it easily if I needed to. I very badly wanted to kill these two guys and I was getting ready to do it.

Stop the clock for a minute. I know that those of you who have not experienced prejudice cannot possibly understand the intensity of our feelings. Until I experienced it personally, neither could I. My friend and I were fully prepared to throw away our freedom, careers, and great lifestyles in the name of honor, pride, and anger. And I wanted to do it. Now I understood why my father punched me in the nose when I called him a wop that night.

Fortunately the guy who took us sensed that things were about to get violent and somehow talked everyone down and pulled us out of the shack. Once I was clear of the danger, the reality of what I was prepared to do, in fact what I very badly wanted to do, rocked my world and gave me an appreciation of what my dad went through and the bravery of what my mom and dad did together by simply falling in love and getting married.

How is it that the intensity of the prejudice and pressures that dad and mom experienced for years was overcome and made invisible to me, the first generation of such a union? I had no idea that this prejudice even existed while I was growing up. How could that be?

The answer was the miracle of the melting pot concept that our founding fathers invented that is now losing ground to the new notion of cultural diversity. E Pluribus Unum (one out of many) was the magic from which our founders made America. When Augusto and Rome came to the US, they came to be Americans despite the prejudice. They learned English as quickly as they could. I remember my dad telling my grandmother when she spoke Italian at family gatherings, "you are in America now, and you must speak English." While we reveled in Italian things—great food, music, and history—there was no doubt that we were Americans and that English was our language.

And being an American was not stolen or taken for granted by my dad and grandfather. Augusto came here legally through

Ellis Island sponsored by his brother who played the oboe for the Chicago Symphony Orchestra and Chicago Opera Company (we have the Ellis Island documents). My father, grandmother, and aunt had to wait six years before joining him legally. Rome went to school and learned English and the family became proud Americans.

In order to become a US citizen, my father joined the army and risked his life for his country fighting the Japanese in China, India, and Burma with the Flying Tigers and Army Air Corps. He did not slink in to the US illegally or expect to be given American citizenship; he earned it. And then he went to college on the GI bill to get a degree and started a career and became a manager for Motorola. And he married the "belle of the ball" (more about mom in a minute!). Then this Italian immigrant who came here with nothing and his wife raised three kids, and sent them to college. Who would have thought that the sons of an immigrant would grow up to be business executives responsible for tens and hundreds of millions of dollars and the careers of hundreds of people? Or a daughter who conquered crippling Crohn's disease and then graduated from college and raised a beautiful family. That is the American dream done the right way.

I feel compelled to contrast this version of the American dream (which millions have lived over the decades) against what we see today. Today, being an American citizen does not hold the magic and honor that it did or should. We have cheapened it and defiled it. Today, much of our culture thinks it is okay to sneak into America illegally. If you can sneak in illegally and have a baby, that baby is automatically given citizenship (we are the only country in the west where a baby born on our soil is given citizenship even if the parents are here illegally). Now many of our elected officials are talking about rewarding those who broke our laws by coming here illegally with citizenship. If we insist on people learning English as was envisioned in E Pluribus Unum, we are labeled as racists. It used to be that you had to earn American citizenship. Now it can be bought or stolen. That which is not earned is not treasured, and will be lost!

With that background on half of the miracle of the melting pot, let me talk about the other half, my mom, Verna Legg. What a complete contrast to Rome. Mom's family was primarily British, with some German and American Indian ancestors, and they were here at the beginning of this country. Robert Morris, who signed the Declaration of Independence, Articles of Confederation, and the Constitution; is part of the family. Protestant and raised on a small farm, mom was regal, brilliant, and full of grace. Verna was the very model of the American heartland. How on earth did Verna and Rome get together? Easy! Love and the great melting pot made it possible. And as you will find out later, Verna was the type of women who blazed her own trail. If she wanted to be with Rome, then nothing and nobody was going to stop her!

While I have explained what kind of prejudice my father experienced in his life, I am proud to say that I never heard of or felt any prejudice from my mom's family toward him. It would have been easy given the differences in cultures and backgrounds, but I have never heard of it. My mom's family is honorable and reserved, and I think they understood her love for Rome. And I think that these very reserved, very proper people enjoyed the vivacious Italian from Chicago who said and did things that their reserved culture did not allow them to do or say. Rome was just fun to be around!

The fact that these two people from very different backgrounds and cultures got together, fell in love, and prospered despite the clear cultural pressures against them is a testament to the power of the melting pot. Was it easy? No. But was it worth it? Absolutely, as they and I would say. Like Nietzsche says, "That which does not kill you makes you stronger." And I say, that which you earned the hard way, you treasure. Mom and dad stood their ground, fought, never gave up, and took their hits. But they had the ultimate satisfaction of a joyful and productive marriage with three kids who prospered and took it to the next level. They followed a process that millions have followed with similar results over the years in America.

Contrast that with today. Now when someone calls another person a dago, wop, or some other ethic or racial slur it is a hate crime. Police, lawyers, the judicial system, the press, and everyone gets involved. Are those names wrong? Of course, but things have gone too far. Today we can't even tell gentle good-natured ethnic jokes because we might hurt someone's feelings (I like a good Italian joke as much as anyone). Our whole culture is focused on being neutral about everything because we don't want to hurt anybody's feelings. And because of that, our nation has turned into a bunch of whining, sniveling wimps and victims (sorry, you will find that I do have a few strong opinions, but it is my book!). We are no longer responsible for our own results. It's not our fault. We are a bunch of coddled pansies who will not be able to survive the tough brutal world that will always be there. People like Rome, Verna, Augusto, and millions of other "battle-tested" Americans in past generations who created the greatest country on Earth have largely been replaced with whining wimps.

But I was one of the lucky ones as many generations before me were as well. Because my parents stood tough and did it the right way, I have the honor of being an American with American values and skills but also the joy of living in two cultures and environments. I know the joy of an Italian background and the excitement of the big city. I know the great lessons of a rural farming community and the values and heritage of a classic American background. I have had the best of all worlds and I was taught when to use the lessons from each in the right ways at the right times for maximum benefit. I was taught by people who learned it the hard way and earned their success which was then treasured and passed on to their kids. And because of that, I was able to live the American dream to the fullest.

A word of warning based on history. I am the son of an immigrant and I wish nothing but the best for all legal immigrants from any country who follow the process that made America great. Come here legally, learn English, get educated, work hard, and be responsible. God bless you! But we will destroy what is America and "there will be blood" if we don't change the course that we are on now sanctioning illegal immigration and killing the great melting pot with ethnic diversity.

If we continue to allow twelve million illegal aliens to stay in this country, allow them to suck dry our schools, hospitals, and other infrastructure resources and cheapen American citizenship, there will be violence. Why? Up until August of 2008, our unemployment rate has been roughly 5 percent which is historically very low and life has been very good compared to history and to the much higher unemployment rates in Europe (although the biased media would never admit that). But as the recent dramatic collapse of the stock market and prior historic economic cycles indicate, we are about to experience one of those periodic severe recessions and we are probably going to see much higher and painful unemployment rates of 7-8 percent or more as the recession hits full force.

When American citizens and legal immigrants can't get jobs because companies would rather pay illegal immigrants 10-25 percent less and those American citizens, and legal immigrants can't feed their families or pay the rent, there will be violence as there has been in the past like in the New York City riots during the civil war where hundreds died.

Who gets hurt by illegal aliens? Certainly legal immigrants and any blue collar worker whose pay is 10-25 percent lower than it should be because illegal aliens are willing to work for less and can't complain. Anybody who pays taxes. Today schools and hospitals in many parts of the country are incredibly over crowded and out of money because 25 percent or more of their clientele is made up of illegal immigrants who use their free services (mandated by law). Unbelievably, in many states a pregnant illegal alien women gets public aid and her baby is immediately covered under welfare (they are not suppose to be here yet we are giving them taxpayer money!). In some states, illegal immigrants get free college tuition which some American citizens don't qualify for. I recently read about an illegal immigrant who had four liver transplants in L.A. There are US citizens who will die because they can't get one liver transplant. That is nuts!

Besides the damage to our institutions, our taxes, and the value of being an American citizen, there is one more huge cost. We are either a nation of laws or we are not. If we allow illegal immigrants to break the law, which other laws do we get to break if we choose to? Anarchy and the destruction of the rule of law are around the corner on our current course.

These facts are simply not debatable. Knowing this, who is promoting this illegal immigration and why? First, the business community and the Republican Party (disclosure: I usually vote Republican) which the business community pays off in campaign donations for obvious reasons. The presence of millions of illegal immigrants who cannot complain about unfair wages or working conditions drives down the wages for anybody competing for those lower-level jobs and increases the profits of those companies. These companies are driving up our taxes which support the illegal aliens, and ruining our schools and hospitals so they can make more profit. Any blue collar worker in the restaurant business, hotel business, or other low-paying jobs would be making 10-25 percent more if twelve million illegal aliens were not here to drive down wages. My favorite line is that illegal aliens take jobs that American won't take. That's right; an American would not take a menial job at five dollars or less an hour. But they would take that job if it paid a fair wage. But a fair wage is not offered because illegal aliens drive down the wages.

Democrats support illegal aliens because they know that if allowed to vote, illegal aliens would vote overwhelmingly Democratic. Why not? Democrats would allow them to stay, award them citizenship, and give them free health care and services at taxpayer expense. In the meantime, our country, our culture, and the value of American citizenship will be destroyed. So Democrats are risking our culture and our quality of life for an increase in their power.

Let me close this chapter reinforcing my position. God bless all *legal* immigrants from any part of the world. Join the melting pot and enjoy the opportunity that this great country offers. And to all of the illegal aliens in our country no matter where they come from, I say I understand and sympathize with why you want to be here, but you have to play by the rules just as the millions of legal immigrants who have come to our country before you over the last two hundred years like my dad did. There are hundreds of millions of people in Latin

America who want to come to the US and live according to some opinion polls that I saw. We cannot take you all without destroying our country. We must be a nation of laws or we will face anarchy and the destruction of what is America.

Chapter Two

A Family History of Rebellion and the Joy of Being Italian

It seems that rebellion is in my genes from both sides of the family and I am so thankful that it is. How boring it must be to feel like you must conform even when you know something is wrong. I have never been able to do it and it has gotten me in trouble many times. But I have never regretted standing up for what I believe and I am so glad that behavior was encouraged by my family and our history!

I will start with the obvious and most famous rebel in our family. Robert Morris. First, a quick history lesson: Robert Morris came to America from Liverpool, England at the age of thirteen in 1747. He grew to be an incredibly successful businessman and eventually became one of the, if not *the*, wealthiest men in America. Rich, well respected, and powerful, he risked it all when he rebelled against England in the cause of freedom and signed the Declaration of Independence. He is known in the history books as the Financier of the American Revolution.

He was close friends with George Washington who stayed at Robert's house many times when he was in Philadelphia. As the politicians in the colonies dithered and would not provide the resources that Washington and his army needed to fight, Robert Morris provided over a million dollars of his personal credit to keep the army fed and armed (and that is when a million dollars was worth something!). When the army was about to mutiny at Valley Forge because they had not been paid for six months, Robert Morris provided $50,000 in silver of his own money to pay the troops and save the army. In all he personally provided $800,000 of his own money toward the pay of revolutionary soldiers as well as contributing 150 ships at his expense, which were lost in the war to bring supplies around the British blockades (more than some of the colonies provided in the whole war). And when the new nation wanted to build a navy to fight the British, it was Robert Morris who raised and secured the funds and provided the first ship of the line. He also established a spy network against the British using his business contacts.

Robert Morris was at the heart of the formation of our government and he was one of the few people who signed the Declaration of Independence, Articles of Confederation, and the Constitution. He also started the first bank in the United States which became the Bank of North America.

His fall from grace is tragic and, in my view, a stain on the honor of the United States. After his enormous service to our country, he entered into a huge land deal in the westward expansion of the country and in Washington DC for which he arranged a loan from Holland. And just as his debt came due and he was about to get his loan from Holland, Holland declared war on revolutionary France. Europe then went to war which destroyed land value everywhere and eliminated the source of the loan he structured the deal around. Unable to pay his debts, the Financier of the Revolution was put into debtor prison (no good deed goes unpunished) with no help from the nation that he risked his fortune for. Broke and sick, Robert Morris eventually got out of prison and he and his wife finished their days living with Bishop White, his wife's brother in Philadelphia. Robert Morris lies buried today in the same burial plot as Bishop White and his wife at Christ Church in Philadelphia because he could not even afford his own grave. Thus is displayed the gratitude of the country that came into being in large part due to his bravery and financial support.

For years I had heard the story of Robert Morris in my family but had not known where he was buried or the details of his contribution to our nation. So when I lived in Virginia as a salesman for a division of American Hospital Supply thirty years ago, I decided to research him and find his grave. I finally did find it and went to visit Grandpa Morris. It was an unbelievable rush to stand next to the burial crypt of this great man, my great, great, great, grandfather. I felt that he was there and could hear me as I thanked him for his service and told him how proud I was of him (yep, I really did). I just visited Grandpa Morris again last year while on a business trip in Philadelphia and felt the same strong connection. People kid me that I am financially very conservative and always plan for the worst-case scenario. While my friends don't understand, Grandpa Morris understands.

On my mom's side we have all kinds of explorers and frontiersman in the family history since the family has been here so long. Seven members of our family were massacred by Indians in one day on their wilderness farm. And one of my relatives married an Indian (of course the rumor is that she was a princess). So I understand both sides of the Indian issue.

Like all other people, American Indians had good qualities and bad. Warfare was a way of life before the white man came and Indians constantly fought and killed each other, enslaved each other, and that is how manhood was established in their culture. Whites were warlike as well but they used war to realize their "manifest destiny" and spread their culture and economy. The bottom line is that these two warlike, aggressive cultures fought and in this case, the whites won. Just like Alexander conquered Persia, the Romans conquered the Greeks, and on and on. The world is and has been a dangerous place since the beginning. Get over it and move on!

The family history is made up of lots of farmers carving out a living in the wilderness and moving up from Virginia, Pennsylvania, Ohio, and Tennessee to Illinois over time. We have relatives who fought with Sherman on his march to the sea and we have a relative hung as a horse thief. But mainly, the family is made up of tough, honest, hard working farmers who worked the land. My mom's family is a fascinating piece of American history.

The last rebel on my mother's side is mom. In those days, a woman's role in her culture was to get married to a good Protestant boy from the country, raise children, run the household, and obey her husband. Not Verna! First she was one of the rare women in those days to go to college and live away from home as a single girl. And then she had the audacity to fall in love with and marry a Catholic Italian immigrant from the big city. She became a teacher for the mentally handicapped and an aggressive advocate of women's rights when that was unheard of. And then she got her master's degree at a time when few men, let alone women, achieved that level of education. She dedicated her life to fighting for the rights of the women and the handicapped. She was brilliant, loving, brave, elegant, regal, and fun loving. She insisted that we stand up and fight for principle as she did.

I have no doubt that she chose my dad because he was fun, vivacious, intense, loving, determined, and was also a rebel. I think dad represented the fun and gregarious side of life that was simply not a part of the honorable but reserved culture that she came from.

And she was the bravest person I have ever known. She got breast cancer and fought and survived for twelve years. You would have never known. In those days breast cancer was a sure death sentence. But to us kids, she made it seem that it was nothing more than a nuisance. And she continued to live life with joy. And then it spread to her lungs and she had to go to the hospital and be put on a respirator. The doctors said that she would die off the respirator, but my mother made it perfectly clear that she would not live the rest of her life tied to a respirator. Writing on a pad of paper, she told every doctor, nurse, child, relative, and Rome that she wanted to be off the respirator. And her wishes were honored.

She was a devout Christian and had no doubt about where she would be going after death. And then she prepared for her death with us in absolute calm and determination writing her wishes on her pad of paper. She told us what dress she wanted to wear, that she wanted to be cremated, where she wanted to be buried, and where to have the dinner after her burial. She told us not to spend too much money on her funeral and to rent a casket to save money since she was going to be cremated. She asked that they hold off pulling the respirator until her brother Lowell could join us to say goodbye.

I know now that she did all that to keep control of her life until the end just as she had lived it and to save us the agony of having to make the hard decisions. She did it for us. And then the time came. We all said goodbye individually and alone with her and I cried when it was my turn. She was facing death and yet she comforted me in calm and reassuring words on that pad of paper. She then told them to pull the tube and in seven minutes she was dead. Regal, brave, elegant, and thinking of others to the end. Nurses and doctors openly wept. These people who see death every day had never seen anything like that. I can only hope that I will have half of her courage and class when I face the end.

We don't know as much about my father's side before Augusto, but what we do know is extremely interesting. First, of course there is Augusto. I don't have proof of the following, but what I know was from stories told by Augusto, his brother Guido, Rome, and others. He went to college and just one semester before he graduated, he fell in love, got married, and left college to make a living. He did not talk much about his World War I service to me but his brother Guido did. He is the one who told me about Augusto being in the Alpine Corp. I researched the battles that the Alpine Corps fought against the Austrians and that was as tough as it got. Fighting in the Alps under miserable conditions with high losses was the norm. So when I learned that Augusto had been shot three times, poison gassed, and that he was the only survivor of his unit after the gas attack, I was not surprised. Augusto downplayed the story and did not talk about it much with me, although he showed my brother the scars of his bullet wounds after I moved away to college.

Somehow Augusto became an official of the railway union after the war (maybe his war hero status helped). This apparently was a high profile position in Italy as the railroad represented the most visible example of modern progress. As I said, Grandpa was surely a socialist and probably a communist although I don't have any proof of that. Then Mussolini came to power and formed the fascist party. Fascists hated socialists and communists and Mussolini's "black shirts" made a regular habit of killing communists and socialists. You would think that Augusto would go low profile in this environment. Apparently not Augusto. He was enough of a problem that they wanted him dead. But if you knew Augusto, you would expect nothing less. I like to think that he got in trouble by fighting for his union's rights despite the risk, but I don't know that. Principle was worth the risk to Augusto; I do know that. Apparently, one day he was informed that the black shirts were going to kill him. This was not an idle threat as it happened every day. Augusto had to leave or die and he left, leaving his family behind. The story is that somehow Al Capone was paid a large sum of money to get Augusto out of Italy. I doubt it, but it adds some spice to a story that doesn't need any.

Then Augusto lived in the US without his family, as a laborer and carpenter facing the prejudice that I already discussed. Leaving a high-profile job with high respect in Italy he was now at the bottom of the ladder in the US and facing prejudice. Knowing Augusto and his past, I expected nothing less than a relentless fight for his principles and the six foot Swede who got beaten by five foot five inch tall Augusto was just one of the casualties along the way. Six years later Augusto was able to legally get my father, grandmother, and aunt to the US. Eventually he became a successful contractor, built a large home in Chicago, built a vacation home in Lake Geneva, and provided a good life to the family. The great melting pot! In the end, Augusto was also put on a respirator. Determined not to end life that way, he ripped it out of his throat. A fearless fighter to the end.

Uncle Guido is another of the family "rebels" but in the opposite way. A true unorthodox artist, he broke all of the mores of the day. He studied art and music at one of the oldest universities in Europe, Bologna University (over a thousand years old). Upon coming to the US, Guido became an oboe player in the prestigious Chicago Symphony Orchestra and the Chicago Opera Company which are still world famous today. He played with Toscanini and other icons of the time, and was asked by Toscanini to accompany him on his tour of South America. Rubbing elbows with the rich and famous, Guido bragged of fathering hundreds of children in his days on tour. He bragged about his sexual experiences with the famous ballerina Pavlova. And he loved to brag about his wife's three nipples. He spoke about these things with me, my brother, and my sister when we were kids at a time that you simply did not talk about married sex, let alone unmarried sex. But while Uncle Guido was a world-class artist, he cared not a twit about social rules. He talked about these sexual exploits with the same open passion in front of his wife Mary and us kids who he would also talk about the beauty and powerful meaning of Dante's *Inferno* and Vivaldi's *Four Seasons*.

The last rebel I will talk about is my dad, Rome. On one hand, he was the perfect example of the melting pot aggressively adapting to American expectations and success. On the other, he took huge risks and fought for the principles that he believed in, and it cost him dearly. I have already talked about how he aggressively fought even the slightest prejudice. But he did not complain or whine or let it get in his way, he just fought back and never gave up and in the end, he won. He did not sue anybody, or claim a hate crime; he just fought and soldiered on. And he only talked about the good things as I was growing up (until the day he punched me in the nose). He only talked about his friends, the fun they had, the good times. No whining!

I have already talked about how he joined the army to fight the Japanese. He did not hesitate to risk his life for his country and to earn his citizenship. But like so many World War II vets, he did not share the bad times, only the good times.

Growing up, all he ever talked about was the great friends that he made in the war and the exciting non-combat things that he saw in China, India, and Burma. Not the danger, the death, the fear, the inhumanity of the enemy which I learned about later.

It was not until I was married and when he was in his fifties that he started to talk about the brutality of the war he experienced. How they would capture one end of an airfield and the Japanese would hold the other end and bomb them every day. The number of planes that crashed and pilots killed on the runways. Or about seeing poor Chinese peasants throwing their babies under the US trucks to kill them because they did not have enough food to eat. Or how a poor Chinese peasant simply tired of life intentionally walked into the spinning prop of a Flying Tiger P-40. Or how he caught malaria and almost died in China. He told me about flying over the hump (Himalayas) and losing an engine and preparing to parachute out of the plane at 20,000 feet.

But the real clincher was in the last year of his life. Rome had dementia in the end but occasionally would have moments of complete lucidity. It was in one of the moments of lucidity in the last month of his life that I got a true appreciation of his experiences that he quietly endured. He suddenly looked at me intently and said, "When you are in a trench and the Japanese drop a bomb on your position, it always looks like the bomb is coming straight at you." I could see that he was actually reliving the moment and got a small glimpse of the emotion that he must have felt at the time.

On a side note, I find it totally amazing how much critically important experience is lost from just one generation to the next. The lessons that my father and his generation learned about the realities of war and the cost of not being prepared were enormous and intense, yet many in the next generation are not aware of those lessons or don't believe them. That was driven home in spades after this discussion with my dad and shortly thereafter in another discussion with a college student and his mom who is my age. Sitting together at a dinner put on by our investment broker, the woman's son talked about a thesis that he just wrote about how criminal and unjustified it was that the United States dropped the atom bomb on Japan. The mom agreed and asked me what I thought.

I am an intense amateur historian and I have taken over twenty college history courses in the last five years just for fun. This was an interesting topic for me and I had researched it in depth. Millions of Chinese, Asians, Europeans, and Americans were brutally murdered by the Japanese in World War II. Just read *Flyboys* by James Bradley and you will get a flavor of the extremes of cruelty that the Japanese would go to for their cause. Based on the actual Japanese and American casualties suffered in Tarawa, Iwo Jima, and Okinawa (98 percent dead for the Japanese and 25 percent wounded and killed for the US), US experts estimated that an invasion of Japan would result in 1 million US and 10 million Japanese casualties. After four years of war and four hundred thousand dead Americans, Truman would have been impeached if he did not use the atom bomb to save American lives.

Some people say that the Japanese were ready to surrender just before the atomic bombs were dropped. But that is not true. The Japanese war counsel refused to consider termination of the war and murdered any members that proposed surrender. Even after both atomic bombs were dropped, the war counsel was at a stalemate over surrender and it took Hirohito to break the tie and order the surrender. We knew this is true because we cracked the Japanese code and we knew exactly what they were going to do.

I explained all of this to the college student and his

mother but they just did not get it. I explained that while it was tragic that three hundred thousand Japanese died from the atomic bombs, that it was a hell of a lot better alternative than the 11 million Japanese and Americans who the experts said would die with an invasion of Japan. They still did not get it. Finally I relayed what my dad described in his experiences in the war and the fact that he would have been on a troop ship headed for the invasion of Japan. He might have been one of the 1 million US casualties and I would not be here today if Truman did not drop the bombs. At that point I did not care if they got it or not. You just can't fix stupid!

What scares the hell out of me is that these well-documented truths occurred just one generation ago. The kids of the parents who experienced these incredible tragedies are alive today (baby boomers). Yet many of them learned absolutely nothing and reject the overwhelming facts to naively and ignorantly pretend that if we are just nice to bad people, they will be nice to us. The forever truth was best said by Plato; "only the dead have seen the end of war." The only question is whether you will be ready and win the next war, or be naïve and lose your freedom and way of life. But it appears to me that human beings just cannot learn the hard lessons of history and each generation has to suffer because of that. What a pity!

Where dad was a real rebel was in his choice of a wife and his rejection of the rigid Italian rules. The rule was you married a "good Italian Catholic girl" and you followed your father's wishes. Not my dad. I guess after his war experiences, he decided he was going to do what made him happy. When he met Verna, he fell in love and married her. She was not an Italian girl, and Rome married her contrary to Augusto's wishes. And to make it worse, he moved away from home to independently pursue his future.

Verna always said that she was not accepted by my dad's family and that they blamed her for his departure from the Italian way. Seeking a religious compromise, mom and dad became Episcopalians which is sort of a compromise between Catholic and Protestant. Sometimes the family rejection got bitter and caused mom and dad much pain, but they never let us see it. The real pain came in the end when Augusto died (it may have been after Grandma died as well, I am not sure of the sequence). We don't know why for sure, but Augusto left virtually everything to Rome's sister and almost nothing to Dad. She followed the accepted Italian life. She married an Italian and lived under Augusto's roof and rule until he died. Rome was devastated by the apparent rejection of Augusto upon his death. We were told that Dad's sister would not consider what he thought was a fair redistribution of the inheritance. In Dad's opinion, this was the second time that our side of the family was cheated out of a rightful inheritance from that side of the family, and it hurt and embarrassed him badly.

After what my dad indicated were several bitter fights over the subject with his sister, my father and mother brought my brother, sister, and me together and told us what he wanted to do. He was so angry at his sister in that his kids did not get their rightful inheritance (in his opinion), that he was afraid that he would hurt his sister or have a heart attack if he ever saw her again. He wanted to pronounce her to be dead to him and us, and he asked for our permission and agreement. That meant that we would not see them again. Each of us saw his pain and understood his position and we supported his decision. In large part, after that decision we did not see that side of the family again except at two funerals. They were in fact dead to us with the exception of my cousin Ron and his family who remained close to my dad and mom until they died.

I really don't know the details of the dispute or how it all really happened. Dad did not share that. I only know that he felt cheated and it broke his heart. And I know that whatever the details were, it tragically broke apart what was a close-knit family. I suppose the issue won't be properly resolved until Rome, his sister, and Augusto meet again in the next world. I would pay to see that!

There is a funny side to this story. Right after this experience and to make sure that this would never happen in their family, my mom and dad made a list of all their possessions. They then gave the list to my brother, sister, and me and asked us to indicate what we wanted and how badly we wanted it. After getting our responses they made a final list which indicated who got what and they put tags on many of the articles so that there would be no confusion. And this was probably ten years before they died! While it was weird, we had a lot of laughs as a family with pretend arguments as to why someone was getting this or that thing or when someone would spill something on "my" carpet or someone would scratch my "brother's" piece of furniture. But I will tell you this, as the executor of their estate and with the help of my brother and sister, every single penny of their estate was distributed precisely to their wishes without one single fight. All of us understood how important that was to Mom and Dad and we made sure that things were settled as they wanted and in the spirit they wanted.

So in the end, Rome was a real rebel rejecting the easy ways and sticking to his principles. Unfortunately, in his last seven years he developed dementia and much of his fun-loving side was lost and we lost sight of all the great earlier years. But as I think of him now, the sixty-five years of his life before dementia, it was the life of a brave, fun-loving, fighter who risked all for love and honor and duty.

I have painted a somewhat negative side of being Italian in our family history. But there is a powerful positive side. In fact, I think everyone really wants to be Italian, as we live life better and fuller than any other people I know. I am convinced that Italian is a dominant gene over any other nationality and if you have even 10 percent Italian in your blood, you are Italian (sorry, I know that is not politically correct, but truth is truth!).

Before the family rift, I remember holiday dinners with my Italian family. There were hordes of relatives with everyone talking at once and with high emotion. Fun, intense, and crazy, we all had a great time. And the food! Every dinner was a six-course meal of extraordinary flavors and everyone cooked and contributed. The Italian bread and antipasto as a starter is incomparable to anything else. Proscuito, mortadella, olives, and all the best tastes in the world! Then homemade tortellini soup. Fresh pasta made that day whether it be spaghetti, penne, rigatoni, or gnocchi. Then turkey, roast beef, and veal cutlets. And then, endless desserts and cookies! It was a common practice for everyone to loosen their belts to make room as the dinner progressed.

And were we proud to be Italian! After all we had an Augusto, Guido, and a Rome in the family! War heroes and artists! We were the people of the Roman Empire that ruled the known world for a thousand years and invented law, architecture, and the highest quality of life that would not be matched for a thousand years—the people of Cincinatus, Caesar, Cicero, Augustus, Trajan, Marcus Aurelius, Constantine, and Marconi. With artists like Vivaldi, Albinoni, Verde, Michelangelo, Dante, Rossini, and an endless lists of greats that no nationality can possibly match. We were the people who brought the world out of the dark ages with the Renaissance. The best cooking in the world (the French learned everything they know from Italians). How on earth could you not be proud!

Part of my love of history started with exploring my Italian heritage. I simply cannot read enough about the Roman Republic, Imperial Rome, the emperors, and the great heroes like Cincinatus, Cornelius Scipio, or Aetius. Everything that you need to know about the future can be learned from the past and Rome.

Read Edward Gibbons' *The Decline and Fall of the Roman Empire* written in 1776, which historians say is the best history book ever written. It is the story of the greatest empire the world has ever known which collapsed because its people became decadent, self-centered, and lazy. They invented "outsourcing" by having Egypt grow their grain because of lower cost which resulted in the collapse of the small farmer and then the republic. They outsourced their military to the barbarians who eventually conquered them because the citizens did not want to do the hard work of defending their country. And they created a spoiled populace that came to expect free bread and increasingly decadent entertainment in the coliseum. Finally they opened their borders to the barbarians who were willing to do the menial labor that its citizens were no longer willing to do. Then they were conquered by those very barbarians and the world was plunged into a thousand years of the dark ages.

Any of this sound familiar? Are there any lessons to be learned from Rome that apply to our country and the issues in our news today? It certainly seems apparent to me. But what I find amazing is that most people do not have a clue about any of this. The ignorance about the lessons of history is epidemic and overwhelming. And unfortunately, I am afraid the famous line of "those who don't know history are doomed to repeat it" is tragically true.

Anyway, back to the glory of being Italian! If you have not been to Italy, you simply cannot understand the over-powering extent of its greatness, especially if you are Italian. The eternal city of Rome with the Coliseum, Forum, St. Peters, and other incredibly famous great landmarks is endless. On our first trip there, my wife and I were blown away by the fact that you would see the cutting edge Gucci store on one corner and the 2,500-year-old Forum on the next. On a later trip, after spending one day at the Forum, we walked to a non-descript street and ate at a local outdoor restaurant (I never had a bad meal in Italy and I have been there a dozen times). Looking across the street, there were some ruins twenty feet below street level with beautiful buildings, temples, and walkways. It wasn't in the guide book or labeled. Intrigued, we asked Evelyn's cousin who lived in Rome what it was. Turns out that this ruin was the Campus Martius and the Theater of Pompey where Julius Caesar was assassinated (he was not assassinated in the Forum but was cremated in front of it). There are so many great historical sites in Rome that it did not make the cut in the guidebook!

Rome is just one fabulous city in Italy. Italy has unimaginable and endless wonders. Beautiful Florence, Venice, Milan, and Sorrento are just a sample of the places that must be seen to be believed. Art, history, and greatness are everywhere. One day at the Vatican museum or at Pompey and you will be under Italy's spell forever and you could take a lifetime and not see it all. But the people are the real treasure.

My wife and I went to Italy on our honeymoon. We were dirt-poor college students and given a choice by my parents of getting furniture or airfare to Italy for a wedding present, we chose Italy! We backpacked through Europe and took trains, buses, and hitched rides. We stayed at pensiones and college dorms to save money. But we were unprepared for the incredible friendliness and zest for life that we experienced in Italy versus home, Switzerland, France, or Germany.

Relatives in Italy who we had never seen or even heard of before welcomed us with incredible warmth and expensive wedding presents and made us stay at their homes in Bologna, Rome, and the family resort in San Marco. I remember feeling completely at home with people who I did not know and being surrounded by joyous laughter and warmth. People on the street all over Italy went out of their way to help us wherever we went.

All of this cemented in me forever what it means to be Italian and you cannot help but be proud of that heritage. Don't get me wrong, I am incredibly proud to be an American, which today is the greatest nation on earth. And there is no doubt where my loyalty lies. But I am also Italian and very proud of it! It is in my genes and makes up part of who I am.

Chapter Three

Growing Up with John Wayne

I feel so sorry for young boys and young men today. Metro sexual is good, sensitivity is good, dodge ball is bad, guns are bad, hunting is bad, Boy Scouts are bad (too judgmental!), having hairy arms and legs is bad (did you know that boys now wax their legs and backs?). What on earth does it mean to be a boy today? How do you have fun and excitement, and where do you look for role models? No wonder the scientific data indicates that more boys are screwed up, dropping out of high school, and choosing not to go to college. I say that the problem is that there are "no more lions to kill" to earn your manhood and boys today are lost. It is an identity crisis!

When I grew up, life was simple. If you wanted to know what it took to be a real boy and then a man, all you had to do was watch a John Wayne movie. Guys were tough, they liked guns, they liked action, they fought bad guys, were courteous to ladies, honor was everything, you never let your buddies down, and you were a patriot. Straight talk was the key; you said it plain and direct and if someone didn't like it, tough. If someone called you a name or treated you badly you didn't call your lawyer or the cops to file a "hate crime" or whine, you took care of business. And sometimes you got your butt kicked and sometimes you won. But the main thing is that you stood your ground and that was all that counted. We grew up following John Wayne's script.

We were never indoors and our parents did not know where we were until dinner. Everyone watched out for each other's kids and we were safe. Nobody bothered kids back then and there were no creeps hanging around little children (at least it was not visible). And if you misbehaved away from home and another adult saw you, you got spanked. And when they told your parents, you got spanked again. Today, of course, they would go to jail for child abuse (is child behavior better today or back then?). If the cops caught you doing something wrong, they would not arrest you and take you to court, they would smack you, tell your parents, and they would smack you again. Crime was lower, no court costs, and no permanent record for the kid!

We were well treated by our parents but we were treated like guys expected to handle things like guys. I remember my dad teaching me how to swim the first time at Lake Geneva when I was about five or six. He picked me up and threw me in the lake and told me to swim back to him. Given the choice of swimming back or drowning, I swam. And then he threw me in again, and again. No namby-pamby stuff, just tough it out. Today I love swimming; swam a mile a day for twenty plus years, became a lifeguard, and continue to be an active scuba diver. The Nietzsche "that which does not kill you makes you stronger" school of swimming really worked!

We played baseball, football, went swimming, played army, or went hunting or fishing all day. We were always outside and active. I remember going to camp when I was seven for the first time. We learned the manly arts like shooting a gun, shooting a bow, woodworking, and making a camp fire. At seven, there was simply no doubt about what being a boy was all about. And in case you were confused, you went to Cub Scouts and Boy Scouts and you were reminded again, scouts honor! And as a scout you got merit badges for doing the right boy stuff. There just was never a doubt about what being a boy was all about and it was a good time. And because you were outside running all day long, you collapsed and went to bed when it was nine o'clock. I lived this lifestyle when we lived in the city and moved to the suburbs, and on the farm (the farm really raised the "being a boy" bar which I will cover later).

What a contrast today is. Today, all you hear about is boys being indoors and on the Internet. The primary all-day activity is the latest video game about stealing cars or massacring villages. Of course now, actually touching a gun or going hunting is seen as psychotic and immediately makes you un-cool in today's "metro male" world. In fact I recently heard on the news that a young boy who drew a picture of someone with a gun was suspended from school! Holy cow, all we did was draw pictures of army guys and cowboys with guns when we were kids. They were our heroes.

Of course we were not always good boys. We got in to fights, shot off illegal fireworks, and created general havoc and destruction in the neighborhood and the cops had to set us straight once and a while. And my brother wants me to fess up to some of the rotten things I did to him like when my buddies and I hung him by his heels pretending that he was a captured Indian, or shooting him with my sling shot, or sticking him with a dart from time to time.

We also got hurt from time to time but that was part of the deal. Like the time I fell out of my two-story window while goofing around and got knocked unconscious. Or the time that I got knocked unconscious playing catcher when I stepped in front of the batter to pick off a guy stealing second as the batter swung at the ball. Or the time that I got knocked unconscious running into the garage playing hide and seek and did not notice the rope that my buddy had strung across the garage which caught me at the neck and lifted my feet right out from under me and I crashed on my head on the concrete floor. Or the time riding my bike that I turned right in front of a car without looking which then hit me and threw me twenty feet and knocked me out when my head hit the street (I will never forget the look on the face of the poor driver when I came to because I am sure he thought that he had killed me). By the way, in the second or so that it took from when I saw the car to when it hit me, my short life did in fact flash before my eyes as the saying goes because I was sure that I was about to be killed. I have heard that being knocked unconscious multiple times can be a cause of Alzheimer's. What is my name again?

We did have fun and we did take chances. One of my most vivid memories is at about age fourteen on one of our suburban hunting trips at the edge of the local golf course. There were five of us walking across a frozen pond in late winter. Suddenly the ice started breaking and one by one, we started falling through it. I suspect that only a few people have experienced that extraordinary sensation so I will share it with you in some detail.

Fear was not the first emotion that I felt when it happened. As I was going down, one of our friends was the last to be on top of the ice and he was laughing at us thinking that he was not going down. Time stops when you are scared to death, but I remember feeling deep satisfaction as he suddenly broke through the ice too. My first emotion was revenge!

You would think that when falling through the ice into ice-cold water, the first physical sensation would be extreme cold, but it wasn't. It felt as if I was being scalded by boiling water and stuck by a thousand heated needles! I think the senses are so overloaded that they just don't know how to react. Being a very strong swimmer (remember my dad's Nietzsche swimming technique?), I was not worried about drowning. And for about four or five minutes (it could have been longer or shorter, I lost track) I would launch myself back up on the ice with great energy and it would break and drop me down again, and again, and again. My legs became completely numb and I began to worry that the sharp edge of the ice was cutting my legs and my private parts to shreds (a bad thing at that age when you could think of nothing but the day of sharing those private parts with a girl).

And then hypothermia set in. What a strange feeling. Utter exhaustion and total calm. Suddenly I had absolutely no energy and I realized that I was going to die. But that was okay. No fear. I was ready. Hypothermia is not a bad way to go if you have to go. And then something inside of me said quitting was not acceptable for a guy (after all, what would John Wayne say?). So I tried again and finally made it on top of the ice and crawled on my belly to where the ice was thicker.

But that was not the worst part. All of us got out except one: my brother Mark. He looked up at me and asked me to help him. Although I wanted to help, I knew for certain that if I went back into the water, that was it, I would never get out. I was afraid—deathly afraid—I did not move to help him for what seemed an eternity. But then I thought of going home and telling mom and dad that I did not have the guts to save my brother. I decided that I would much rather be dead than have to admit that I was a coward. And I went back to the edge and got him out.

My brother and I did not talk about that for twenty-five years. And over the years I wondered if I remembered it correctly until one Christmas morning when my brother and his family stayed over at our house for the holiday. I overheard Mark telling my son Ben how I saved his life at the pond. He never noticed my hesitation and just talked about how I risked my life to come back to him (I did tell him later that I had to think about it!). The next Christmas Mark reminded me of all the rotten stuff that I did to him when we were kids. I asked him if I saved his life before or after all of that rotten stuff. When he said that it was after, I asked if we were even now. I was greatly relieved when he confirmed that there was no balance due!

That was my second potential brush with death (getting hit by the car was my first). Little did I know that there would be at least twenty more to go! Nor did I know that Mark would be the first of at least four lives that I would save over the years.

Chapter Four

The Glory of Being a Boy on the Farm

For a boy, it just didn't get better than being on the farm. Boys were kings and could do manly things at a very young age that city boys could never do until they were eighteen, or possibly may never be able to do. Whether it was driving trucks and tractors at twelve or thirteen, riding horses bareback, or swimming with water moccasins in ponds, the farm was a constant action high for a boy.

The farm taught you the hard facts of life first hand and with stark reality in a way that folks from the city cannot possibly understand. Life, death, danger, responsibility, and hardship as well as beauty, joy, excitement, and deep satisfaction are all openly present on the farm. There are lessons that you never forget, which prepare you for the rough and tumble world and give you a confidence and independence that you simply can't get in a city environment. I am convinced that the farther man goes from the farm or wilderness, the more naïve, ignorant, and dumber he gets.

My mom's family farmed in deep southern Illinois. It is more like the Deep South in attitude and language than you would expect in Illinois. This was the boonies and the closest town had 600 people and the only attraction was the pinball machine at the drug store. The closest movie theater was twenty miles away. These were good, hard-working folks. No pretense, no show, just good folks. Some of them were millionaires in land value like my uncle Lowell, but you would never know. Uncle Lowell was a hard-working, serious, and incredibly honest man. And he was kind of a pillar of the community. I stayed with Uncle Lowell and his family during the summers when I worked on the farm.

The view of life from the farm is incredibly different than it is from the city. Take a core component of humanity that has been true for millions of years. We are meat-eating animals and in order for us to eat, animals have to die. Living in the sheltered world of the suburbs or city, you could go through your entire life without actually seeing proof that steak, chicken, or pork actually comes from living animals that are killed so that we can eat. I can hear the animal rights groups whining now. In the city we buy meat in nice packages and as far as you can tell from the looks, it could grow on trees.

On the farm, you are reminded every day of the facts of life in the harshest terms possible. As a young child, I remember being on the farm and being told that we would have chicken that night, and then I watched with amazement as my grandmother caught a chicken that was running around the yard and killed it for dinner. I remember Grandpa butchering a pig that he had been raising. When we needed milk, we went to the barn and milked the cows (and squirted milk from the cow's udders in to the mouths of the cats that always hung around during milking). Side note: most people have not experienced milking a cow. They are big, dumb heavy animals with huge udders and multiple nipples, and they can break your foot if they step on you. There is certainly no glamour as you grab the large nipples the size of a grown man's thumb and squeeze down to force the milk out and into the pail. But there is something timeless and natural about it as well. And fresh milk is as good as it gets!

On the farm, life and death and the tougher components of life are in your face every day. It is not good or bad, it is just the way it is. I remember the first time that I helped birth a calf. It is not a pretty sight with sticky fluids everywhere, but it is a magical moment. The reality is that later, that same calf with the huge brown eyes is then slaughtered so that we can have steak. I have seen all ends of the process. As little kids we saw animals having sex, being born, growing up, and then being slaughtered for food. It is just life. We raised pigs and there were always new litters being born. We would watch them be created, born, and then we had to castrate the young males (that is nasty but required), feed them until they matured, then sell them or kill them and eat them. Nothing personal, it is just the way it is and has been for a million years. It goes on thousands of times a day for the city folk as well, but they can pretend that it doesn't happen because they don't see it.

Even though we knew that our animals would eventually be our food, we liked them and treated them well while they lived (right up until we killed them to eat them!). I can picture 75 percent of the people reading this cringing at the ugliness of it. Sorry, it is reality and they are being killed every day for you and in your name. Many people probably just don't want to know because it is too uncomfortable to deal with. But the folks on the farm knew that it works both ways. Some of those animals would kill you and even eat you if they could.

A six-hundred-pound sow can suddenly turn on you and she could kill you. It happens. And most certainly if allowed to, she would then eat you because pigs will eat anything. My mom, and later my brother were chased by a bull and under the right circumstances, it would have killed them. Nothing personal, just the way it is. But if you did not know that or if you did not watch out for that danger all the time, you were at risk and there was no second chance, no little beeper that warns you that they are about to attack (like when trucks back up in the city). You were responsible for your own safety and you had to stay alert or the penalty could be pain or death. But that also made every day exciting and intense. And it made you sharp and more alive.

People have this "cutesy" image of farm animals. We liked them too, but we knew the other side and had a balanced and realistic view. Here is a story that will drive animal rights activists like PETA nuts. I was young and my cousin Dennis just got a real cute Shetland pony named Bucky. The kind that city folk just fawn over! As my cousin walked by, the pony suddenly and without provocation, bit him big time on the arm. Much pain and agony! As a city boy, I did not know that cute ponies would bite you and I was shocked. But then Dennis got the pain under control, walked to the edge of the corral, picked up a two by four and calmly hit Bucky in the middle of the forehead so hard that I thought for sure that he killed him. Bucky sat down on his haunches and shook it off after a few minutes. Dennis explained that he needed to do this every month or so because Bucky forgets that there are repercussions to biting. Then all ill will was forgotten, Bucky behaved and we all went riding and had a good time until the next lesson was needed. That's just the way it is.

From an early age (ten and on) we rode my grandpa's horses, Lady and Peaches, bareback. Lady was my favorite. I am sure an image pops in your mind of a majestic, beautiful horse. I liked Lady, but she kept trying to kill us. Whenever we would go for a ride, she would first try to rub us off against the barb wire fence. You see, she would rather be in the cool barn eating than out in the sun with us on her back. Then we would get far down the pasture and Lady would start to gallop at full speed back to the barn running directly at a large post in the corral. Reaching that post she would slam on the breaks and rear up hoping to throw us off. It took some time for me to understand that you needed to make sure that Lady knew you were the boss and that there would be consequences to bad behavior (the farm boys knew). Then she would be fine. Nothing personal, it's just the way it is.

The farm was also hard work and responsibility. I worked on it during the summer and every day we got up before dawn, had breakfast, and then hit the fields until sundown. Hard work, and at the southern edge of Illinois, it was hot work. But it was man's work and at thirteen or fourteen, I was expected to do it and I did.

I remember cultivating a field in the bottomland as part of my job. My uncle had a thousand acres of river bottom land and he dropped me off in the field and left me to cultivate the field alone as he worked another one. I am responsible for a big tractor (no air conditioning or umbrella in the hot sun, 95-degree temperature, and 95-percent humidity) and cultivating between the endless rows of corn or soybeans to loosen up the soil and remove the weeds. Not another soul for miles around. It was a big responsibility for a young kid, but very cool! And very, very lonely.

To give you a sense of the loneliness and vastness of a thousand acres, one day I was cultivating alone and I heard a huge explosion in the sky. This was during the cold war and fall-out shelters, and I began to think that the Russians had dropped the nuclear bomb on us. The longer the day went on and I did not see another person, the more I became convinced that I was the last American alive in the country and I wondered how I was going to live. I started to go nuts. And to add to the drama, a large whirlwind hit the field (looked like a small tornado) and then I was sure that the end was here. You can imagine my relief at the end of the day when Uncle Lowell came to pick me up. Turns out that the huge explosion was from an Air Force jet that broke the sound barrier. But for a while, I was the last living man in America!

There were some very tough jobs too. One of the tough jobs was chunking. That is where a field that had just been a forest is cleared of all the trees which are then burned in massive piles. The chunkers walk the field (still smoldering) and pick up any "chunks" of wood still in the field or pull out tree stumps with a chain and truck. Remember, it is 95 degrees, 95-percent humidity, there's no shade, and the field is still smoldering in some places.

The evening before my first day chunking I had all but cut my toe off (right through my work boots) while cutting fodder for the horses with a hand sickle. So I was already hurting. While chunking that first day, I learned the importance of hydration. Feeling poorly with my almost-amputated toe and with my gym shoes semi melted due to the heat of the burning embers (my boots were ruined by the sickle), I passed out with heat exhaustion. Who knew! When I came to, the guys gave me salt tablets and told me that I had to drink a lot of water, and then get back to work. So I did. No whining allowed on the farm!

So as you can see, water was real important. But the problem was that we shared a common jug of water and a common cup, and old Joe kept fouling them. Joe was about sixty, had no teeth, and loved sardines. I am here to tell you that there is nothing more awful than being as hot as hell and going to drink water from a cup that smells like a toothless old man and sardines! Well we tried several times to get old Joe to quit eating the sardines, but we could not get through. Finally at our wits end, Ed and I decided to make a demonstration. We climbed up a thirty-foot sapling until it bowed to the ground. Then we created a sling shot out of the tree by placing Joe's lunch box in the limbs and we let her go. That lunch box may still be in orbit! Joe did not bring sardines after that.

Of course we had to discipline Ed too. Ed used to think it was funny to drive the truck out of the field into the shade during lunch breaks without waiting for us. We were then forced to walk to the truck (still 95 degrees, 95-percent humidity, and smoldering field!) to get our water and lunch. Ed thought it was funny as hell and would laugh at us all the way as we walked to the truck. Right up until we put him through the windshield!

We were at the edge of a field and we knew that Ed was about to take off and head to the other side without us. So we quietly took the one hundred feet of chain that we used for pulling stumps and hooked one end to the biggest tree around and the other to the frame of the truck. When we walked away from the truck, Ed hopped in and took off like a bat out of hell. Right up until the end of the chain. It was a sight to see and I was afraid that we had ruined the truck when it snapped to a stop and flew straight up into the air. Ed got to experience rapid deceleration first hand and never took off without us again!

We worked hard but had fun too. I remember often taking a break in the heat and skinny dipping in the salt ponds formed by the oil wells that were ubiquitous (who knew that there are oil wells in southern Illinois!). I also remember climbing the oil pump arm and riding it through the fifteen-foot trip it made every thirty seconds. One wrong move and we could have lost our hands, but it was fun. Or climbing one of the thirty-foot-high oil storage tanks and sliding down the piping like firemen. Sometimes we would swim in the local creeks. It did not bother us that there were water moccasins and leeches in there with us and black/blue mud up to our shins. It was a way to cool off and have fun. And Ed would burn the leaches off us with his cigarettes when we were done. Of course old Joe would steal our clothes and we would have to run around naked looking for them.

Another fact of life on the farm is that with all of the danger around every day, bad things do happen. We used to regularly swim in a pond by my grandfather's house. Deep black/blue mud, snakes, and leeches, but it was fun. But when my little cousin Todd drowned there one day (he was with his little sister), it reminded all of us in stark terms that life can be hard. Working with heavy tractors, large animals, and heavy machinery, farming is one of the most dangerous jobs in America. It was common to hear of farmers being killed on tractors that had tipped over, or farmers losing their arms in the power train link of a piece of equipment. I remember when three people got killed at the grain elevator in town when it exploded from the grain dust. I used to go to the elevator when we dropped off truckloads of freshly harvested wheat and we knew that it could happen at any time. That is just the way it is. Like life, the farm is beautiful, fun, and exciting, but it is hard, dangerous, and it can hurt you or kill you.

That lesson hit hard on one of my other tough jobs on the farm. I was working for my Uncle Allen. A tough cigar-chewing guy, he ran a drag line. Using huge cranes, they would create drainage canals that would drain the farmland to eliminate flooding. Creating twenty-foot levies (at least they seemed that big to a fourteen-year-old kid) which framed the canals, our job was to burn the huge piles of dead trees on top of the levies. My uncle took great joy in telling me that I would be working with Fuckenheimer who was going into the army the next month. I remember wondering how he would make it through the army with that name. But after Fuckenheimer almost killed me, I became less concerned! By the way, I just found out from Uncle Lowell this year that was not his real name!

Here is how it happened. Fuckenheimer was in charge of the tractor with a platform on the back which held a fifty-gallon barrel of diesel fuel. I rode on the back and our job was to spray the huge pile of trees with diesel oil and then burn them. Being thirteen or fourteen, I did not think much of it as Fuckenheimer ordered me to spray both ends of the levee that we were perched on. We were twenty feet high on a narrow and steep levee. To our left was a huge pile of diesel-soaked trees and the same to our right. And then Fuckenheimer lit the piles of trees. Suddenly we were surrounded by walls of flame and it was incredibly hot. Fuckenheimer and I got on the tractor and we went left and then right looking for escape. I was on the platform with the fifty-gallon barrel of diesel oil and I realized with certainty that it was going to ignite and I was going to die.

Fortunately, I was suddenly put out of my misery. Fuckenheimer decided to head the tractor straight down the steep levee. No warning to me and as the tractor headed down, I was thrown over Fuckenheimer and the tractor and down the levee in front of the tractor. As I was airborne, I realized that Fuckenheimer and the tractor were going to run me over and kill me. And then the lights went out.

When I came to (another knockout), I was in the middle of a blackberry bush. In case you don't know it, blackberry bushes are full of very sharp thorns. Needless to say, I was in intense pain in every part of my body. But, I was alive! Somehow Fuckenheimer avoided running over me and we went back to work.

Speaking of blackberries, the farm also offers subtle forms of simple pleasure that city folks can never experience. One of my favorite things to do was to go blackberry picking with my cousins and Aunt Dorothy. Now you had to pay attention because of the thorns and there was the possibility of rattlesnakes, copperheads, or water moccasins that you had to watch out for. But once you got those fresh blackberries and brought them home, you knew that Aunt Dorothy would make the absolute best fresh blackberry cobbler that you have ever tasted. Simple, exquisite, and earned pleasure! Kids today have no idea.

Speaking of snakes, the reality of snakes hit home pretty hard one day on the farm. I brought a friend from the burbs out to the farm one holiday so that he could share my adventures (and to prove that the stories I told were true). We decided to take a rubber raft down the Skillet Fork River and look for excitement. I brought a pistol just in case. We might as well have been in the Amazon River because we could see nothing but the river bank and low-hanging trees and brush. No people and no civilization. Cool! Eventually we saw this huge water moccasin (five feet long and really fat) on the bank. It was not moving, its mouth was wide open, and it looked dead. My friend Larry wanted to pick it up and take it home. Having lived on the farm and seen the hard side of life, I suggested that he use a stick to make sure that it was dead. He did and I had the pistol ready to go.

When the stick touched the snake all hell broke loose (it was spring time, cool and the snake was just coming out of hibernation). It started hissing, spitting, and struck out at us repeatedly. And it almost got us. I unloaded the pistol into the snake (at least all around it) and it rolled and hissed all the way down into the river and disappeared. We assumed that I had killed it. Well, it took a while for us to calm down and we got back into the raft. We decided to drink some water from the leather water bottle that we tied to the raft and kept in the river to keep it cool. When we were about to drink from the bottle, we were shocked to see two fang marks where the snake bit through the bottle. We were sitting on the rubber bottom of the raft that was no thicker than a balloon as we realized that the snake could still be alive and bite us through the bottom of the raft just like it bit through the water bottle. Needless to say, we broke the sound barrier getting the hell out of there. Larry had a good story to tell when we got back home and suddenly people believed the stories that I had been telling!

You can do things on the farm that you can't do in the real world at thirteen and fourteen. My cousins had a go-cart that would go sixty miles an hour. So we took an empty field and with a tractor, we groomed a quarter-mile oval race track for the go-cart. I remember taking my brother for a ride and going flat out. I flipped the go-cart on a turn (that is suppose to be impossible to do) and we ended upside down, trapped, with gasoline dripping down on us. Why we did not get killed is beyond me. Another life lesson that you can't get in the city or the burbs!

There were also tons of interesting history and traditions on the farm. Farms are usually in the family for generations and the history stays alive. My grandfather told me about Indian tribes that lived on or passed through our land. Or gypsies caravans (my mom saw the gypsies go through when she was a girl). One of our favorite activities was arrowhead hunting after a rain storm had just washed off a freshly plowed field. The Indians would camp on hills near a water source, so that is where we would go hunting. It is a kick to find arrowheads, tomahawk heads, banner stones, or other tools used by Archaic, Pottawattamie, or Cherokee Indians who lived on our land one hundred or a thousand years ago. Today I still have quite a collection of artifacts that we found on the farm and it got me turned on to history. Now I am addicted to collecting ancient Greek, Roman, Persian, and Indian artifacts and it is one of the passions which give me much joy. It is really fascinating to hold a tomahawk head and imagine the Indian who held it five hundred years ago and maybe used it in battle or even against one of my ancestors. And that life-long passion started when I was thirteen or fourteen, on a hill overlooking a creek where Indians once lived on our family farm!

After a summer on the farm, I would try to explain my experiences to my friends back in the city or the burbs. They simply could not understand and I don't think that they believed me. Even today, I try to explain my experiences to folks who have never been on the farm with no luck. If you have not been there and done that, you simply don't understand. For me, those experiences are indelible and shape everything that I do. I understand that life is both beautiful and dangerous and I prepare for both in everything that I do. I know that danger can be managed and there is satisfaction in managing it. But most people simply can't understand me when I always prepare for the best and the worst. And I can't understand them when they naively ignore the possibility of the dark side and only assume that everything will be fine. In the real world which is always lurking around the corner, they will not be prepared. And I am afraid that there is a major whuppin' coming and most people are simply not ready today.

One last note about the folks on the farm: A few years ago, we went back to the farm for my aunt's funeral. It was during the presidential election and the "elite" liberals of

New York and California were making fun of the heartland. They liked to refer to the middle of our country as "fly over country." They made fun of the values that are held in that part of the country like patriotism, honor, hard work, self-sacrifice, faith, etc. and they liked to call the people Hicks." I remember looking around me in the little country church in the middle of farmland where the service was being held. Many of the folks there wore their best bib overalls because that is the best they had, and the service was very simple, plain, and genuine. The meal afterwards was of fried chicken, biscuits and gravy and such. I remember thinking that if the elite could see this service; they would laugh and make fun of the hicks.

I have worked with the elites in San Francisco and New York City and I have worked hard with the folks on the farm in fly over country. I know the folks on the farm real well. There is no doubt in my mind about who has got it right and who I respect. They are the ones wearing the bib overalls!

Chapter Five

Hunting from the Arctic to the Swamp and How a Wild Boar Hunt Can Cure a Mid-Life Crisis

Like the farm and like life, hunting is on the one hand beautiful, exciting, and wonderful, and on the other hand dangerous, ugly, and terrible. Like the farm, hunting prepares you for the reality of life in a stark way. You must pay attention and know what you are doing and follow the laws of nature or you will be seriously hurt or possibly killed and eaten. The penalty for failure can be severe, but the joy of success and survival in the face of extreme challenge is intense. Quite frankly, the adrenaline rush of survival in extreme circumstances is absolutely addictive.

Hunting is not about killing, at least not for me. That is the least enjoyable part. In fact, when I killed my first animal, I cried. I was about six and I threw a rock at a robin and killed it. I felt terrible and ran to Mom. Even today I take no great pleasure in killing an animal although I have killed hundreds. So the question is, why do it?

Hunting to me is about experiencing the beauty and the challenge of nature—of testing your skills against nature and your prey. Can you survive and conquer the Arctic, Rockies, desert, or the swamp? Can you outwit your prey in the oldest competition in the history of the world? Can you make that four-hundred-yard shot? Can you control your fear, stay steady, and make the shot when you have only one chance, two seconds, and the price of failure is death? Actually killing the animal is sad, but it is the way of the world, natural competition, and life for a billion years. It is the way it is: in order to eat, we have to kill. Hunting is also multi facetted. It is the simple and relaxed joy of walking a cornfield with your dogs and hunting pheasant, and it is intense like hunting wild boar with a pistol where everything in the swamp is trying to bite you, cut you, sting you, kill you, and eat you every second that you are there.

To start this chapter off, I am going to share an article that I wrote for *Field and Stream* (they did not print it, but my buddies loved it) about a bear and moose hunt that my buddies and I went on in the Borealis Forest of Manitoba, Canada. Near the edge of the Arctic Circle and near the Northwest Territory, it is in beautiful territory. It gives a good flavor for the elements of a hunt.

They Ate My Tree Stand!
A true (most of it anyway) story about bear hunting in the subarctic

All hunters are liars. That accepted fact is fair warning to the reader. It all started when my two good hunting buddies (Drew and Mike) and I went to the Safari Club meeting in Wisconsin to look for our next out-of-body hunting experience. We hooked up with an outfitter who offered a good deal on a combined moose and bear hunt in the subarctic of Manitoba. After checking their references, we are in. Months of anticipation, working out to get in shape, buying gear, checking gear, studying bear and moose behavior and anatomy; we did all the normal pre-hunt prep and fidget.

After an 1,100-mile drive from Chicago and two hops in airplanes, we are 1,500 miles northwest of Chicago (I did not know that you could go 1,500 miles north of Chicago!). Finally I am walking in the woods with our guide Roy who is going to drop me off at my tree stand (for bear) and then take my buddy Mike out to moose hunt for the rest of the day. I am comforted by the fact that Roy and Mike promise to come back eventually with the boat (camp is five miles away by boat). Roy is commenting that they have been seeing significant bear sign and that there is a big guy in the area. As we are walking in the woods, I have to constantly make sure that I don't step in the bear sign which is purple, as they have been gorging themselves on the blueberries that are everywhere. This is cool! Then I see a pile of bear sign that is as big as a house. "That is the big guy," says Roy. No kidding. He is either the big guy or he needs to see a doctor.

As we get to the tree stand, a good-sized bear suddenly pops up twenty-five yards away and decides to check us out. Roy warns me that the bears up here are not afraid of humans and can be very aggressive. But he tells me that this is not the bear I want (it is only 300 pounds). The one I want is twice as big and I only have one bear tag! I remember the normal bear sign that I had seen compared to the big sign and realize if this is the normal guy, then the earth will shake when the big guy shows up. Whoa! And then contrary to the bear behavior books that we read, this bear shows no fear and starts walking right up to us to check us out. Mike and Roy wish me luck, split, and the bear follows them. I listen for screams and don't hear any so I assume that they made it. I hope so since they are my ride home.

Now I am alone in the subarctic, I know that there are bears, and I know that there is a big guy. This is going to be good. The Borealis Forest is beautiful with rolling hills and a white and pink carpet of lichen (moss) which covers everything on the ground. I am a little concerned about the bear's aggressiveness and lack of fear, but I am confident that I can handle it. Suddenly another bear pops up at thirty yards. I didn't hear him and he was just suddenly there—again, good-sized at 300 pounds, but not the big guy. He decides to stick around and I enjoy watching him. This is great. I turn around and behind me is another good-sized bear about twenty-five yards away. I didn't hear him either. He decides to stick around too. It seems like a lot of bears in one place. I turn to my right and there is another bear. I did not hear any of them coming. I am starting to feel like Custer at the Little Big Horn and I count how many cartridges I have. Eight does not seem like enough. Bears are everywhere.

Naturally, I am paying real close attention to all of those bears, but after an hour of no bear attack on my tree stand I am comfortable with my new friends. Since I have decided not to shoot them cause I am waiting for Big Guy, I enjoy watching them sun themselves, wrestle each other, and scratch their backs on my tree (we are talking real close). Suddenly all three of my new buddies stand up and face the same direction, stare, and then bolt. Big Guy. I see him now in the heavy brush and he is huge (at least to me anyway). He is a cinnamon color and he is probably seven feet from nose to tail and 600 pounds (this is my first bear hunt so all you guys who have shot ten-footers have to give me a break). I decide that I will not chance a shot yet because of the heavy brush that could deflect my bullet. The last thing I want to do is wound him and end up in that purple pile of bear sign. My heart is screaming and I promise myself that I will not blow this shot or shoot too early. He walks toward an open shooting lane thirty yards away. Twenty yards. Fifteen yards. Ten yards. The safety is off and my finger is on the trigger. Ten more feet and he is in the clear and mine. Then he sniffs the air and walks back into the bush. Wind shift and I am busted!

It takes about half an hour for the adrenaline to come off full throttle, and then my bear escorts return. And now that the big guy is gone, they are feeling spunky. They walk up to the tree stand and check me out. I have a camera in one hand and my rifle in the other. I got some great pictures as the bears are only ten to fifteen feet away. Then the biggest bear, at about five foot five and roughly three hundred pounds, decides to stand up. Both my hands are on the rifle now and the bear starts pushing my tree to knock me out of the tree stand. I am suddenly feeling like an apple during harvest. I don't like it as he is only seven feet from my boots! I push back, call him some nasty names and prepare to shoot him. And then he backs off for a minute. This is really fun!

I suddenly realize that it is dusk and it will be dark in half an hour or so. As much as I am enjoying the company, I decide that it is probably not a good idea to be walking out of the woods in the dark surrounded by bears. So I make a racket and get aggressive to move the bears and climb down the tree. As I start walking, I notice one of the bears about thirty-five yards away starts to follow me. Since I unloaded my gun to climb down the tree, I decide that this is a good time to reload. As I walk, my bear friend starts to close the gap. Thirty-five yards, thirty yards, and then twenty-five yards. At twenty yards I realize that I am now potentially part of the food chain. At fifteen yards the safety is off but I don't want to fire because I am saving the tag for Big Guy. At ten yards I decide that I have to fire and my finger is on the trigger. I try one last thing. Those bear behavior books said that when charged by a black bear, puff yourself up to appear bigger than you are and yell at the bear. A black bear will often back off. However, never do that with a brown bear because they will always attack if you do that. Or was it the other way around? Oh well, I would try it and hope for the best.

Fortunately our hunt is in Manitoba and not Quebec because when I yell "back off or I will blow your brains out" it is clear that the bear understands English and he backs off about ten more yards. I have had enough fun and get on the radio to see if my ride is on the way. Our other guide Dave answers that he is ten minutes away. Dave is a real pro and has been guiding bear hunts for twenty years. I am a little embarrassed to admit that I am concerned by the aggressive behavior of the bears, but I decide to ask Dave anyway. So I put on my best Tom Cruise, Top Gun *radio voice and ask Dave if it is normal for bears to try and knock you out of the tree stand and follow you out of the woods. I am expecting him to say that they always do that. I did not expect to hear, "holy shit, how close is he?" When I tell him that he is ten yards away again, Dave shouts "take the safety off and shoot him if he takes one more step closer to you." That is not the response that I am looking for.*

The bear and I do this dance another three or four times with me stopping, taking the safety off, yelling, and being prepared to shoot. Fortunately, each time the bear backs off at the last second. I am almost to the water when suddenly the bear disappears. In thick cover, I realize that I like things better when I can see the bear. Now I am real unhappy. About the time my heart is about to jump out of my chest, Dave tells me over the radio that the bear is at the edge of the lake eyeballing him. Nice sized bear says Dave. Don't I know it!

I am thrilled to be on the boat and heading back to camp as the sun goes down. Of course the guys love the story over drinks and we plan the next day's hunt. I tell Roy that I have decided to wait for the sun to come up before going in the woods again because the bears are so aggressive and I want to be able to see them. Roy says he understands but points out that I will be reducing my hunting time. Besides, he thinks that I will be safe in the dark. I like Roy; he is the salt of the earth, so I am seriously considering what he says. Then it occurs to me that Roy is a fireman for Winnipeg in his real job and he thinks that it is safe running in to burning buildings every day. Roy is clearly nuts and his opinion does not count. I tell him so and I think he gets a kick out of it.

Next day after the sun comes up, Dave drops me off at the edge of the lake. And this time I bring more ammo. After getting in my tree stand, I spend four more hours surrounded by bears but no Big Guy. But the local bears are regularly taking turns walking to my tree stand and checking me out like I look at a good T-bone steak at the grocery store. Eventually the bears and I take a lunch break and Dave meets me at the edge of the lake to take me to camp for lunch. When he brings me back and drops me off at the edge, he asks me to radio him to let him know all is okay. When I get back to the tree stand I call Dave before climbing the tree and tell him all is okay. We agree that we will meet at the edge of the lake just before sundown.

As I prepare to climb up, I notice green foam all over the place. While I wonder what it is, I am climbing the fifteen feet up and the tree stand is gone! The metal parts of the stand are still there, but the wooden seat and padding are gone. The bears ate my tree stand!

This was a plot. Just like the Alfred Hitchcock movie The Birds, *this is* The Attack of the Bears. *For two days they have been scouting me out, testing my defenses, and checking out my resolve. And now, they have forced me to the ground where they can charge me. I climb back down, reload my gun, and recount my cartridges. I brought twenty this time but I am beginning to think it is not enough, but at least I will go down fighting. Just like Custer.*

Now I am on the ground surrounded by bears that have made a habit of walking right up to my tree stand. They have always been so silent that I never heard them so now I have to constantly do 360-degree scans to make sure that they are not sneaking up on me. After about an hour of spinning I am getting a neck burn. I decide that I am no longer waiting for Big Guy. No doubt he will send a scout just before the attack so I decide to take the scout down when he shows up just to show them that I am not a pushover (easy for you to call me paranoid sitting in your nice and safe easy chair).

And here he comes, the scout, just as I thought! He is about 250-300 pounds, five feet six inches from head to tail, and thirty yards away. I hold off for a perfect broadside shot. The last thing that I want to do is track a wounded bear in the bush while his buddies are waiting to ambush me. I wait and wait for the right shot and suddenly realize that I have been so focused for ten minutes that I have not done my 360-screening check and the big guy could be right behind me ready to eat me. I do my 360 review one more time and decide to take the shot before I have a heart attack. This is really fun!

The sight picture is good as I pull the trigger and I am sure that the bullet will hit the heart/lung zone. The bear spins and for a second he seems to be charging right at me but then heads for the brush and disappears. Great! I jack another shell into the gun and go to the impact site looking for a blood trail and I see zip. Impossible. I saw the exit wound when he spun around right where it should be. Having no choice, I start to track him. I am really having a good time now and I paid big bucks for this! I say my thanks when after only twenty yards I see him lying motionless in a depression in the ground that I could not see from where I shot him. He is down hard with a perfect shot.

After confirming that he is dead by pressing the barrel of my loaded gun against his eyeball, I consider the fact that his buddies are really pissed now. I count my shells again. Nineteen does not seem like enough for the mass attack that I know is coming (I am not paranoid!). I have two more hours until Dave is back. So I get comfortable and sit on the dead scout and decide to talk to the other bears. "Nobody else has to die," I say to the bears that I know are out there. "Just leave me alone and we will all see the sunset." I keep this up for two hours and then the cavalry arrives! Dave calls on the radio and he is on the shore headed my way. I made it.

Over the radio, I tell Dave about the tree stand, the attack, and the dead bear. He tells me to stay loaded and immediately shoot any additional bear that I see. He sounds pretty excited which surprises me since he does this for a living. When he arrives, he is carrying his rifle which guides never do and he tells me not to take my eyes off the brush and to shoot any bear I see while he skins my bear. Apparently, this is extremely aggressive bear behavior and not normal. Hibernation is only a week away and the bears are desperately trying to pack on calories to survive the long winter and I represent 250 pounds of calories. These bears have never seen humans before and have no fear. This is exceptional behavior from the bears that most hunters never see says Dave. Aren't I lucky?

Well it makes a great story back at camp and Dave confirms what happened. I did not get the big guy, but I got more than my share of thrills. And now after the hunt and safely home, I am starting to miss the adrenaline rush. I know that those bow hunters who take 1,200-pound brown bears are saying what's the big deal? While I respect their courage, I have no doubt that they are nuts. But I do want to go back. Big Guy is still out there!

Okay, that is one of a hundred hunting stories but it shows all sides of a hunt. The beauty of the Borealis Forest, the excitement, danger, and ultimate reality of the laws of nature are all represented. By the way, that only represented half the hunt that trip; the other half involved moose hunting. While I did not get one, it was a magnificent experience. I will share one unforgettable moment with you. My guide (a Canadian RCMP state policeman or "mountie") and I found the tracks of a large bull moose and started to follow them. For several miles we followed him over magnificent hills, gorges, and across streams and bogs. We were at the top of the world next to the Arctic Circle and suddenly my guide stops and says to me, "You know, the odds are, no human being has stood on this ground before." How cool is that!

Let me talk a little about hunting and shooting. I have been hunting now for about fifty years. As I said, I first learned to use a gun at seven years old. I figure that I have fired 100,000 rounds over the years and I have been within a hundred feet of other people shooting over 3,000,000 rounds at shooting ranges, sporting clay, or trap ranges. I also figured that over the years and in all of my hunting trips, I have walked over 7,000 miles carrying a gun. To me, guns are simply a tool which one has to treat with respect. On the farm, there is a gun in every house and it is a tool like a shovel, ax, or hammer. Like any other dangerous tool, it has to be handled with respect and skill and it is. No big deal.

But like everything else in life, they can be dangerous. I have been at the wrong end of a gun four times (not bad out of 3,000,000 opportunities; that is better than six sigma!). The first time I was hit by a ricochet from a rifle when I was fifteen. I was with my buddies and loading my gun when I was hit in the groin and right where it counts. My friend who fired the shot did not understand when I suddenly dropped my rifle and shells and stuck my hand in my pants to check for blood. I decided right then and there that if my private parts were shot off, I was going to kill myself. I mean what is the point of living at fifteen if you can't have sex with girls? I had just discovered that year that sex involves two people!

Imagine my relief when I found no blood. I dropped my pants and there was a hell of a bruise but my zipper (which was ruined) stopped the momentum of the bullet (which I found) and prevented penetration. Well, my friend is wondering what the hell is happening and when I show him the bruise, bullet, and zipper he starts laughing. Now I am pissed. He shoots me (accidental ricochet that he could not have avoided), I am prepared to kill myself, and he thinks it's funny. I guess things could have been worse!

The other time I got shot was during dove hunting. I was hunting with a new hunter (very nice guy) and positioned myself at what I hoped was non-lethal range from his position because he was a novice hunter. I warned him about any shots toward me. Unfortunately I watched him track a dove that headed right to my position and I watched him pull the trigger and then I was hit. A Dick Cheney experience!

A few fascinating facts at how fast the brain works became apparent in this experience (now that I can calmly reflect upon it). I was maybe forty yards away and the shot was traveling at roughly 1,000 feet per second. That means that I was hit one-tenth of a second after I saw him pull the trigger and saw the smoke and shot leave the barrel. Let me catalog the thoughts and observations that went through my head in that brief span of time:

1) I am going to die.
2) My life does flash through my mind (not the first time if you will recall).
3) I should duck.
4) I distinctly remember hearing the shot after I saw the shot (speed of light vs. speed of sound).
5) I hear the shot hit the corn (I am two rows into the corn to hide from the doves).
6) I get hit.

All of that within one-tenth of a second. Amazing! The good news is that my judgment was correct and I was not within lethal range. I got hit in the chest and arms, but because I was wearing a heavy canvass hunting jacket, the shot was embedded in the canvas and did not penetrate. That makes two times that I have been shot and I don't really care for it. I was nearly hit on two other occasions and as a result, I am the safest hunter that you can imagine. Now some people might say, "Why don't you give up guns because they are clearly dangerous and you have nearly been killed by them." My response is, "Life is dangerous. I enjoy hunting and guns, and if I gave up everything that is dangerous, life would not be worth living." It is just the way it is. That is life!

I enjoyed hunting birds from an early age. It is hard to hit them, they can escape if they are good and you are off, and it is fair. Besides, there is no better eating than fresh pheasant, grouse, or dove. My friend Drew wanted me to move up to deer but I did not think using a gun on them was fair and I was not sure that I wanted to kill them. So we compromised on hunting them with bow and arrow in which you must get within forty yards to make a shot and that makes it very fair. So I practiced with my bow, put on my camouflage, found some good deer trails and rubs, put on fox urine to mask my scent, climbed up my tree stand at four in the morning, and spent six days and ten or twelve hours a day in the freezing sleet and rain waiting for the deer to get in range.

I saw a lot of deer but they knew exactly what forty yards is. The bucks would stand just out range, snort, paw the ground, look at me, and laugh. The does would come and lay down right under my tree stand (does are dumber than dirt) but I did not want to shoot a doe; I wanted to shoot a buck! That is what John Wayne would do. So I was forced to stay perfectly still for hours (in the sleet and wind) while a dumb doe was ten feet away. If I moved or coughed or did anything, she would jump up and run, scaring away the bucks that were just out of range. I hate does!

Well, I did not get my buck that year. But what I did get was severe walking pneumonia which lasted six months and made my life truly miserable. I bought a deer rifle the next year. I would have bought a grenade launcher if it was legal! And I have been deer hunting ever since. It is a thrill; the bucks are really smart, and if you get a buck, you deserve it. They are magnificent animals. You would have to see the miracle of a 250-pound buck with a huge rack of antlers running at full speed in deep brush in the dark without touching one tree or bush to believe it. Their sense of smell and hearing is simply awesome. They are majestic. And they are very tasty.

For those of you who have never been deer hunting, let me describe what it is like for responsible hunters (which are the majority). First, you are honor bound to do it right and legally. Second, it is not about the killing. Most important, it is about being with friends and sharing the joy of being in deer camp. The excitement and challenge is palpable as is the competition of who will get a buck playing by the rules. Nothing is worse than a cheater and there is no honor getting a buck improperly. So everybody does it right (or you find a different group of guys to hunt with).

Then there is the prep for the hunt, which builds the tension. Like taking your rifle to the range to make sure that you are on target. Getting your deer tags, camo, ammo, and latest scent to fool and draw in the bucks (my wife never got used to keeping fox and doe urine in the refrigerator prior to the hunt!). Next, you create your pre-hunt packing list (so that you don't forget anything like your rifle) and pack everything including gun and shooting supplies, clothes, survival gear, knife, binoculars, range finder, GPS, and maps, etc. Then there is going on-site before the hunt looking for deer sign, deer trails, and scrapes so that you can put your tree stand where the deer will be.

It is now opening day. You get up at 4:00 a.m. and it is pitch dark and probably twenty degrees outside. All the guys get up and have breakfast and the tension and excitement is high. We all get in trucks and head to the woods and get dropped off a quarter of a mile away from our individual tree stands so that any nearby bucks are not scared away by the truck.

What follows is hard to explain, but let me try. You are now alone in the woods. It is pitch dark and there are deer, bear, and coyotes around and you can't see any of them. You hope that you can find your tree stand in the dark and it is a good bit into the woods. A compass and the occasional reflective marker seem inadequate to getting you there. And you hear movement in the woods all around you. Is it a bear? Admit it or not, you are nervous. You are concerned about getting lost and being embarrassed. And you are worried that the noise to your left is a hungry bear with her cubs (very unlikely but we are talking emotion here).

Finally you get to the tree stand. It is fifteen feet high and you are alone. There's a slippery, flimsy metal ladder with a flimsy, tiny little seat (especially if you weigh 250 pounds). You know that most hunters that die during the deer hunt die from falling out of their tree stand. You tie your unloaded rifle onto the haul-up rope and you start your climb. When you get to the top, you put on your safety harness, pull up your rifle, load it, hunker down, and wait for the sun to rise an hour from now. You want an hour of quiet before the sun comes up to settle the bucks down. The woods are alive with noises that you think are deer, although the odds are it is squirrels looking for acorns and sounding like monster deer.

Finally you relax, and really take note of your surroundings. If you are lucky, it is clear, cold, and crisp with a light covering of snow (helps make the deer stand out, but not enough to muffle their footsteps). You feel intensely alive and your senses are at 110 percent. The stars and moon are incredibly bright and you feel as though you can touch them. You now have an hour to wait and you feel a sense of awe with nature and you reflect on the beauty of your surroundings. Even if you are not deeply religious, you feel closer to God and like you are in His presence. In my case, more so than I have ever felt in church.

The sun gradually comes up and shadows turn into clear images. At first your adrenaline is high and you know that your best odds for a buck are in the morning of opening day. Gradually your intensity dulls with time and you have to force yourself to stay sharp. If you are very lucky, a magnificent buck now walks within range. Your heart nearly jumps through your chest. Will it come into range? Will you get a clear shot? Can you control yourself and make a steady shot? Finally the sight picture is right, and you know that it is a safe shot (critical as your bullet can travel three miles) with a high probability of a clean kill. And you take it.

The best way that I can describe how you feel when you kill a magnificent buck (at least me) is to refer to the movie *The Last of the Mohicans* with Daniel Day Lewis. He shoots a magnificent elk and as he approaches the dead animal with his Indian brother, they apologize for killing it, praise its majesty, and thank it for providing them food. Exactly! You also feel proud that you mastered the hunt, found the right spot, found your tree stand, stayed alert, drew in the buck, and made the shot despite being on an adrenaline high (buck fever).

That is one type of hunt. To give you some contrast, let me share an article I wrote on a wild boar hunt in the swamps of Savannah. It shares the intensity of the feelings that you experience on a dangerous hunt. It is from the hunter's perspective and no doubt the intensity of the emotions of the time color the memories of the experience. I am not sure that an unbiased observer would have seen things exactly the same way as I did, but the following is my perspective of an exciting hunt.

Wild Boar Hunting
The Perfect Antidote for a Mid-Life Crisis

Remember the Peggy Lee song, "Is That All There Is?" Something about turning forty makes us all temporarily insane. It certainly happened to me.

Here I was forty years old with a great wife and son, and an interesting and well-paying job as executive vice president of a multi-million dollar company. You would think that I would be happy with my lot in life. I was not. Somehow I thought that there should be more, that I had not reached my full potential, and that I was now on the down side of my life. Mid-life crisis!

Then my hunting buddy Drew called me up and asked if I was interested in wild boar hunting in the swamps of Savannah, Georgia. He said we would use pistols and that it would be pretty dangerous. These aren't just feral (escaped domestic) hogs; these are genuine and wild Russian boars from stock imported a hundred years ago. My reply was "Perfect, it is just what I need to get out of my funk." I asked approval from the boss. She knew what I was going through and said that if it was a choice of chasing strange women or hunting wild boar to get through the crisis, I had better get my gun. What a wife!

Next was the always fun part of the hunt—buying the gear. Snake chaps, swamp boots, speed loaders, and jungle fatigues were the order of the day. We had a great time at Gander Mountain.

Drew's friend was going hunting with us and he was an old hand at boar hunting, having gone ten times. He told us that it was very dangerous and that he would not take us until we could pass his marksmanship standards. He wanted six out of six rounds to hit an eight-inch target at twenty-five yards. I am an okay shot but not that consistent. So we spent a fair amount of time at the range. After a while I could meet the standard with my Smith and Wesson .357 magnum with a six-and-a-half inch barrel. I was sure that the .357 was adequate for the job (wrong, bring a .44 magnum).

Well, we were ready, trained, and outfitted. It was time to go. When we arrived in Savannah, we had some interesting surprises, like when we got picked up by our guide at the airport. If you saw the movie Deliverance, *you knew our guide. Then my buddy Drew made things interesting. Drew is a good hunter but also a very civilized and European kind of guy (he likes his luxury and creature comforts). So our guide does not understand that Drew brought his "purse" with him. But when the guide refused Drew's request to take a picture of him and Drew asked if he is afraid that the camera would steal his soul, I sensed that we were off on the wrong foot.*

In fact our guide lacked some of "the customer is king" attitude that we have all become used to in the civilized world. For instance, he told us that he was not happy about this trip. It was September and still hot, which means that the alligators were still very active. He was very concerned about losing a prime hunting dog to the gators. There was no mention of our well-being. He also warned us that if we accidentally shot one of his dogs if attacked by a boar, we would not come out of the swamp alive. This is not the kind of customer service approach that I was accustomed to in the Chicago area.

Somehow we avoided a gunfight with our guide and headed to camp. Remember Deliverance. *I kid you not, that was camp. Dinner was being prepared by one of the guides who had just lost three fingers to a boar that he thought was dead the prior day, which then attacked him (boar tusks are razor sharp). We are talking bloody stumps and bandages while cooking our food. Drew started things off in a friendly way by making fun of this poor fellow's bad luck. I pulled Drew away and suggested that it is usually not a good idea to piss off the cook. After all, who knows what nasty things he might do to our food? Drew didn't get it, so I walked over to the cook, apologized for Drew, and suggested that if he felt that he needed vengeance, please don't mix up Drew's food with mine. Every man for himself in the swamp!*

After dinner, one of the guides asked Drew and me if we wanted to go gator hunting that evening. Now I don't know anything about gator hunting, but I figure that if the guide is suggesting it, it must be okay. So we expressed interest in joining him and we started getting ready for the hunt. Right up to the point when he said, "when we are in the middle of the swamp (in the dark) if I start running, it is critical that you keep up with me because I won't come back for you." I was confused and asked him why he would do that. "Well," he says, "sometimes the DNR (Department of Natural Resources) shows up and we don't want to get caught." Turns out that it is illegal to hunt alligators and there is a $20,000 fine (more or less). We elected to pass on the gator hunt. Picture Deliverance. *You can hear the banjos playing.*

I woke up the next morning to see our guide wrapping duct tape around the top of his boots. When I asked him why, he told me that it is to keep out the leeches. Now we are having fun. I have some experience with leeches and I don't like them! We had breakfast (fresh gator and eggs, no kidding) and moved out to the swamp.

The hunting ground is a vast salt marsh that used to be a rice plantation a hundred years ago. It stinks from rotting vegetation (swamps and rotting vegetation go hand in hand). There is seven-foot-high razor grass everywhere. Razor grass is as sharp as its name suggests and any exposed flesh gets nasty, painful cuts that tend to fester. Because it is a tidal swamp (water level goes up and down with the tide), there is mud everywhere. The mud is at least six inches deep and in some places the mud is four feet deep (I got to experience that personally). The razor grass is so thick that you would not see a wild boar, alligator, or poisonous snake until you stepped on them.

We piled in to a john boat and started cruising the swamp. The prime hunting dogs piled in with us. They are the ugliest, foulest dogs that have walked the earth. Our guides get them from the dog pound and they turn them loose on the boars and the swamp. Those that are aggressive, that track and attack boar, will come home. Those that don't, become gator food. Our guide reminds us of the penalty for accidentally shooting one of these thoroughbreds in the heat of battle. While he can get us to the swamp, he doesn't have to bring us out. Again, a clever adaptation of customer service.

Traveling the swamp, we saw numerous gator slides where good-sized gators had slid down the banks to get to the water. This added some interesting ambience. Suddenly the dogs picked up the scent of a boar and we piled out into the swamp, mud, and razor grass. Delightful. The boars were there and you could hear them, but not see them. They were popping their jaws in anger and warning and it sounded like there was a herd of them. Ominously, the razor grass started moving as the boars made their move. We were nervous, couldn't see anything, and we were worried about gators, poisonous snakes, and boars. I was most worried about two nervous guys (my hunting buddies) with cannons in their hands. Having been shot twice, I was concerned that the third time would not be good.

It was about this time that our guide decided to tell us where to shoot a boar when we get a chance. First he says, don't bother to shoot them in the head because they have armored skulls to protect them from the tusks of a rival boar. Second, forget the front of the chest for the same reason. This is important information that nobody told us until now! This is getting better all of the time. To make it even better, the guide tells us about how smart boars are, and how in Europe they would get wolves to follow them and the boars would encircle them, kill them, and then eat them. Great!

Somehow the boars got away that time. We were in seven-foot razor grass with no visibility. We started walking. It was now 90 degrees and 100-percent humidity. The razor grass was cutting us everywhere. Everything in the swamp wanted to bite us, cut us, sting us (poisonous millipedes and spiders), and eat us. We are really having fun now. And we paid for this!

After several hours of this delightful hike, I was hoping that someone would accidentally shoot me in the head to put me out of my misery. I was dying. We decided to split up to increase our odds. Drew and his buddy got in one boat (two guns and a buddy) and I was alone with the guy from Deliverance *and I have the only gun. Great. We start to cruise the shore again in the boat. My guide pointed out a ten-foot gator in the water as we passed it (how could you miss a ten-foot gator?). It was huge and fat. I have seen plenty of gators before but they are usually in the five-foot range and much skinnier. At ten feet, it was much more than twice as big overall. It had my full attention.*

We went a hundred yards and the guide said that this is where we would get out of the boat. It was waist-deep water. I wanted to be one of the boys, but I had to ask him about that ten-foot gator that we just passed. "What are you worried about?" he says. "You have the gun." Now that is true. But the water is murky and I could not see the gator until he had me in his jaws. But I am not going to let this cracker get the best of me, so I press on. I decided that if we get attacked by the gator, I am going to shoot the guide first, then the gator. After all, I have nothing against the gator; he is just being a gator. For the rest of the afternoon we covered a lot of swamp and I hear about how Yankees (that is me) usually pee their pants when things get dangerous. I was beginning to come to the conclusion that the guide is about to have a fatal accident.

It is then dusk and time to head home. I have spent thirteen hours in the swamp. I am cut to shreds from the razor grass, and am having muscle cramps in my legs from walking in the mud and from the heat, humidity, and dehydration. I also desperately want to kill my guide much more than any boar! We got in the boat and started heading home. And then that fine specimen of a hunting dog caught the scent of a wild boar. He leapt off the boat and started pursuit. I jumped out of the boat on the other side and landed in mud up to my armpits. Excellent! It took everything that I have to get out of the mud and I followed the dog's path through the razor grass. My legs were cramping badly and I wondered if I was going to make it. It seemed to take forever.

And then I saw the wild boar. He was an excellent boar with a huge head and large tusks; a blue boar (dark coloring with a bluish tint) which is the prize. At about 275 pounds, he was all head and shoulders. He was in a creek fighting the dog and did not notice me. I could tell that both the boar and the dog were already exhausted from fighting each other in the deep swamp mud, but he was still plenty dangerous (remember the cook who lost his fingers to the dead boar that attacked him). Suddenly I am not tired. I went temporarily insane and decided that either I was going to kill the boar or he was going to kill me. No other outcome and nothing else mattered. I jumped into the creek right behind the boar and the guide called the dog off. The boar was six feet away and then started to turn around to get me.

This is where time stands still and nanoseconds turn into hours. I am sure that from the time the boar started to turn until the time that I shot him could not have lasted for more than two seconds. And in those two seconds I experienced an hour's worth of thoughts and observations. First, I debated with myself where I should shoot the boar. Even a perfect heart/lung shot would take too long to kill him. He could be dead on his feet and still rip my guts out with his tusks and kill me before he dropped.

The adrenaline had kicked in and I noticed that my senses were incredibly sharp and I was struck by how intense all of my surroundings seemed. The stench of the swamp was overpowering. The sky was deep blue with incredibly white puffy clouds. The boar looked and sounded meaner and nastier than imaginable. I could feel the blood surging through my veins. There was a coppery taste in my mouth and I felt like I had the strength of ten men (called the "fight or flight reflex"). I felt invincible. I thought about all of these things in the two seconds it took to make a decision as to where to place the shot.

I decided to shoot him in the brain stem before he completed his turn. It would drop him instantly and it was an easy target to find at the base of his skull. If I was successful, that is. If I missed, I assumed that he would probably kill me. I had one chance and I took the shot.

The boar dropped instantly like a load of cement. Perfect shot. I pulled back the hammer of my pistol in case I needed a second shot but I knew I didn't. And suddenly a great wave of reality washed over me as I realized that I could have been killed. And part of my insanity was driven by this damn guide that had been driving me nuts all day. With the hammer pulled back on my .357, I looked him right in the eye and very quietly asked him if I needed to do any more shooting today.

This old boy was smarter than he looked. He knew exactly what I meant and how I felt. He said, "No sir Mr. Rossi. That was a fine shot. As good a shot as I have seen. Why don't you rest on the creek bank and let me field dress that boar for you." He then pushed the boar's head under water to make sure that it was dead. I am not sure what I would have done if he had lipped off. I worry about it sometimes.

We dragged the boar to the boat (did I mention the mud?) and headed home. By now the sun is at the horizon and it is beautiful—big and blood-red. I am alive and I have an excellent blue Russian wild boar.

I should be thrilled. But I am not. I am numb. Not because I was afraid of the boar, but because I realized that I had been prepared to risk everything for a stupid pig. That is what was scary.

We met back at camp and Drew and his buddy were excited for me. They did not get a boar but had some pretty hairy times as well. Drew's buddy told us that six months from now we will want to come back because we will miss the adrenaline rush. Drew and I pulled aside and decided to call our wives. We agreed that we would never come back because this was nuts. I called Evelyn and told her that if I said that I wanted to go wild boar hunting again, she should bench-slap me. And I meant it.

Next morning all was well. We had fresh venison and eggs for breakfast that was shot the night before (no, it was not deer season). Time has softened my bad memories from the day before and I am reveling in the fact that I got a prize boar. We headed out to hunt again and I was excited again. I have nothing to prove and I can relax. We headed for the swamp. This time it is a traditional bayou type of swamp with trees and Spanish moss. We are wading in about two feet of water. I ask if we should not wear our snake chaps since this is perfect water moccasin territory. The guide says not to worry about it because the boars eat all of the snakes in the area (these are tough critters). We find that there are deep gator holes in the swamp as we occasionally go under water when we step in one. Leeches are the side benefit of this experience.

Since I have gotten my boar I am an observer and helper although I do have my .357 in my shoulder holster in case I need it. Suddenly the dogs catch the scent of boar and we are off to the races. When we catch up to them we see that they are fighting a nice-sized wild boar. One of the dogs has been slashed across the throat by the boar's tusk and is bleeding like crazy. No doubt that he will fall dead in a few minutes (he doesn't and the guide sews him up later). It is a terrific fight between boar and dogs and Drew sneaks up to get a shot. He uses a tree to shield him and gets within a few feet of the boar. The guide calls the dogs off and Drew takes a perfect heart/lung shot. I am thirty feet away and directly in front of the boar and I have a perfect view of the action.

When Drew takes the shot, the boar immediately looks straight up—at me. We lock into each others eyes and he takes off like a freight train right at me. Again time stands still. My first thought when I looked into those eyes is that they look like the eyes of the devil. Black, beady eyes that say I am going to kill you. The only thing I can compare it to is the eyes of a shark. For anybody who dives and has looked into the eyes of a shark, you know what I am talking about.

My second thought is hey, why are you mad at me? I did not shoot you, Drew did. Go after him. My third thought is that a wild boar is charging me and my pistol is in my shoulder holster. Don't I feel stupid! In the one second that has passed I think all of this and I then see Drew step aside from the tree and swing his .357 in an arc toward me. The arc of his swing carries the gun toward my head. Looking into the barrel of a loaded .357 that is pointed at you is not a pleasant experience especially if you have been shot before. I am no longer worried about the boar; Drew is going to put me out of my misery. But Drew continues his swing and fires as the arc of the swing has the .357 in line with the boar. Suddenly the boar collapses. A perfect shot to the spine that instantly drops him.

It takes a second for me to get my act together and I notice that I had reached for my pistol, released the safety strap, and started to pull it out. I had not even been aware of the fact that I had done it. I would not have made it though; the boar was too close and coming too fast. Drew probably saved my life.

Suddenly, my mid-life crisis is over. The overwhelming feeling was one of joy. Just being alive is a wonderful thing. All of those other worries were silly and irrelevant. I was blessed! I have a great wife and son, good friends, and an interesting, prestigious, and well paying job. What else could anybody ask for? I have never had those mid-life crisis blues again. And I still get a kick out of just being alive.

But we are not through with the excitement yet. Our wonderful guide (that I should have shot the previous day) thought it would be funny to try and pretend that he was lost in the swamp. So as we headed out of the swamp, our genius of a guide tried to confuse us by taking different routes and then he really did get lost. We are in the middle of a swamp, the sun is going down, and I am looking for a dry spot to spend the night. Right after I shoot that SOB. Our fearless guide climbs a tree (you can't see anything because you are under a solid canopy of trees) and sees a plane heading for the airport far in the distance. Now that he has his bearings, we get out of the swamp and are soon headed home. Important lesson: always have a compass and maps even if you have a guide. Don't trust anyone.

We got home and I promised my wife that I would never hunt wild boar in the swamp that way again. And I meant it at the time. But then after about a year, I got my boar back from the taxidermist and as I held it and remembered the thrill of the hunt, I remembered what Drew's friend told us: "You will miss the adrenaline rush and you will want to come back." And he was right!

Well I could tell a hundred more hunting stories but this chapter is getting long and I will cover some of my other tough hunts in the next chapter. Let's close this chapter with the simple pleasure of bird hunting and then why after fifty years, I have stopped hunting.

Bird hunting can be a civilized and gentlemen's form of hunting. It can be a day hunt walking a corn field hunting pheasant or it can be in the woods hunting ruffed grouse or woodcock during the fall with all of the glory and beauty of changing autumn leaves. Walking with your friends, you may cover five or ten miles depending on the day, but it is good exercise with spurts of excitement when the birds burst from the ground. We tried to do it ten times a year if we could. Possibly the best part (next to being with your friends) is being with our partners, the bird dogs. They are phenomenal and they are like little kids. They live to hunt. When they are let out of the truck they will run around for five minutes with pure energy in anticipation of the hunt. But when it is time to hunt, they are pure business and they work hard.

These dogs have incredible noses and they will run back and forth sniffing the air for microscopic traces of scent but always staying within twenty yards of the hunters. We generally used pointers (German Short Hairs and other breeds) that are trained to not flush the bird when they find them but to "point" them out to the hunter. They freeze facing the bird with their tail held rigidly behind them. And they will hold that position until the hunter bumps them to proceed. As I said, they are like little kids and it takes every bit of will power for them not to jump the bird. They actually shake with excitement while they are pointing. Once the hunter says okay, they will charge the bird and if all goes well, a beautiful cock pheasant with long flowing tail feathers bursts into the air with a fury of feathers and sound to make his escape. The pheasant is soon flying at twenty or thirty miles an hour and you have just three to five seconds to make the shot before he gets out of range.

There is excitement and everybody has to be disciplined so that nobody gets shot but the bird (including the dog!). Your heart is pumping with excitement, your friends are watching, and you don't want to blow it. It is bad enough to be embarrassed in front of your friends, but if you miss, the dogs will humiliate you. They look forward to finding the downed bird and bringing it back to their master after the shot. There is nothing worse than missing the shot and having a dog look at you with the clear message that you are a twit for missing his bird!

My best story on bird hunting is when four friends and I took Duke ruffed grouse hunting in northern Wisconsin. Duke is a great German Short Hair professional and Drew and I took the 5th place with Duke in the Southern Wisconsin Pheasant competition. It was early in the season and we hunted all day through the woods and got several grouse. By the way, grouse are absolutely the best-tasting bird there is. And when they suddenly burst from the cover of the woods, you swear you will have a heart attack, and they always manage to put a tree between you and them in less than two seconds! Anyway it was the end of the day, and we were walking back to the truck when suddenly Duke could not walk. He whined and tried hard, but he just could not walk. We were afraid that we must have accidentally shot him or simply worked him too hard. We should have known better, you don't work Duke hard, he works himself hard!

We took Duke home and he would not eat. Now we were worried. So five, big bad hunters take turns sleeping with Duke in a bunk bed to make sure that he makes it through the night okay. The next morning Duke still can't walk. We decided to go hunting and leave Duke in the cabin so he could rest. But as Duke saw us getting our guns and gear, he started walking on his "elbows" because he wants to join us on the hunt. That rips it. Our hearts are broken and we decide to skip hunting and take Duke to the vet. It is embarrassing to see five big guys choking up over a dog. But he is our hunting buddy.

We get Duke to the vet just as the vet is putting another dog to sleep. Duke sees this and doesn't say anything. Then the vet asks us to put Duke on the table so he can check him out. He explains that there is a lubricating gland in a dog's ass that gets clogged occasionally causing constipation and he wants to check it out. So he puts on a rubber glove, sticks his finger up Duke's butt, and suddenly Duke jumped off the table and ran around the room wagging his tail in frenzy. You can almost hear Duke saying "between putting a dog down and sticking a finger up my butt, I have had enough of this crap!" The vet told us that all was well; Duke was just out of shape this early in the season and just needed an aspirin. You have never seen happier guys!

The other great bird hunting memory is when I took my son Ben hunting for the first and last time. Not an elaborate trip, just a day trip on a bright sunny day in Wisconsin. Ben was about thirteen and although he had been shooting BB guns, this was his first hunting trip. He was excited (not as much as me) and I let him use my 20 gauge to keep the recoil down. I watched him like a hawk and was never one foot from his side. He did great and knocked down two out of the four pheasants that the dogs put up for him. Now Ben was like all teenagers and he would argue about everything, but on this trip he was perfect. He was safe, handled the gun like I asked, and he never argued once. Afterwards I complimented him on his great behavior. He said, "Dad, of course I behaved. You had a gun"! He enjoyed that hunting experience, but with his sports and his school interests we never went together again. And now with his career and girlfriend there just isn't time. But for one day I got to be the proud dad who showed him how much fun hunting can be and watched him knock down his first pheasant.

Finally, why did I quit hunting after almost fifty great years in the field? Here is the deal. We were on my second elk hunt in Colorado last year. Our camp was at 12,000 feet; it was November and cold, and we had had a bear in camp that had tried to break into the cabins. The first night I got up at 3:00 a.m. with food poisoning and had to walk outside to the outhouse which was twenty-five yards away from camp. Feeling lousy and in my long johns, I put on my boots and strapped on my .44 magnum in case the bear showed up. I am sitting on an ice-cold steel toilet seat having terrible cramps and other "stuff," and I am holding my flashlight in my mouth pointed at the door because I have my .44 pointed at the door in case the bear decides to join me. Suddenly I have an epiphany. I am fifty-five years old, I am freezing my ass off, I have to worry about being eaten by a bear again, and I paid big bucks for this! I suddenly realize that I could be sailing in the Mediterranean with my wife drinking a rum and coke and sitting on a warm toilet seat for less money!

Just to make sure that I got the message; fate had me spend most of the next day with my pants off doing that same nasty business in the rain, sleet, and then snow. I felt horrible from the food poisoning, plus I was cold and wet and I did not give a damn if I ever saw an elk. Finally after having enough fun and freezing my ass off as the sun went down, I built a huge bonfire to stay warm until it was time to leave the field. As a hunter you have to know that is not a good way to attract elk and our guides were to say the least, very unhappy. I did not give a damn (one of the benefits of being an old fart!). I was done.

That is the official version and it is all true. But that is not the only reason I quit. In addition to that, I decided that I have just killed enough game. I was not driven to make the kill like I used to be. Part of it was that my shooting skills were not what they used to be as my eyesight got worse with age. My physical stamina was not what it used to be at 12,000 feet. And if I can't excel at something, I don't want to play. Finally the ambiance was gone. My last two hunts were with too many guys, the wrong kind of guys, the wrong kind of behavior, with too much drinking and driving, too much drinking and guns, and just too much drinking. The total focus was on killing animals any way possible, not the simple and quiet joy of being in the wilderness and hunting in the spirit that I like to hunt. I simply did not want to be part of that style of hunting. And I really would rather be sailing in the Mediterranean with my wife now.

But those fifty years in the wilderness or on the pheasant fields were great and I loved every minute of it even when I was part of the food chain. Who knows? Under the right circumstances, I may be back!

Chapter Six

Mother Nature Is a Bitch and She Will Try to Kill You

Those are pretty hard words and I mean no offense to Mother Nature. But they are true. Of course everybody talks about the beauty of Mother Nature and that is true as well. We have all seen the beauty of a sunset or sunrise (you should see it at 12,000 feet in the Rockies or in the middle of the ocean). On TV there is always the focus on the beauty and innocence of the mountains, forests, etc. That part of Mother Nature is well known and it is obviously true. But those of us who spend time in the wilderness or on top of, or under blue water, know that if you are not paying attention, if you are not prepared, or if you break the laws of nature, Mother Nature will kill you. Hell, she may kill you if you do everything perfectly. Nothing personal, it's just the way it is. That side of Mother Nature is usually not well publicized in the media and most folks simply don't understand that it is always there. But everyone needs to know about the other side of Mother Nature.

I will share a cosmic truth of the universe with you: Once you have looked into the eyes of an animal that is trying to kill you to eat you, your life changes forever (assuming that you survive). You suddenly understand that you are nothing special, you have to survive in the food chain like anything else, you are mortal, and death is always possible. It is the ultimate reality check. You understand that in the natural world you don't have any inalienable rights; there is no appeal, no do-over. If you fail, you can die. And Mother Nature has an endless number of ways of killing you.

That sounds scary, but it is not so scary once you understand it, accept it, and prepare for it. In fact, it is stimulating. Our ancestors knew this truth and dealt with it as a basic part of living because it is a fact of life. Unfortunately, most of us live in a technologically sheltered world and we have lost touch with the laws of nature. But as the folks in New Orleans and those that survived the tsunami now know, the laws of nature are always out there waiting.

The wilderness and blue water are always potentially hostile. The most consistently threatening environment I have been in was the swamp. As I said earlier when describing our wild boar hunt, every minute I was in the swamp, I felt something was always trying to bite me, cut me, sting me, kill me, and eat me. But all of the wilderness can be dangerous whether it is the desert, mountains, the north woods, or the Arctic. You can fall, starve, freeze to death, get eaten by animals, drown, get poisoned, or just get sick and die because the nearest doctor is 500 miles away.

Gosh, how can that be fun? Because you can conquer the wilderness if you are strong, if you are prepared, if you are equipped, if you have the knowledge, and most importantly if you can control your fear and do the right thing (luck helps too)! And there is no greater rush than beating Mother Nature when she throws her best at you.

Wild boar hunting in the swamp was one story of a very tough environment. But let me share another, and that was our caribou hunt at the southern edge of the Arctic Circle in Quebec. More then 1,600 miles north of Chicago, we landed by float plane at the water's edge of our camp. With no other humans for many, many miles, we were on our own in the tundra when the plane left us for the week. It was beautiful but stark rolling country with almost no cover. The largest trees were about ten to twelve feet tall because the growing season is so short.

I found out on our first day how hostile the environment can be. We had all four seasons that day and every day: snow in the morning, sunshine and maybe fifty degrees for a few hours, and then thirty-knot winds, sleet and rain, and then snow—and then all over again. They say that there is no weather forecast in the Arctic because that is where the weather starts.

Just two days into the hunt, all my survival skills paid off. I was five miles from camp and alone. I was walking in some treacherous and craggy limestone covered with slippery lichen resulting in real bad footing when the wind kicked up to thirty knots and the sleet began. I was wearing a frame backpack and just as my foot got caught in a limestone crack, the wind kicked up behind me and blew me over my own leg. I was certain my leg would break but I could do nothing about it because my backpack was acting like a sail in the strong wind. Suddenly there was a loud snap, a flash of lightening in my brain from the pain, and I was unconscious.

When I came to I couldn't breathe from the pain, and I couldn't see because of the flashes of light in my brain caused by the pain (very weird experience). I was certain that I had broken my leg. Having gone through first aid training, I also knew that I could have a compound fracture and I could be bleeding to death if the bone punched through my leg and cut an artery. And I was five miles from camp, with bears and wolves in the area, and my buddies didn't know where I was. I could freeze to death. What to do?

When you go to the wilderness, your survival depends on you. So you must be prepared. I was and that made the difference. Survival rule number one is to attack the most immediate threat first. Once I controlled the pain, I checked to see if I was bleeding from the fracture because it is possible to bleed to death in five minutes or less. Luckily, it was not a compound fracture and there was no obvious bleeding. Next, because I was injured and not mobile, I had become part of the food chain. I crawled to my rifle and was greatly comforted by the fact that I had twenty rounds with me (some of which could be used to call for help). I could defend myself.

The next threat was exposure. Wet, cold, and in thirty-knot winds, one can freeze to death quickly. But I had brought a space tent and a space blanket which weighed just a few ounces each and I could survive for days with them. Plus I could make a fire because I had brought fire-making tools and fuel.

The next threat was water but I had a canteen full of water and water purification pills (not really required in the Arctic because the water is usually good because of the cold). Finally food. You can survive for a few weeks without food but I had brought survival rations just in case anyway.

I now had the comfort and security of knowing that I was prepared to handle each of the immediate threats to my life. I didn't panic because I was prepared. And I could now make reasoned, rational decisions because I was in control. Being prepared did not happen by accident. Knowing that the wilderness is dangerous, I have taken survival training and first aid. I had prepared and brought the tools needed to survive. But the key was that I understood that bad things can happen and I prepared for them (thank you days on the farm).

Panic and ignorance is what usually kills people in the wilderness. Simple things can save your life if you can just stay in control and come prepared. Now that I was in control, I decided to cut down a small tree and make a crutch and then try to walk back to camp. I did and found that I could, in fact, walk. And just to put icing on the cake, one of the camp guides suddenly showed up and I was no longer alone. It was not pretty or quick, but we made it back to camp before dusk and life was good. But for thirty minutes or so, I was alone and hurt in the Arctic and I thought that my survival depended on staying in control and making the right choices. There are not always happy endings in the wilderness!

Turns out that I did not break my leg, but I did rip several of the muscles and ligaments in it. We kept cold water from the lake (forty degrees or so) on the leg all night and I took some muscle relaxants that we brought just in case (along with first aid kits, and other meds). By next morning the swelling was down a lot although the bottom of my foot was completely purple from all of the blood that drained down from the tears in my muscles and ligaments. But I was alive and I could even hunt. That next day I walked sixteen kilometers on my crutch looking for caribou (I paid cash money for this hunt)!

A few days later I was once again alone (still walking with my crutch) and about five or six miles from camp. No cover and suddenly the wind kicked up again to about thirty knots accompanied by sleet. After about thirty minutes of this, I became worried about hypothermia. Then I spotted a huge boulder in the distance. About eight feet high, it was magnificent and it was dropped there by the last ice age. It looked better than the Ritz! I got to the lee side of the boulder and I was then sheltered from the wind and rain. I built a fire, ate some lunch, and life was good. Hypothermia can kill, but if you know what to do, you can survive. I have stayed at a

Doge's palace in Venice and I could not tell you what it looked like now. But I have pictures of that glorious boulder and I will never forget what it looked like!

At the end of our trip, Mother Nature wanted to remind us again who the boss was. We were out of food (more important, we were out of beer) and the float plane was going to pick us up early the next morning. We were anxious to get home. Winter was due in about a week and then the Arctic would be uninhabitable (at least for us) until spring. The next morning the wind was over fifty knots and heavy with sleet. They told us over the radio that the float plane almost crashed taxiing out for a takeoff and it was unsafe to fly. No plane today. Remember the part about being out of food (and beer) and the coming uninhabitable winter in the Arctic in a week? Well, we gathered some blueberries out on the tundra, scrounged for food in camp, and fortunately the plane was able to come the next day. But it doesn't always work out that way!

If you are with Mother Nature enough, you will see her fury and you will know that she can kill you any number of ways. For instance, my wife and I have been through two tornados. One went right over our tent while camping and another one went over our sailboat while we were tied at the dock. And yes, it is true that it sounds just like a freight train! Because we have wind instruments on our boats, we know that the wind speed reached about ninety miles per hour at our dock. As tornados go, that is a mild one. But for ninety seconds or so, we thought our 8,000-pound boat was going to go airborne. The noise was horrific and the boat was heeling at least forty-fivedegrees, and that ninety seconds seemed like an eternity. After the storm passed, I remember thinking "thank goodness I paid the extra bucks for those thicker dock lines!" I bought them assuming the worst case scenario!

The power of Mother Nature is indescribable and I will share another example of it. While sailing in the Caribbean with four friends, we got caught in hurricane-force winds. It was a bright and beautiful day, the forecast was good, and we were thirty miles from land sailing between two islands. Suddenly the sky turned completely black to the northeast and we could see three(!) water spouts dancing across the front, and that is not good (even though I knew we were in trouble, I had to take a picture because it was so awesome). We knew that this was serious and we turned on our VHF radio. We immediately picked up a Mayday call from a fifty-foot trawler with five souls on board. They said the wind was at hurricane force, they were taking on water in heavy seas, and the pumps couldn't keep up with the water which was approaching their batteries (once the water hit the batteries they would lose power). They were pleading for help. And then the radio went dead. We found out later they were all lost at sea.

We tried to pass on the word about the trawler on the radio and reached a sailboat that we had met earlier in the day. They had just been hit by one of the water spouts which ripped off their boom. They were fighting to stay alive and they told us that they couldn't talk anymore. So we knew what was coming and we knew that we were in deep trouble. Our boat had a hull speed of six knots so we couldn't run away from it. What to do?

Each guy reacted differently to the coming threat. For me, since we couldn't run or hide, a peaceful calm settled in. What would be would be. So we battened down the hatches, shortened sail, did all the preparation that we could, and then popped a cold beer as we waited for our fate to be decided. It could be our last beer and it was damn good. There was nothing else that we could do.

Since very few people have experienced sailing through hurricane-force winds, I will share the experience. When it hits, the blue sky turns to a deep and dark grey. The calm seas suddenly grow to fifteen-foot breaking waves. It would have been worse but we were in relatively shallow water (ninety feet). There is nothing like looking up at dark green water as it breaks over your stern! The wind is incredible. We had a hand-held wind speed indicator with a maximum readout of seventy-five miles an hour which represents hurricane force. I brought it out because I was curious what the wind speed was, and it pegged at seventy-five miles an hour so we knew that we were in hurricane-force winds. Thirty miles away on shore the wind hit about ninety miles an hour according to the paper the next day and they reported extensive wind damage on shore.

But that does not begin to describe the sensations. Picture this: It is raining very hard and the rain is completely horizontal because of the wind. The wind is blowing the top one or two feet off the waves creating a solid wall of white spray all across the ocean. The wind is blowing so hard that it feels like it is sucking the breath out of your lungs and you feel like you can barely breathe. But the most overwhelming sensation is the noise. It is overpowering and actually painful. As the wind blasts through the rigging, it sounds like a woman screaming at the top of her lungs right into your ears. All of our senses are on overload. Sight, hearing, touch, and even taste because of the sea water spray, everything tastes like salt. It is exhausting and exhilarating. I felt our odds of survival were fifty/fifty.

It is interesting to see how people react differently to life and death stress. Our "skipper" (he had the most sailing experience of the group, although he was not really a skipper) was cool as a cucumber, showed no emotion at all, and was pure business. On the other hand, one of the guys was petrified with fear and was totally helpless. He stayed below and hid throughout the storm and did not come topside even when he could have helped us as we tried to keep the boat intact (I felt sorry for him because he had to know that he had lost our respect for him, even though we never criticized him or discussed it). Another member of our crew was scared to death and stayed below most of the time, but when we needed him, he managed his fear and did his duty. We respected the fact that he could overcome and manage his fear (you can't be brave unless you know fear and then conquer it). And our crazy Viking friend was totally fearless to the point where he was careless and was about to go overboard in the wind and waves as he went to secure our storm jib on the foredeck.

I was in the middle of the spectrum regarding emotions. On the one hand I was pretty scared and as I said, I gave our odds of survival at fifty/fifty. On the other hand, I was in awe of the power and majesty of nature and it was incredibly exhilarating to experience that power. I wanted to stay topside and experience everything. Plus, if we went down, I did not want to be trapped below. I drank in the experience, helped prepare the boat and fought the storm on deck where I could, took pictures, and brought out the wind speed indicator so I would know for sure what I was experiencing.

When the crazy Viking went to the foredeck to secure the storm sail, he was being careless and I was sure that he would be blown overboard. There was no way we could get him if he fell overboard, so even though I was putting myself at risk, I went with him on the foredeck and held on to his belt with one hand and held on to the shrouds with the other. You can't imagine what it is like trying to walk upright in winds exceeding seventy-five miles per hour! I am pretty sure that I saved his butt. He never said anything, but when we got back to the cockpit, he gave me a silent nod of gratitude and respect. That was enough for me.

As we approached a reef near the harbor entrance, I

walked back to the foredeck and stood at the bow pulpit as the lookout to make sure that we did not run aground on the reef. I almost got knocked off the boat as we turned in the channel and jibed the storm jib. The force of the wind slammed the sail over me with incredible force and it took every bit of my strength to hang on the forestay and stay on the boat. I was real happy to get back into the cockpit after that!

To add a little more excitement, we faced a final unplanned threat as we had to turn dead in to the wind to make our final run into the harbor. Preparing to turn the engine on, our skipper discovered that the ignition key had broken off as guys were slammed around the cockpit in the heavy seas and he could not turn on the engine. There was no way that we could get into the harbor without the engine. We were totally exhausted and so close to the safety of shore that we actually talked about intentionally driving the boat onto the beach just to get back on land. But then it occurred to me that part of the key was still in the ignition, so I grabbed a screw driver, jammed it into the ignition, turned it, and miracle of miracles, the engine started.

Long story short, we made it and had one hell of a survivor's party that night. As it turns out, we had just survived the worst nor'easter' in those waters in twenty-five years. Several boats and crew members were lost. It helped build my confidence in my personal sailing because now I know what it takes to survive and that if you react rationally and you are prepared, you can make it through almost anything. I would not have missed it for the world!

Mother Nature can be pretty nasty. Most city folks have no idea because they are simply not exposed to the true harshness of the natural world; they live in a technology-cushioned and artificially protected world of civilization. That became crystal clear to me when I was hunting antelope in southeast Colorado in the high desert a few years ago. I got my antelope on the first day (very cool animals as they are the fastest hoofed animal on earth which we clocked at sixty mph and they have the eyesight of a man looking through 8X binoculars). When we went back to camp, the owner asked me and the other hunter who got his antelope on the first day to go kill a mountain lion that was in a canyon on his ranch. He had killed ten so far that year, but this one was elusive and it was the biggest lion that he had ever seen at around 190 pounds. Now normally, I don't hunt anything that I won't eat. And I don't really want to kill predators like mountain lions, wolves, or coyotes because I think that they are majestic animals. But I did not tell him that (not cool in the Badlands); I just politely declined because I did not have a mountain lion tag and it would be illegal.

Holy mackerel did he set me straight and explain the ways of the world to me! First, he said that he didn't give a damn what those sissies back in Denver said about what is legal on his ranch. He explained that mountain lions and coyotes kill about 10 percent of his cattle which costs him a hundred thousand dollars a year. In addition, those damn lions kill for fun. He found a group of dead mountain sheep (the rams are prized hunting game) slaughtered by mountain lion. They did not even eat them, they killed them for fun. But, finally, he said that the local ranchers can't leave their kids or dogs out alone on their property because the mountain lions will maul or kill them. He closes with, "those wimps in Denver don't live in my world." The passion and common sense of his argument was overwhelming and we agreed to try and take the mountain lion in the canyon.

The next day we went to hunt the lion and broke a few laws of nature that could have killed us. Let me back up a minute and give you some perspective. The previous day my hunting buddy Drew got out of his truck at sunup and stepped on a rattlesnake. Fortunately it was cool, the snake was lethargic, and it did not bite him. My hunting partner and I also ran into a rattlesnake which we killed that day. The bottom line is that there are rattlesnakes everywhere and that should be top of mind. But my new hunting buddy and I are so amped up about hunting the mountain lion that we seemed to forget the laws of nature. We drove to the canyon where the lion lived before the sun rose and headed out into the desert. It was only after a few hundred yards that it occurred to me that there were snakes everywhere, it was dark, and I couldn't see them. Oops. Well we walked very carefully the rest of the way to the canyon and we climbed halfway up (in the dark) and settled down under some boulders and a tree. It was still dark and we took out the electronic predator call that the rancher gave us. It makes the sound of a wounded rabbit and would draw the lion in to us. We loaded up our guns and turned it on and waited for the lion. We were pumped!

Then I had another epiphany! We were in the dark, sounding like a helpless rabbit, under some boulders and trees where we knew that a 190-pound mountain lion was hanging around and killing indiscriminately. Really stupid. For the city folks in the crowd, let me explain. Unlike the city where everything is designed to protect you and warn you of danger, mountain lions are not equipped with warning devices. Generally a mountain lion will soundlessly creep up behind you, climb above you (like the boulders and trees above us) and then jump down on you and instantly break your neck so he can eat you. You see, he does not care that I am the president of a company, or that I have a wife and son. I am simply part of the food chain. Breakfast as it were.

I immediately told my new hunting buddy to turn off the predator call and explained what we have just done. He is a veteran hunter and as embarrassed as I was at our foolishness.

What were we thinking? We were quite pleased when the sun finally came up. At the end of the day we did not get the lion, but he did not get us either!

That trip had several reality lessons for us. One of the hunters at camp got introduced to the reality of bison behavior. He drove into a blind canyon that a 1,500-pound bison called home. Apparently the bison either thought his truck was a sexy gal or he was pissed over the intrusion and he charged the truck. But he did not figure on the .300 Win Mag. that settled the issue. Take a note: don't corner a bison in the wild unless you are well armed and mean business.

Then we explored the ranch (hunting was over since we all got our antelope) and our guide explained the long history of the ranch which reinforced the reality of the harshness of Mother Nature. We passed several empty stone and mud cabins in excess of a hundred fifty years old and he told us of their history. Some were abandoned because the harsh conditions of the desert drove the settlers out. No water, hard winters, starvation, etc. At several cabins, he explained that the settlers were killed in their cabins by attacking Apache or Comanche Indians in the mid 1800's.

I have been around a lot, but that hunting trip served as a timely reminder of how tough the world can be. On the other hand, it was beautiful country with canyons, rivers, bison, eagles, blue sky, cactus, antelope, bear, rattlesnakes, and mountain lions. I wouldn't have missed it for the world. But like life, you just have to be prepared, be strong, stay alert, and take responsibility for your own safety.

Nature is not just tough on people. As a deer hunter, I have seen years when we had mild winters and the deer herd became enormous (the deer population in the US is now greater than when Columbus discovered America because of the decline of natural predators—despite human predators).

And then a hard winter suddenly hits and as much as a quarter of the deer population can starve to death. Tough on the weaker deer! But the strong ones survive. That is how natural selection works.

Or take the seven-year ruffed grouse cycle. The grouse population starts to grow because the predator population is low and life is good for the grouse and hunters. Then the predator population begins to grow and they reduce the grouse population (tough on the grouse and hunters). But after a while, there are too many predators and not enough grouse and the predator population drops off dramatically (tough on predators). And the cycle starts over. The whole process lasts seven years and then repeats. Somewhere there is a lesson for us humans. Nature is tough and you need to be strong and prepared to survive when civilization fails. Ask the folks from New Orleans.

Once you fully understand that the world is a dangerous place and you need to be prepared to survive, you just make that an everyday habit. If you go into the wilderness even for just a few hours, there are a few simple basics that you should always follow:

- Tell people where you are going and when you will be back.
- Always carry basic and simple survival gear including a compass, knife, the means of making a fire, water, signal mirror, whistle, and a space blanket or space sleeping bag (I always have some kind of protection against animals but that is me).
- Always carry a small first aid kit.
- If I am going for more than a day I take a copy of the SAS (British Special Air Service) survival guide. It's great.
- If you are going on blue water, make sure that the

following is on the boat or don't go:

PFD (personal flotation device) for everybody

Life raft

EBIRB (tells a satellite/rescuers where you are)

VHF radio

Plenty of flares and signaling devices

A seasoned and responsible skipper!

If you go to the wilderness or blue water on a regular basis, take a survival or basic wilderness skills course and a first aid course. They are a lot of fun and they may save your life. In fact, I think that any responsible adult should take a first aid course, water safety course, and CPR course. I have saved four lives with the knowledge that these courses provided me and I can tell you that there is no greater thrill in the world. Take it seriously because if and when it happens, it will be too late to learn and it could cost you or a loved one his life.

Finally, one more suggestion from the crazy man! Remember the deer and grouse cycle and the nasty surprises Mother Nature can throw at you? Remember New Orleans or the tsunami? Well, add to that equation the bird flu. In 1917-18 it killed anywhere from 100-200 million people worldwide and it mathematically will certainly happen again and could shut down our cities; read *The Great Influenza* by John Barry. Just to make it interesting, add to that threat terrorists and a dirty nuclear bomb or a biological warfare attack. The bottom line is that our nice cozy lifestyle is due for a dramatic interruption. Anyone who has studied history knows that it is true. Be prepared and do what FEMA and Homeland Security recommend. Have the following at home to protect your family:

- 3-7 days worth of water (I would have more, but that's me)
- 3-7 days worth of food (ditto)
- First aid supplies
- Some cash
- Other (check their Web sites)
- And I would have a weapon in case the world goes nuts. (Give me a break! I have had men, animals, and nature try to kill me so I am sensitive, okay?)

Bottom Line: it is a dangerous world. Your safety and the safety of your family is your responsibility, and nobody cares more than you do about saving your life so be prepared to do it yourself. Don't trust the most important thing in the world to anybody else!

Finally, I will give you one last hunting experience to partially explain my self-defense position. You may remember several years ago when a guy (Hmong) shot and killed about six deer hunters in Wisconsin. I was there. It was near Hayward (closest sort of big town near where it happened). I was in my tree stand which should be miles from anyone or anything. Suddenly I heard several rapid shots from a semi-automatic rifle. That is not unusual, some hunters get carried away. I didn't think much of it until an hour or so later when a medical evacuation helicopter went right over my tree stand at a very low altitude and then landed maybe a half mile away. You cannot believe how loud they are when they are right over your head! Thirty minutes later it left.

I stayed in the tree stand until dusk wondering what that was all about, and then went back to camp. As I walked into camp, the guys said, "thank God you are all right; call your wife and tell her that you are okay." Naturally I asked what the heck's going on and they said that there were six dead, six wounded, and twelve missing (not correct, turned out it was six dead and two wounded). What? Then they explained that two guys in a silver Nissan pickup truck with an ATV in the back were shooting hunters in the woods (they were wrong, it was one guy)! The helicopter that landed near me was picking up the wounded hunters that survived. I called my wife and as I was telling her what was going on, a silver Nissan pickup truck with two guys and an ATV in the back pulled into our camp!

I yelled to my buddy Drew (yep, him again) to load his gun and get ready, and I told my wife that I had to go, and I hung up. I got my rifle, loaded it, jacked a shell in the chamber, and positioned myself with a truck as cover. You see we were way in the boonies; nobody ever comes to our camp except the guys in the camp, and the odds of a coincidence are one in a million. The odds are in fact, that these are the killers and Drew and I are prepared to shoot them in self defense if we have to.

Despite the probability that these are the guys, neither Drew nor I pointed our guns at them but we were ready. When they stopped and got out, we watched for guns and didn't see any. We asked them who they were and fortunately they told us that they were the father and son of one of the guides in our camp and wanted to make sure that he was okay given what was going on. They answered enough of our questions that Drew and I realized that these were not the guys. Thank goodness.

Later at the bar, the father said, "I noticed you boys had your guns out. Were they loaded?" We said, "Yes sir, they were." And then we asked him to repeat the description of the killers. He almost fainted when he realized that he fit the description of the killers and what could have happened. Now some people may criticize Drew and me for loading up our weapons and being prepared. But maybe if the six dead hunters had been more cautious when they ran into a stranger on their property, they might still be alive. I am just glad that we prepared but showed restraint. The world is a dangerous place and any seasoned hunter knows that from experience!

I want to make one last note on that hunt. That night, we did not know that the police had already caught the killer. Most of us in deer camp stayed indoors concerned that the killer was still out there in the woods and in the dark hoping to pick off more hunters. I went to bed that night with my loaded pistol just in case. But two of the guys in our camp were cops and also trained SWAT officers for their departments. As most of us went indoors looking to protect ourselves, they went to their cars, got their SWAT gear and AR15 rifles and went into the dark woods to look for the killer. They have my everlasting respect!

Chapter Seven

Living in the Age of Aquarius

I guess I need to confess at this point that I have not always been a good guy. I think I am a good and responsible citizen now, but in my youth (it is decades past the statutes of limitations, Officer!) I did a lot of things that I am not proud of today. I was not a mean or bad guy, but it was the Age of Aquarius, and it was all about seeking thrills and excitement any way that you could.

Thank God I grew up, survived, never seriously hurt anyone, and never got caught! But I cringe to think about the irresponsibility of my actions. Of course, watching the media now, we were just amateurs compared to what we see in today's kids. But I am afraid that we, the baby boomers, have started a decline in our culture that is spiraling down at an accelerating rate. I am appalled at what I see today and I am an ex-scumbag!

It was the dawning of the Age of Aquarius, Woodstock, and Kent State! It was free love, dropping out, tuning in, and turning on, and I was in college at the height of it. On the one hand I regret many of my actions; on the other, I feel sorry for anyone who did not grow up in the intensity of the emotions and the explosion of the senses that were happening at that time! I got to see and be in riots, took over the ROTC building, drank barrels of Ripple and Old Milwaukee, had a great time with my girl, smoked dope, did crazy stuff, worked hard, and yet still graduated with distinction. We did it all.

I was a weird combination of cultures that did not exactly fit in anywhere, but could reasonably fit in almost everywhere. I was a red-neck (strong on defense, rural interests, hunter), and I was a long-haired hippie, philosopher, and student who worked his ass off and fell in love with and married his high school sweetheart in college. Now that was an unusual combination. Hippies hated guns, the military, red-necks, hard work, commitment, and hunting. Yet I was both.

The only group that I did not find interesting at the time was the Greeks. The Greeks (in college those kids were the ones in the fraternities and sororities) hated long hair, hippies, philosophers, and red-necks. I felt the Greeks lived in a different world than I did and were completely out of touch with the real world (the movie *Animal House* best describes my view of the Greeks at that time). I suspect that this was an unusual time for Greeks because I knew many people who I respected and who were in fraternities and sororities and loved them. I think at that point in time, Greeks were on the outs because they were seen as part of the establishment, and the establishment was who the protests were all about.

I got to enjoy the best of being a hippie and the best of being a red-neck. During the school year I got to enjoy all there was to being a student and in the summers I worked some of the hardest manual jobs around. I am not going to share the details of my poor behavior escapades (despite the statute of limitations), but I would like to share some of the intense experiences that I had that are representative of a special time in history.

Let me start with a vivid memory during the riots in response to Kent State. I majored in sociology at Northern Illinois University with a focus on criminology (I was a juvenile delinquent and I wanted to counsel kids that weren't as lucky as me—they got caught). I was taking a course in crowd behavior and decided to write my term paper on the riots that were happening on campus at the time. I supported the Vietnam War so I was not a protester (although I did feel that if you are going to fight a war, fight to win. and I felt that we were not fighting to win). In fact, I was going to join the service before I went to college because I was not sure that I wanted to go to college. But my dad talked me out of it (he used a great line, "you can always quit college if you don't like it, but once you are in the service, you are in") and I fell in love with my girl and she was going to college. I had no idea what I was about to experience at the demonstrations when I went to see what was going on.

My first encounter was at what was supposed to be a peaceful march on campus in support of Kent State. As I remember it, thousands of students were there. All was well and peaceful until we were next to the student center building when some of the "townies" (local DeKalb red-necks, not students) tussled with some of the students. Next thing I know, someone went through the plate glass window and the riot began. I was right there when it happened and my crowd behavior text book had it completely right.

The peaceful crowd suddenly and instantly became one crazed animal driven by fear. Irrational violence, panic, glass breaking, fights, craziness, and lunacy were suddenly epidemic. I saw a townie order his Doberman pinscher to attack a group of twenty-five students, and it obeyed. It is impossible to describe the scale, emotion, and intensity of the event. I ran like hell to avoid getting arrested by the police (honest officer, I was an observer writing my term paper). By the way, I don't blame the cops; the crowd was nuts.

My next experience was when several hundred students decided to march into town from campus. The police decided that this was a bad idea (I don't blame them on that either after seeing what happened in the first riot) and set up a roadblock across the bridge over the Kishwaukee River. There were maybe a hundred very large State policemen in riot gear straddling the bridge with a tear-gas gun on a tripod that looked like a fifty caliber machine gun (at least in my memory). I saw them arrive, get off the busses and march to the bridge and these were all very big guys. Each of them had his helmet, face mask, and very large baton.

For a while, all was quiet; the students were sitting in the middle of the road and the cops were standing in the middle of the bridge. I decided to interview the cops for my term paper and get their view of what it is like to be surrounded by hundreds of students. After the previous riot, I was wearing my track shoes, gym shorts, and tear-away shirt in case I needed to escape. The cops were reasonably cool (despite my long hair) and we started to talk, although they had little interest in me.

Suddenly, the students started throwing rocks at the cops—lots of rocks—and I was with the cops and in the line of fire! For a moment, time stood still. Suddenly the cops (a hundred) charged the students (hundreds). I didn't blame them (I was getting hit by the rocks too) but mass hysteria and panic resulted. Everyone was running everywhere. Some students fought with the cops (real dumb move), some ran. I seem to remember the cops beating the crap out of anyone that they caught for a while, both guys and girls (I won't swear to it, but that is my memory). I decide to get the hell out of Dodge because I was a long-haired hippie and could be confused as a protester. I was glad that I was wearing my get away outfit.

I broke free and called Evelyn to report. She was in the dorm and the dorm officials had ordered all the students and their floors locked down. I was the student connection to the outside world and they were shocked at what I reported was going on. Then the riot escalated. Students were roaming the campus and burning cars. Violence increased and there was tear gas in the air. I called Ev again to report and she convinced me that now would be a good time to get off campus and get back to my rooming house in town. I decided that she was right and swam/waded across the mighty Kish (since the cops still held the bridge). She had to stay put and study for some finals, but she told me that it was tough to study with tear gas in the air, a wash cloth to her mouth, and cars burning below her window. I guess!

Neither the students nor the cops can be proud of what they did in those riots. The rioting students deserved to get their butts kicked. They were out of control. The cops did what they had to do but there has to have been a better way with less violence. On the other hand, if I had hundreds of kids throwing rocks at me, I would have kicked some ass too. My crowd behavior book was right on in that a crowd takes on its own wild-animal personality. Riots are incredibly dangerous things and display a dark and scary side of humanity that most people just would not believe. Chalk up another extreme life experience for future reference. Incidentally, I got an A on my term paper and in the course!

As a contrast to that violence, I will describe another

student protest a few years later to show how things evolved. I think that the event was when the public found out that the US invaded Cambodia. This time the protests were peaceful. The students decided to take over the ROTC building and the administration decided to let them have it to avoid violence. I decided to go and see what was happening. Getting there, students were hanging around, smoking dope, and looking bored. I met my brother by chance and after hanging around a few minutes, we decided to split and find something more interesting to do. The students finally got bored enough that they also left and gave the building back. Quite a difference from the chaos and violence of the previous riots a few years ago! I am not sure that the administration did the right thing by letting the kids take the building, but there was no violence.

By now you know some of my extreme life experiences early in my life and you will have some understanding when I say that college was a somewhat weird experience for me. On my very first day on campus, a guy asked me if I wanted to buy "some weed" which was a shock to me. But the real weird part of college for me was the students. No offense to the majority of them (and this is a broad generalization), but from my life experiences up to then, I thought that they were the most pampered, unrealistic, and naïve kids that I had ever seen. In contrast were the tough kids that I worked with in my manual labor jobs during the summer who could not afford go to college. I felt like I was in two different galaxies. The hard working kids (some of whom were illegal aliens that I really respected for their work ethic) were dealing with the tough reality of making a living in the real world. Contrasted with that was most of the college kids that lived in a sheltered and unrealistic world (at least in my view). But I made up my mind to make the best of things and enjoy both worlds, although it made me a bit schizophrenic!

As a "hippie" I enjoyed the laid-back lifestyle, long hair, Ripple and the weed, my girl, and I enjoyed the open attitude toward "free love." I loved the great, great music of the time. On the other hand, unlike the hippie lifestyle, I worked hard in school, took sixteen to eighteen hours a semester, and got great grades (graduated cum laude and made the sociology honor fraternity). I was motivated to excel in my chosen field and I knew that I wanted to get married and provide a good life for my soon-to-be wife. I also took karate, scuba, played racquetball, lifted weights, and swam a mile a day. Not your normal hippie stuff. In the summer, I worked the toughest manual labor jobs around from a night shift at a foundry (really dangerous place), to laying asphalt on a road crew, to a tree removal service (climbing and chain saws). Bottom line, I took the best from both worlds and did not fit perfectly in either. The story of my life!

Speaking of taking karate, that experience was more of a wake-up call than I had ever anticipated. While I thought I had already been around the block with numerous life experiences, karate was a shocker. Our Japanese sensei (instructor) calmly and coolly taught us more than twenty ways to kill a man or permanently paralyze him using nothing but our hands. It was a wake-up call first, because I became aware of how fragile human life is and how easy it is to kill or paralyze a person. Secondly, it shocked me to realize that good, rational, and calm people have been practicing and perfecting pretty horrible ways to kill, paralyze, or maim people for over a thousand years. We were taught how to poke out both of the enemy's eyes and rip off both ears with one move. Another move involved sending the bridge of someone's nose through their frontal lobe to kill them instantly. Karate taught me discipline, the skill to manage pain, and the intense responsibility that comes with the lethal knowledge that we were being taught. The sensei also taught us the oriental view of honor; when it was right and wrong to use the skills that we were being taught. That concept of honor and responsibility in the starkest terms possible are probably the most important lessons that I learned in karate. I must also say that it suddenly turns into a weird world when you are angry at someone and you know that you have the knowledge and the skill to kill that person over twenty ways with your bare hands. Very weird and it led to interesting fantasies in some of the heated board room arguments that I was involved in! But it does add to confidence.

There was one funny time my hippie and red-neck worlds collided at Northern. I missed the first semester as I was working for a tree removal service to make money to go to school. My girlfriend (now wife) was at Northern pursuing her nursing degree (she knew she wanted to be a nurse since she was like three, how lucky is that) and I wanted to visit her on campus so a friend and I borrowed our boss's ten-ton crane truck and drove it to campus to take our girls out on a date. Weird looks from 20,000 students as we cruised through campus with our babes dragging a ten-ton crane behind us!

It is worth a second to compare that job to the life the students were living at NIU. Part of our job was to climb to the top of sixty-foot trees, rope ourselves in, and then cut down the tops of the trees in pieces with our chain saws so that the pieces would fall between the houses (not enough room to drop the whole tree). My biggest fear was that I would embarrass myself and die by cutting my own safety rope and falling sixty feet to the ground (having to explain to St. Peter that I was dumb enough to cut my own rope)! To motivate us to work faster (so he could go to the horse track and place his bets), our boss would start cutting the base of the tree while we were still working up top (interesting management motivation technique). The other part of our job was to cut trees into pieces with our chain saws after cutting them down the traditional way when there was room. In any case, the work was hard and dangerous with chain saws, hand saws, heights, and high-powered shredders which could shred large branches into tiny pieces for removal—remember the chipper in the movie Fargo?

Our boss used the most modern management techniques as I mentioned before to motivate us. Sometimes he would lose our paycheck money at the track so we would have to hide the company trucks until he coughed it up (another motivational tactic). Safety equipment and training were considered highly overrated! Compare that life style to the experience of most of the students at NIU who generally seemed pampered to me and whose biggest hardship was that they got too much homework. Obviously, there were plenty of hard-working kids and some hard luck and tough kids at NIU, but they sure seemed like the minority to me.

Let's talk about drugs for a moment since that is always a hot topic on the news. I did smoke marijuana and I did enjoy it at the time. And yes, I did inhale! I did not mess with acid, cocaine, or the harder stuff. I figured that I was screwed up enough and did not need that baggage. In those days, marijuana was very innocent. We used locally grown stuff or Maui Wowie and it was not connected with violent gangs and all of the horrible stuff that surrounds drugs today.

While I enjoyed grass in my early college years, I began to see the horrible down side of drugs even then. I saw kids freaked out on acid and one guy walked off an eight-story building and died. While on one of my summer jobs, I worked with a heroine addict and saw how it totally dominated and ruined his life. Even then, there was certainly an ugly and insidious side to drugs that was down-played in the Age of Aquarius.

I noticed for myself that while weed relaxed me, loosened me up, and created a good time, it also reduced my drive to push myself hard and excel. Toward my junior year I realized that I had to make a choice in life: stop using weed and achieve my goals, or keep using it and risk not succeeding in my overall life goals. I decided to quit. Some friends could not understand my decision and we drifted apart. I look at those people now and they never achieved anything of distinction. I think that weed sedates the intensity that is necessary to excel and achieve great things. I also know for a fact that it is a precursor to harder drugs (ask any drug counselor) and I thank God that I had the motivation and inspiration (Evelyn) to shoot for bigger things in life!

At the beginning of our senior year, Ev and I got married. We just could not wait any longer and wanted to be together all of the time. We were dirt poor (but in love and having a ball), taking mega hours of courses a semester to finish our degrees, working nights and weekends, and life was very, very serious. I worked at the Greyhound bus terminal and taxi stand in town when I was not in class and discovered a whole new side of DeKalb. Driving a cab or working the bus station introduces one to every dimension of humanity! Ev worked as a waitress for a while when not in class.

We also volunteered at Dixon State Mental Hospital every week during that year to provide attention and human contact to patients who had no visitors except staff. That experience makes you appreciate all that you have and it has always stayed with me. Working with folks who cannot communicate or do anything to help themselves certainly brings personal understanding to the old saying, "there, but for the grace of God, go I." It was an awesome and humbling experience. Evelyn and I were no longer participants in the Age of Aquarius at that point. It had passed us by while we focused on building our new life together in the "real" world.

When I think about how little we had back then and the risks that we took, I am amazed. We owned no furniture except a stereo (got to have your priorities straight). We lived in a tiny furnished apartment off campus. We had no health-care insurance. There were many days when we had no money and we would gather our empty pop bottles for the deposit to buy macaroni and cheese for dinner. Occasionally, my parents would come to visit us and brings wonderful bags of groceries. They would bring delicacies that we could not afford (like steak and wine) and we would feel like royalty. But we were in love, and we were having a blast. Besides, everybody else we knew was poor too.

Chapter Eight

World-class Business Achievements and How We Did It

Well, if you've hung in this far, I am sure that you are wondering how this crazy lunatic got to be a group president of a business and accomplish world-class business achievements. So, I guess I had better start this chapter with our accomplishments first to establish my credentials, and then I will tell you how we did it. It is a story of regular good folks, who together made a great team and accomplished extraordinary things. It is the story of the power of teams, the power of processes, the power of data, the power of a culture that strives for world-class distinction, and the power of setting high goals. And I would like to think it also illustrates the power of effective leadership.

Together, our team at Scotsman consistently delivered profits significantly better than the Fortune 500 average over fifteen years, successfully implemented the Toyota Production

System, and was named in the Top Twenty-five Plants in North America by *Industry Week* magazine in 2002, became ISO9001-2000 certified (first in our industry), was named in the Top Ten Plants in North America by *Industry Week* in 2006 (we don't give up and that was the brass ring), and was named a finalist for the Shingo Prize in 2006. According to *Business Week*, the Shingo prize is the "Pulitzer Prize of Lean Manufacturing." But maybe the highest recognition came after winning all of those awards when I got a call from a very high Pentagon official who saw our awards and asked if we would join the prestigious Pentagon SWAT team used to help improve troubled but strategic Pentagon suppliers. How cool is that and how could you say no? There was no income, mind you; the benefit was that you were doing your civic duty and had the chance to work with other SWAT team members who were "the best of the best."

Before I go into much more detail, those of you in business will hopefully find some value in this chapter as it clearly relates to what you do. But I would suggest that what I am going to share here does not just relate to business people. The experiences that I am going to share relate to any relationship with organizations whether they are business related or not. Whether you are a corporate manager or on your church board or a volunteer to a charity, many of the processes that I will be talking about apply. Because any organization has to deal successfully with people, data, and processes to succeed whatever its mission is. And that is what the following is all about.

First I should explain how I went from criminology to business, although I will tell you that studying criminal behavior is a solid base for doing business! My experiences in this transition to business and my early experiences in business impacted everything that I did later as an executive.

My goal in college was to get my sociology/criminology degree so that I could work with juvenile delinquents. I did not care about making a lot of money; I wanted to save the world! At college I got to study criminal behavior and psychology, saw tough young criminals at St. Charles School for Boys (very serious crimes), and I had the delightful pleasure of hearing the cell door slam behind me at the state penitentiary at Joliet (as a guest!). Before graduation I got a job with the State of Illinois which was to start right after my graduation and I would be working with kids six months before they were to be released from St. Charles School for Boys and then six months after they were released in the Cabrini Green area of Chicago. My wife secured a job as a nurse at a local hospital. We were both set on a path to achieve our life goals.

Just as we graduated in 1973, the economy took a big hit and the grant that I was hired under was cancelled. Four years of school, no money, and no job! I wanted to stay in criminology and I tried to tap into any variation of the criminology field that I could, but I had no luck despite my cum laude degree and credentials. I wanted to save the world and trained to do it, but the world was not interested. I was devastated.

Fortunately, my wife had a job as a nurse and we did okay money-wise as I continued to search for a job in criminology. But my grandfather, Augusto (remember him?), told me that I was a gigolo living off my wife and could not consider myself a man until I had a job. Motivation!

I decided that since the world did not want to be saved by Randy Rossi, I was going to make money and lots of it by going into business. After some research, I chose an entry-level customer service job with American Hospital Supply Corporation because they had great growth, were known to be extremely progressive, and I figured that people will always need health care. I was hired! My division manufactured highly sophisticated dental equipment and instruments. I had my foot in the door of the business world and I was highly, highly motivated. I was sure that the embarrassment I felt when I was unemployed has served as a silent but intense motivator for me ever since and pushed me to excel. Nietzsche!

After six months, I was promoted to sales and given the Virginia, Maryland, and Washington DC territory, including responsibility for the federal government. I had no training, no introductions; no nothing except a piece of paper with the list of accounts and their addresses and phone numbers. My wife and I moved to Virginia and we had a ball. That experience of learning the hard way also shaped me forever. I was responsible for many dealers and all sorts of end-using customers and all of those experiences helped me grow. But the real impact and long-lasting experiences were with the government. I will give a few examples.

Imagine a twenty-three year old guy (kid) with no formal sales training calling on the top level of U.S. Army, Navy, Air Force, and VA dental corps. My first government call was to the top army dental officer who was a full bird colonel and his office was in the Pentagon. Let me describe calling on the Pentagon (before 9/11). It is massive. You are assigned a guard to escort you to your destination. (I was convinced at that time the guard was to make sure that you didn't get lost in the massive building and die of starvation.) In case you are not already intimidated, you walked past the office of the Joint Chiefs of Staff (very impressive). If you are me, you are scared to death and wondering what the hell you are doing here. I was certain that I was going to embarrass myself forever. The guard knocked on the door, the colonel said, "Enter," and my world changed forever.

My instant impressions were that his office was a mess, the colonel was picking his nose at the time, his tie was down, his collar was frayed, and I realized with tremendous relief that he was just a guy, not a god. And it turned out that he needed my help because he had some technical questions about my product which I could, in fact, answer. After that, I called on many high-level military officers including generals and admirals and at every major military and government installation in Washington DC, Virginia, and Maryland. Whether it was Walter Reed, Bethesda, or the Norfolk naval base (largest in the world), I called on every major U.S. Army, Air Force, Navy, and Marine base in that area. The lesson that first day at the Pentagon taught me forever is this: even if you are speaking in front of a board of directors, an admiral or general, or a crowd of five hundred customers, they are just people.

One other lasting experience in DC that built my confidence forever concerned the White House. I connected with President Ford's dentist on a sales call. We hit it off and the White House needed a new dental suite. The deal was done and we were in. Next thing I know, I was at the White House to help install the equipment, going through intense security (they thought I was a secret service agent at first but I figured I had better play that right and I set them straight), and then we took the president's personal elevator down to the secure area below ground. Walking through steel blast doors many inches thick, it sure looked like a bomb shelter to me. There was an area with medical suites and a dental suite and I worked with navy technicians and showed them how to install the equipment. Intense security was everywhere. Although installations were not normally part of my job, I wanted to be there. After all, how could I pass up a chance to be at the White House? As much as I thought that the Pentagon was imposing, the White House simply oozes power. I don't care who you are, you have to be impressed. And you have to be intimidated. The White House was designed to intimidate you and it sure as hell does.

But after that, calls to the Pentagon or anywhere else in the world were no big deal. Lesson learned? Just like successfully sailing through hurricane-force winds, sailing through anything less after that is no big deal. It was the same with the White House and Pentagon. Nothing has intimidated me since then. I learned how to excel in sales, I was motivated, and I did not hesitate to go anywhere that would yield results. It is the Nietzsche school of sales and management development.

I will compress the next fifteen years into a few paragraphs. My success in sales gave me a chance to be promoted to product management and learn the marketing side of business. I took business law, finance, and strategic planning courses through the Wharton School of Business and the University of Wisconsin to give me the tools I needed to do a proper job. Fun stuff and I found that I really enjoyed the intellectual stimulation of competition in the sales and marketing world. AHSC was a fast track and about every two years I got promoted from marketing to sales management and back again to marketing management with increasing levels of responsibility.

My division was bought and sold many times and I finally left for new challenges. While I was doing very well and enjoyed it, I wanted to see if I could take the lessons that I learned at AHSC and succeed in a completely different industry. I went to Scotsman, a division of Household International, and met the man that I will call my mentor who lit a fire under me to settle for nothing less than world-class performance. And he showed me how to do it.

Dick Osborne is his name and he showed me the way while he was president twenty years ago. He took Scotsman from an average company and turned it into a good company. He set the stage and when I got my shot as president, I took the tools that he gave us, added to them, and with a great team took Scotsman from a good company to a great company.

Dick's first goal was to build a great management team and he introduced a sophisticated interviewing process to get the best people by identifying those behaviors that got results. We were all trained on the behavior interview technique and formed cross-functional teams to interview critical candidates. Our hit rate increased dramatically and we developed a great team. I have used that process ever since.

Next, the focus was to convert from a traditional "silo" functional organization to cross-functional teams. If you don't do anything else in your business, introduce cross-functional teams to your critical projects. It increases efficiency dramatically by getting all functions together at the same time and avoids the "throw it over the wall" syndrome that results in continuous do-overs. We were all trained on how to work as a team, and after participating and personally seeing how much more efficient the process was, I became a permanent convert. There is simply no other way to get the same results. And there is nothing more satisfying than seeing a well-orchestrated team perform.

Next, Dick introduced us to the quest of always searching for the new, leading edge, and world-class processes. That quest exposed us to teams before they became popular, lean manufacturing, TQM, etc. The key was to look outside the organization for best in class. His message was, "don't be trapped in your own exhaust, look externally and with an open mind for better ways of doing things."

Dick introduced me through his actions to three critical dimensions of a leader that I believe are the foundation of leadership. They are total integrity, "walk the talk," and the value of an open and challenging environment. In regard to integrity, Dick made sure through his actions and his words that we were going to do things the right way. We were going to follow the law, treat people correctly, treat the customer correctly, and be responsible to our community. We all saw cases in which Dick chose not do something that might have increased our profits, but would have stained his commitment to integrity. That had impact.

"Walk the talk" was critical as well. I have been through many training sessions with professionals on a variety of topics, and the common theme of all of them regardless of the topic is "that it starts at the top." The bottom line is simply this: if the leader says to do X, but does not do X himself, X is hypocrisy and nobody in the organization will support it or do it. People watch what the leader does, not just what he says. The cliché of "actions speak louder than words" is absolutely true for leadership.

Finally, Dick created an open and challenging environment. His feeling was that unless you are the smartest person on earth, you need input from other people to provide solutions to problems that you might not be aware of. He would not tolerate politics and he made that clear. If you had a beef with someone on an issue, that was okay. But say it in the open in front of the person and work it to resolution. No behind-the-scenes attacks were tolerated. Put a public stake in the ground and defend your position.

The best way I can explain how seriously he took the concept of challenge is to relate an experience that I will never forget. It was the day before an important staff meeting and Dick and I were having a beer after work. We began talking about the topic of the staff meeting and it became clear that Dick and I were in absolute agreement. So imagine my surprise the next day when I presented that position to the group for formal approval and Dick ripped me up one side and down another with challenges. After intense debate, the proposal was approved by all.

After the meeting, and bleeding from the wounds of the challenge, I asked Dick what the hell that was all about since he told me that he agreed with my position the night before. "I did and do agree," he said. "I just wasn't sure if you and I were right and I wanted to test our position and challenge it." I then realized that Dick challenges himself more than he challenges others! He walked the talk.

I did learn a lesson from this that I remembered when I became president. Dick's challenge process was right on, but he was so intimidating that few people would challenge him directly. He knew this and one time told me that he needed strong managers who would have the strength to challenge him. But they were rare. There were two of us on his staff who would take him on—Chris Hughes and me. The others would be pretty withdrawn in my opinion. On important controversial issues, Chris and I would draw straws to see who would challenge Dick and take the beating. If you got the short straw, Dick would rip you hard, but invariably the next day he would come back to you and say that upon reflection he agreed with you. He always did the right thing. While it was very painful, I never regretted doing the right thing and those experiences are what motivated me to be outspoken and candid for the rest of my career!

When Dick promoted me to president of Scotsman, I truly was awed by the responsibility that he gave me. A hundred million plus dollars in sales, profits significantly better than the Fortune 500 average, and the incomes and careers of roughly four hundred good people were dependent on me. It was a big responsibility. Plus, while I had sales, marketing, and engineering management experience, I did not have direct operational experience and I had never been a GM before. I had a lot to learn and I had to learn it fast!

I made two promises to myself when I got the job. At a minimum, I would lead Scotsman to be a better company than when I got it and continue the improvement that Dick started.

But my stretch goal was to lead Scotsman to achieve world-class status as judged by outside experts. That stretch goal came from the years I worked with Dick Osborne and seeing how stretch goals can in fact be achieved; that, and the strong commitment that I felt for the team's welfare. You might as well shoot high!

Understanding the value of a challenge environment because of my limitations, but realizing how few people would stand up and take a beating, I made a point of trying to create a more open challenge process. When I became president, I published "safe harbor challenge rules." Anybody could challenge anybody in my organization (including me) with no negative repercussions as long as they followed three rules: 1) it was done with respect 2) it was done for the good of the company, and 3) it was done with data. If anybody following those rules felt that they suffered harm for challenge, they could go directly to the president to make it right. We had a lot of healthy challenge in our organization! Since I am not the smartest guy on earth, I need that challenge and different perspective to excel.

When I became president, I wanted to create a different kind of staff environment. I made it clear to my direct reports that I wanted them to play two roles. First, they obviously had to be their functional experts. But second, I wanted them to also think of themselves as members of the board of directors of the company. Any of us could challenge the other functions on important issues and to make sure that functional solutions proposed by the function worked well organizationally, not just on a functional level. Instead of just me and the function head tackling a material functional issue, I had a total of ten good brains coming up with good ideas and challenges for important functional issues. Invariably better solutions surfaced because of the process.

I worked hard at using this process and arriving at consensus decisions where possible. If we had consensus, I knew the odds were good that the decision was right and I would have strong buy-in and support from the staff. Don't get me wrong, this was not a democracy. I was the boss and if after debate the group and I disagreed (and it was an important issue), I made the call. But those circumstances were rare. Ninety-five percent of the time we did get to consensus and the decisions were good. Five percent of the time I had to pull rank (of course, I was always right!), but the group was okay with that because they had a chance to be heard and they understood that in the end, I had to make the call.

This process created a strong management team, and an effective team simply multiplies the output of an organization. But there were a lot of things that led to our success. Let me step back for a minute and summarize what I would view as the critical components of our success in a concise manner. Learn and do these, and you are on your way to excellence:

Critical Attributes of Success

- It starts at the top (the leader has to lead)
- Strong and visible commitment to ethics
- Walk the talk
- Create a strategic vision that motivates the organization and the tenacity to stick to it (no "flavor of the month" syndrome)
- Data rules ("In God we trust, all others must bring data!")
- Cross-functional team culture
- Constructive challenge culture
- Data-based goals and measures
- Process discipline
- Create a culture that fits your vision

- Sense of urgency
- Customer is king attitude
- Culture of continuous improvement
- Rational, data-based, and fair compensation system
- External benchmarking culture
- Intense results-oriented culture

Establish Data-based Critical Business Measure of Success Goals (external standards)

- EBITA as a percent of sales: 10% is Fortune 500, 15%+ is world class
- Sales per employee goal: $400,000+
- EBITA per employee goal: $60,000+
- Customer satisfaction and customers that "would buy again from you" based on hard data:
  4.7 out of 5 is world class
- FPY (first pass yield) excellence: 97% is world class
- DPM (defects per million) opportunity: 500 or better (six sigma is 3.4 but may have a poor ROI to get to that level)
- Inventory turns
  FG: 24+
  WIP: 40+
  PM: 24+
- Hours-per-unit excellence (industry and product specific)

World-class Processes

- Formal strategic planning process that "lives and breathes"
- Hoshin Planning (execution management)

- Cross-functional teams
- Toyota production system
- Disciplined and documented Stage Gate NPD (new product development) process
- Voice of the customer process
- Benchmarking (external world-class examples)
- Kanban material inventory management process
- Kaisans
- Value analysis
- Process mapping
- Recognition programs for all functions
- Gain sharing
- FMEA (failure mode and effect analysis)
- Shake and impact testing to confirm quality
- Supplier performance measurements, recognition, and partnership
- Warranty reduction process (permanently attack the top ten issues)
- Poka-yoke designs
- 360-degree management review process (input from subordinates, peers, and supervisor)

Open and Clear Communications

- Quarterly employee meetings to share direction and results
- Monthly formal project and process review meetings
- Monthly formal executive staff meetings
- Monthly informal lunch meetings with the hourly team (small groups)
- Aggressive recognition program for all employees
- Monthly newsletter
- Well communicated open-door policy and

challenge environment
With respect
With data
For the good of the company

Books That You Have to Read

- *From Good to Great* - Jim Collins (vision and culture)
- *Competitive Strategy and Competitive Advantage* - Michael Porter (the bible on business strategy)
- *Developing Products in Half the Time* - Preston Smith and Donald Reinertsen (new product development)
- *In Search of Excellence* - Thomas Peters and Robert Waterman, Jr. (vision and culture)
- *Lean Thinking* - James Womack and Daniel Jones (lean manufacturing and lean enterprise)
- *The Goal* - Eliyahu Goldratt and Jeff Cox (vision)

I am sure that I have left out a million things, but I think that if you do these things well, you are almost guaranteed a well-run and effective organization. We openly shared all of the above with our suppliers and customers in the very same spirit that the world-class companies we bench-marked allowed us to learn from them. The goal is continuous improvement for all and the creation of an outstanding value chain all the way to the end-using customer. We showed our partners our processes and helped them improve their processes if they showed interest. That practice of sharing built strong relationships with suppliers and strong loyalty with customers.

People are obviously the key and getting the right ones, motivating them, and getting them to pull in the right direction is the name of the game. We achieved world-class status, yet if you were to interview my team and me, I think that you would find us qualified but not rocket scientists. Let's use me as an example. I am pretty good strategically, and pretty good in sales and marketing. But I am just okay with operational issues. But I don't want to be the expert at those things. My strength is identifying good people, creating a vision that motivates them and me, creating an open and constructive but challenging environment, creating a relentless desire in the team to be world class, and I recognize good ideas when I hear them.

In regard to all of the skills needed in business, I am not a virtuoso violin player, but I am a good conductor who knows what I want the music to sound like and how to create an environment in which the true virtuoso performers can do their thing! I believe that is what management is all about.

I had a great staff that complemented each other and me. It took several years, but we assembled some great people who were team players. We were all different, and those differences were a benefit, not a detriment. The power of teams cannot be over emphasized. Our VP of Manufacturing said it best. He was an old-time, very autocratic manager years ago. As he would say, he used to make 90 percent of all of the decisions at the plant. After he saw the power of teams work at Kawasaki, he became a convert and went 100 percent to teams. Now he will tell you that he makes 10 percent of the decisions (strategic and high-level) and the teams make the other 90 percent of the tactical decisions within the framework that he set up. He likes this better! And the results speak for themselves.

How did we make the turn? What were the keys to our success? Awareness of world-class processes, benchmarking world-class companies, training, and a creating a culture of continuous improvement were the keys. The classic example was our conversion to lean manufacturing. We all read the books, understood the theory, and wanted to improve things. But it all really started to happen when several members of plant management went to see the theory in action at the Kawasaki plant in Lincoln, Nebraska. Seeing it work and watching the people and their enthusiasm in a world-class lean environment converted everyone on the spot. A picture is, in fact, worth a thousand words. We now benchmark best-in-class companies four or five times a year on various processes while constantly looking for the next breakthrough. We always returned from these benchmark trips with good ideas that we had not thought of ourselves. We also went back to the Kawasaki plant in Lincoln every five years to benchmark our progress.

Another great example is when we made the management decision to implement the Toyota Production System. We were concerned that we would get resistance from supervisors and our hourly work force. Change is scary. So we decided to invest in flying ten supervisors and hourly personnel on a chartered jet to the Toyota plant in Kentucky hoping for the same "epiphany" that management had at Kawasaki. You have to understand that we were not an extravagant company and we never chartered jets, but that was the most economic way to get the folks there. And many of the team who went had never been on a plane. For us and our team this was a big deal. Conversion to the Toyota Production System was a strategic priority and the folks had to be on board.

How did things work out? Once everyone saw the TPS actually work, our toughest job was to hold them back! They wanted to know why we could not move faster toward the conversion. They saw how it worked, they saw the benefits, and they wanted it now!

One of the other keys to our success was implementing the

"voice of the customer" process. The goal was to find out what the customer wanted and did not want, and then aggressively deliver the goods! We measured customer satisfaction on a broad range of issues every month and carefully tracked the trends. We recorded and tracked all customer complaints and addressed them in current products and processes and also in our NPD (new product development) process. We constantly reviewed our warranty data and we had a permanent team that worked on reducing or eliminating the constantly changing top ten warranty issues. And we invested in expert outside research to help us understand unmet customer needs for our NPD process. And then, using our cross-functional teams, we met those needs. Sounds simple!

People and motivation is what it is all about. We invested a lot of time and money on our recognition system and "gain sharing" designed to identify what is important and then reward and recognize on a regular basis and in a very public way those folks that did well on what we thought was important. It is impossible to do an accurate ROI on the process, but if you could see the folks get recognized in front of their peers, you knew in your gut that you were highly motivating people to do what they could to help the company achieve its goals. It is simply the right thing to do.

Let me share another benefit of the process. We did a lot of plant tours with high-level sophisticated customers as part of our sales process. We did not have our managers do the tours. We had fifteen hourly people on the assembly lines do the tours. Watching an hourly person who may not have finished high school passionately talk about DPM, FPY, kaisans, TPS, hour-per-unit goals, voice of the customer, and cross-functional teams is absolutely the best sales tool that there is. Customers constantly told us that they had never seen such passion and commitment from the folks. The power of motivated teams!

I could write a whole book on those experiences, but I think that I have covered the high points. I left Scotsman (then owned by Enodis) in January, 2008 after twenty years. Why? Well, I had set four professional goals for myself which I wanted to achieve in my career before I retired and I achieved them. First, I wanted to lead our company to world-class status as confirmed by outside experts. Second, I wanted to launch a new product line that was recognized as best in class and would insure that the company was well positioned after my departure. I was given the responsibility of another division which had serious problems and a negative EBITA. My third goal was therefore to get that division up to Fortune 500 EBITA levels. Finally, I had been working on a strategic relationship with a competitor for four years. My fourth goal was to convert that competitor to a customer and open the door to a broad strategic relationship.

I had reached my personal financial goals, and my wife and I were looking to retire in one or two years. In addition I achieved all four of my business goals by the end of 2007. We won the world-class status and awards that I introduced this chapter with. We launched a broad new product line that won the premier awards in our industry for innovation and best-in-class customer satisfaction which resulted in significant market share gains so goal number two was met. We made substantial progress at the other division that I was responsible for and reached the Fortune 500 profitability range that I had targeted in 2007 so goal number three was met. And finally, I led the negotiations that turned that competitor into a customer and opened the door to a stronger strategic relationship.

Despite all of this, I loved being with my team and hated to leave them. But at the end of 2007, I was faced with a choice from corporate management to make certain changes in my business that I disagreed with or leave. That, of course, is their right. I decided that I did not want to spend the last one or two years of my career implementing changes that I did not agree with. The company and I parted on very professional terms in 2008 and I wish them nothing but the best. I do miss my team. We created that rare miracle in business—a highly productive and efficient team—and I thank them for making it possible for me to accomplish my personal and professional goals.

Now I can focus on my other loves like writing my book, consulting, selected board memberships, sailing and diving, and traveling all over the world with my wife for fun, not business!

Chapter Nine

The Best and the Worst of the Business Culture

Fasten your seat belt because if you are a business executive, this will either pump you up or piss you off. As a former group president and business executive, I am speaking in broad and generalized terms from the totality of my thirty-six years of personal business experiences and observations. But I suspect that what I say here is fairly representative of the business world in the US (and I dare to say, Europe as well). And folks, I am afraid to say that we are in trouble! I will start with the worst because I want to finish on the best.

First let me start by saying that poor executive management is almost always the cause of all problems in business. We executives like to blame workers and staff and outside sources, but usually we, the top management, are the problem. I have met some great managers that I have been honored to work with like Dick Osborne, my staff, and several others. In fact, at various times in my career I have met many very good managers that I respected. But unfortunately, they are the minority in my opinion.

In my rough estimation, 30 percent of the executive managers I have worked with in a variety of ways deserve respect, and 70 percent do not. Unfortunately, in my opinion, what drives the majority of executive management today is short-term personal greed, which then drives executive actions that damage shareholders, employees, and our national strategic competitiveness. These actions are, in my opinion, destroying America's business heart and soul as we ship our high-paying manufacturing jobs and critical technology to China and India for short-term profits, bonuses, and stock options. We are watching the wholesale slaughter of the great American manufacturing engine that drove progress and greatness in this country and created "the arsenal of freedom" for the world. And we are building a house of cards in its place that is empty and will collapse under its own weight if we don't wake up. Lou Dobbs, you are right on target. I got to see it from the inside over the years.

First, let me share my personal standards which are out of sync with today's business world. I believe that the business executive has seven critical constituents which must be taken into consideration and served. They are the law, shareholders, customers, employees, the local community, your country, and yourself. Each is very important and each represents an obligation of the executive.

The three constituents that all executives fully understand are the shareholder, the law, and self. Regarding the shareholder, my opinion is that too many executives focus on short-term actions that fool the shareholder to make them temporarily feel good in return for immediate personal gain to the executive. After getting that bonus or stock option, many of those executives get out of Dodge just before the shareholder realizes that he now owns a house of cards. In my opinion, the majority of high-level executives will throw the customer, employee, community, and even his country under the bus for personal gain if he feels that he can get away with it. Watch the news. It seems to be happening every day now. Very few executives will chance breaking the law because that will land you in jail. But I have been amazed to see over the years that some executives were prepared to break the law either out of ignorance or desperation. Standing up to that and saying no as a subordinate is the true test of personal courage in business.

The overwhelming driver today in public companies is short-term quarterly profits. And in my opinion, that drives incredibly bad short-term executive behavior that is destroying our economy and America's strategic strength. Let's compare a theoretical publicly held US or European company against a theoretical well run and well financed privately held company, and then against a Chinese company. In my opinion, a well run privately held company or the Chinese company will almost always win the long-term battle against the publicly held company. The following explains why.

Let's assume that all three companies are $1 billion in sales and all are making $100 million in EBITA (10 percent). Suddenly we go into one of the periodic recession cycles that will always occur. Immediately the public company will cut advertising, investments in NPD, execute deep personnel cuts, and anything else that does not contribute to short-term profits so that they can hold the original anticipated earnings promised to shareholders or analysts. That is as certain as the sun coming up tomorrow.

Now the well run and well financed privately held company will be able to position itself for future success against the public company. The private owners are already paying themselves a great salary which they live off of and they are willing to temporarily see their profits go from let's say $100 million to say $90 million because they know that they are making an investment with a huge long-term pay off against the public company during the recession. For instance, they maintain advertising investments because they know that their ads will have two to three times the impact because public companies are cutting back. That builds a long-lasting brand strength that will pay back in spades later on.

The privately held company keeps its long term NPD development going because they know that will put them ahead of the publicly held company that cut back NPD for short-term profits. That is a sustainable and strategic advantage that can last years. And when the economy turns around, the privately held company will reap the benefits of the investments made in the downturn. In addition, the privately held company will scoop up the good employees who were either let go by the publicly held company during the downturn or left because they were demoralized or disenchanted by the actions of their company. Unfortunately, our economy is driven by publicly owned companies and we have seen our strategic advantages shrink away to foreign competitors, especially in the manufacturing sector.

The Chinese competitor perspective is even scarier. Let me share a story. I have a close friend who was asked by the Chinese to run a company that they had purchased in the US for them. He had worked for US and German companies and knew what was expected from them regarding profitability, returns, and cash flow and he asked the Chinese what their expectations were. He was shocked when they said that as long as he was cash neutral and broke even, they were satisfied as long as he continued to grow the business. Anything else was a bonus. You see, they had a real long term plan. This was China incorporated. And as long as he broke even, Chinese peasants were being employed back in China and did not have to be supported by the government. The national interests and company interests were both considered in business strategy. And because we have shipped most of our manufacturing to China, they have accumulated tremendous strategic strength against us. We are surely dumber than a box of rocks!

Let's talk a little about China. Many business leaders and even our government talk about the value of free trade. They criticize anybody who suggests that maybe it is not healthy for our nation to ship our critical manufacturing jobs and technology to China. They call us "protectionists" and "isolationists" and tell us that it is just too complex for us to understand. Well my response is that it is no more complex to understand than baseball! In baseball, competition is good and cheating is bad. We follow the rules in our version of business baseball and the Chinese are using cork bats, spit balls, and drugs to improve their performance to win the game. That is wrong. It is just that simple. China cheats and we let them!

China cheats like hell, and our government and our executive business leaders just don't care because they are making more money that way. How do the Chinese cheat? Take currency first. The Chinese manipulate their currency so that their products are always cheaper than ours, all else being equal. Right now experts believe that China intentionally manipulates its currency to be 30-35 percent undervalued to the US dollar. That means that if all else was equal on efficiency, quality, and everything else, China has a 30-35 percent price advantage. Not too complex is it? And clearly to anybody who is not comatose, it is not fair. It is cheating. But that is not all.

In the US, we mandate that our manufacturing companies follow strict rules that reflect our core national values. Those US companies must comply with minimum wage rates, safety standards to protect employees from injury, environmental standards to protect our environment, compliance to intellectual property laws, and we have to conduct business following very strict laws designed to protect the consumer and investors. These are all good things because those laws and rules support our national values.

Yet we allow Chinese companies to break all of those laws and compete in the US against our companies that have to follow the law. Chinese companies abuse workers and abuse the environment in China and ship that product into our country with no penalty against them as they compete against our own companies here in the US that bear the burden of following the rules. And I can tell you that the costs of a fair wage, safety standards, environmental protection, and so forth, are enormous. They probably add at least another 15 percent of cost against a Chinese competitor that does not follow those ethical laws. I support those investments mandated by US law because they reflect our national values. But by not forcing the Chinese companies to play by the same rules that we mandate for US companies, we are putting our US-based manufacturing businesses out of business. If our stated goal was to shut down American-based manufacturing and give it to China, we could not have been more effective.

In total then, the Chinese cheat like hell and because of their cheating, they have a 45-50 percent price advantage over US companies. Shame on them. But then our government allows that to happen because our business executives (who donate money to the politicians) don't complain because they make more money by shipping jobs to China (US employees are such a burden!). And we the American public are dumber than a box of rocks (I know it is repetitive but it is so accurate) by allowing it to happen because we get cheaper products at Wal-Mart (just an example). And while we have no penalties for Chinese products coming to the US despite their cheating, in my business there was a 35 percent duty when we sold products into China to protect Chinese companies. You can't make this stuff up! The Chinese get it, our government does not.

We are giving away our good paying manufacturing jobs, giving away our children's future, giving away our technology, and weakening our nation for cheap prices at Wal-Mart! There will be hell to pay unless we wise up. Read *The Coming China Wars* by Peter Navarro a Harvard PhD in Economics. It will scare the hell out of you. People like to say that China is our friend and that we are fear mongering when we bring up these facts. That is so incredibly naïve and ignorant when one considers the never ending and repeating cycles of history

Those of us who know history know about the constantly changing cycles and shifting alliances and the need to forever stay strong at home. We know about the need to control our own destiny. Example: Japan and the United States were very close allies starting in the mid 1800's and right up to 1930. Then in 1936 through 1945 Japan slaughtered millions of innocent people including Americans in war and we had to drop two atom bombs on them to stop the slaughter in 1945. The world is, and will always be, a dangerous place! And we must control our own destiny to control our security.

And to those who say that it is okay to lose manufacturing jobs to China and convert our economy to service jobs I say, what is the first thing you do when you lose your job? You cut services. A service economy is a house of cards because when the recession/depression really hits, service jobs will be cut first at a rapidly increasing rate until we find ourselves in a deep and long lasting recession/depression. Wake up America!

Lou Dobbs, keep it up! Bill O'Reilly, please take this issue on like you have taken on so many other important causes—before it is too late!

Back to business executives! They know all this. We talked about it all the time and it worried them too. They were personally very uncomfortable with our nation shipping jobs to China in general, and they worried about what impact it would have on our own kids. But many of those same executives still worked very hard at moving *their* manufacturing from the US to China because the company could make more short-term profit and they could make more personal bonus and more on their stock options. Employees, the community, the nation, and even their kids were thrown under the bus for short-term company profits and personal gain.

Companies today are losing the long-term loyalty of employees. And they deserve it! Companies used to offer long-term careers, pensions, health care, etc. to foster long-term tenure, stability, and loyalty. Now companies have pitched pensions, reduced health care support, and they are shipping jobs to China and India as fast as they can. I think it is hilarious when I hear fellow executives complain about job-hopping employees, high turnover, and the lack of loyalty. What in the hell did we expect?

As a side note, I fought with every fiber in my being to keep our jobs in the US and we were successful. By investing in training, infrastructure, and world-class processes, we were able to effectively compete against anybody from anywhere. Our employees knew what we were fighting for and they knew what was at stake. And that was part of the motivation that helped us achieve those world class distinctions. We were all on the same team fighting the same enemy—and to keep those jobs in the US.

While we are talking about executive greed, let me

talk about another common executive action that I came to detest. And that is when executive management would lay off employees just to make their short-term bonuses. I saw it happen time and time again at various organizations and it is epidemic in American business today. And the employees know it. How on earth do you build loyalty and motivation when employees know that they will be thrown under the bus so that the high-level executives can make a higher bonus? I must say that I was immensely proud of my staff one tough year when they voiced the opinion that they would rather sacrifice their personal bonuses to retain good people who we knew would sustain our success in the future. I completely agreed with them and that is what we did. Now that is management you can be proud of!

I understand the need to lay off people if the company is truly in trouble and I have done it. I understand that you sometimes have to fire people (after appropriate training and counseling) if they are not doing their job. I have done it. I also understand the need to let people go if their jobs have been eliminated through sustainable efficiency improvements that make good business sense. I have done it. Those are always painful steps, but they are appropriate business actions. But letting good people go who the company needs to get the long-term job done, simply to max bonuses for the executives or to make a short-term earnings projection, is wrong in every way. In my view it is bad business, damages long term shareholder value, creates expensive employee turnover, and it is immoral. And it happens frequently today. Watch the news!

While I have talked about executive greed, let me now talk about another thing that I found appalling, and that is the extent of executive cowardice that I witnessed time and again. I wish there was another less aggressive word, but cowardice is the only appropriate word I can think of. I won't go into detail, but over my thirty-six years in business as a manager I have witnessed dozens of cases in which top-level management was doing things that were inappropriate or harmful to the business (in many cases it may have just been bad judgment, not bad intent). I have been with fellow executives who knew these things were wrong, strongly disagreed with management, and wanted to change things. But then when it counted, when they could stand up and make a difference and inform or put pressure on top management to reconsider their actions, they were silent. From most, there was nothing. Zip. Nada. It was downcast eyes, folded hands, and silence—pure unadulterated cowardice.

Why? Because they did not want to challenge top management and put their careers, compensation, bonus, or next promotion at risk. I understand that people are afraid and that there are a certain percentage of cowards in any population (remember sailing in that nor' easter and one out of five of the crew being a coward). But what appalled me was the very high percentage of executives who would simply not stand up even on issues that they were personally passionate about. At least 70 percent of executives in my opinion would not take the personal risk, and on really tough issues in which the personal risk was high, it was 90 percent of executives who would clam up. I knew that they thought management was absolutely wrong because they personally told me so, but they did not have the personal courage to stand up for what they knew was right. That lack of personal courage that I observed in executives over thirty-six years was truly shocking and disappointing. I expected more from my fellow executives.

I just could not live that way. I guess it is in my rebellious family genes that I talked about earlier, or the fact that I viewed it as a case of personal duty and honor to speak up. I have always spoken up and voiced my true position on important issues even if it was politically unwise. I suspect that I could have even gone further in my career, wherever I have been, if I had just played the game according to the generally accepted executive rules of political correctness. But that just ain't me and I would not have done it any other way even if I could go back in time. Self esteem, pride, and honor are worth more than bonuses, stock options, and promotions to me.

I will share some advice I gave one of my staff members who tended to swing in the political winds, but was basically a good guy. I told him that I knew from experience that when you are about to kick the bucket, your life does indeed flash before you. Suddenly at that moment, how much money you made, how many houses you own, your title, etc. were not important. What is important is the answer to only one question: was I a good and honorable man? The first time it happened to me I did not like the answer. But I got a do-over and survived the situation. The last time it happened I was satisfied with the answer and I now know what is most important in life. My advice to him was to always do the right thing and be a good and honorable man. So when the time comes, you are comfortable with your answer to the most important question that you will ever have to answer (see my chapter on Life and Death and what it is all about).

Now let's talk about the best business experiences, because I saw those in spades as well and they kept me going. While there was the occasional outstanding and inspiring top-level executive like Dick Osborne, he was by far the exception rather than the rule in all my years in business. The real joy of business came from "the folks". Because I found that if properly led and given the right tools, most folks want to do the right thing and do a good job. I have found that to be true in a union environment and a non-union environment. And "the folks" can include hourly people and managers below the top executive level.

My best business experiences involved my staff. I have had many excellent managers work for me and together, we have done some outstanding things. But my staff in the last five years has been magical. It has been a joy. Each one was highly ethical, team oriented, and an expert in their functional area. Most had MBAs (I did not) but generally got their MBAs while they worked so they had real world experience. Each of us had our strengths and weaknesses, but rather than create conflict, we created an environment in which those differences complemented each other and created great opportunities that would never have happened if we were more homogenous.

My staff took their cross-functional role very seriously. They thought not only of their function (which they took full responsibility for), but of the total business and aggressively challenged each other and me on broad business issues. I had the luxury of occasionally sitting back and watching ten very smart people challenge each other and I could cherry pick the great ideas that flowed. What a great team!

The other great experience was watching that team's moral courage. Even though I created an environment of challenge, I am assertive and passionate (and sometimes a jerk). It is not easy to challenge the boss, but they did and they made a difference. And I am proud of the fact that my team became known within the corporation as a group that would challenge anybody on important issues. They would take on risky issues at high levels even if it put them at personal risk.

Maybe that is why more people were promoted out of my organization to other corporate positions than any other division. There is no greater pride a manager can have than to have one of his/her people promoted within the corporation. Don't get me wrong, it is a pain in the ass too because now you have to find a replacement, but it is part of the unwritten contract that you have with your managers. Do well, and you will be recognized and promoted. I also found that when trying to attract good people, that became known and it led to a constant flow of very good people to choose from.

The other real heart-warming experience was working with the hourly folks. Once we started the teams and gain sharing, they became highly engaged in the business. They had input and impact and they took it seriously because they got a piece of the action. We were getting hundreds of suggestions a month from the hourly folks on how we could improve the business. They ran the kaisan events because they knew best how to improve their areas. And they cared. And while the goal of a kaisan event is to reduce waste on the production line (time, motion, inventory, etc.) and possibly eliminate jobs, our employees participated at full throttle because it made their jobs easier and we promised that nobody would be let go as a result of a kaisan event. We let attrition reduce the work force in order to retain trust and cooperation. And we kept our word.

To get close to the production folks and because I did not have extensive operational experience, I started having regular lunches with groups of three hourly people on a regular basis. I really enjoyed those lunches that I had with the hourly team at the plant. It may have been one of the smartest things that I did over the years. The first year or two, they were nervous and somewhat guarded because of my title. But they spoke their minds and I was straight with them. After the first year or so they found that nobody was hurt for what they said and in fact we listened and made many changes on the good ideas that I heard during the lunch. And we always responded to their questions and requests, even if the answer was no.

What surprised me over the years is how reasonable they were. Did they ask for more money or benefits? Sure they did (don't you with your boss?). But when we explained the fair and competitive process that we used to determine their pay and I asked for their feedback, they understood and respected our position. And sometimes they made good points on compensation or benefit issues and we made changes based on their input.

Because the process worked so well over the years, it got to the point that once it was announced who was going to have lunch with me, those people would be bombarded with questions that they were suppose to ask me from their peers. And I always asked them what rumors were making the rounds and what people were concerned about. It gave me a chance to squash untrue rumors, address fears about our competitors in China and Japan, or address why continuous improvement was so important, or whatever hot issue was making the rounds in the plant. For the measly price of three lunches in rural South Carolina, I got to talk directly and/or indirectly to all of the hourly employees in the plant about what was important to them and what was important to us. And I enjoyed it. Eventually, I had lunch with the great majority of our hourly production folks. These are good people just trying to do a good job.

One of the greatest pleasures that I got professionally was when we were able to combine our business responsibility with civic responsibility each year. Dick Osborne showed me through his energetic support of United Way that you can combine both. It was moving to see, and it was addictive. Once I became president, I increased our support of the United Way and provided increased incentives for employees to encourage them to support Untied Way as well. No pressure, we just created the opportunity and made it fun to participate if you chose to. Nothing made me prouder than to see the enthusiastic support of a good cause by the folks. And we matched employee donations with company donations. There were lots of volunteers and a surprising level of contributions from employees and managers at every level. Together, we provided hundreds of thousands of dollars of support for the United Way over the years, and we were always in the top contributing companies in our county.

Upon that reflection, I should also talk about the positive experience of working for an inspirational leader like Dick Osborne. We knew that he was pushing us for continuous improvement and introducing us to new world-class tools and processes. And he clearly gave me a foundation of skills and experiences from which I could build and accomplish the things that my team and I did when I got to be president. But I did not appreciate it at the time; maybe because he was tough and demanding and we had a lot of conflict. In fact, when he was considering me for president and had me shrunk with the psychologist, I thought he was getting ready to fire me! Fortunately, I recently had the chance to thank him and to tell him how much I benefited from his mentorship. As I told my staff when I announced that I would be leaving, it is sort of like the Joni Mitchell song, "Big Yellow Taxi," . . . "Don't it always seem to go that you don't know what you've got till it's gone,"

Finally, a special thank you to two extraordinary people: Anmarie Andresen, my CFO and Cary Charles, my VP of HR. Both are outstanding managers for their functions, but they are also outstanding cross-functional managers for the business, both strategically and tactically. They are the two most honest and ethical people I know. They had the moral courage to stand up to anyone including me when it had to be done. There were many times after a staff meeting when they would close my door and challenge the way that I handled something, and they were usually right. On top of that, they had to carry a special burden. As I struggled with my strategic issues, I needed someone that I could vent on and bounce my ideas and problems off. I would not want to share some of these issues with a broader audience. Anmarie and Cary were always rock solid, gave good advice, and kept me from going nuclear many times. Thanks!

In closing, the best business experience and the greatest pleasure a manager can have is watching his or her magnificent team perform at world-class levels. It just does not get better than that!

Chapter Ten

Thank God for Bill O'Reilly and Fox News

Bill O'Reilly saved my sanity. It is as simple as that. After years of watching the news on ABC, CBS, NBC, and PBS I began to think that I was living in a different country. The values, morals, philosophy, and virtues that I grew up with were gone. I felt like I was the last responsible and reasonable man in America. I was actually getting depressed and disheartened. And then my hunting buddy Drew introduced me to Bill O'Reilly! And every day after that, Bill reminded me that I was not alone and that the America I knew was still out there and fighting back. But I would not have known if it were not for Bill.

Before Bill, I watched the news intently because I am highly interested in world events. I would watch ABC's *World News* and PBS's *McNeil Lehrer Report* every night, and *60 Minutes* every weekend. According to them, everything bad that happened in the world was our fault. According to these guys, everything we did was wrong; white males were all bad, all business people were bad, and our heroes were now suppose to be the immoral actors and actresses that I despised. Christians were considered Neanderthal barbarians, and if you were a patriot and loved your country you were a hick. In short, everything that John Wayne told us was good was now bad! If you were not a metro sexual, whining liberal who constantly apologized for being a white male, from the USA, and for the abuse that was heaped on Indians and blacks two hundred years ago by our ancestors, you were archaic. If you believed in a stable marriage, the family, patriotism, and appropriate behavior you were a moron.

And then I found Bill O'Reilly. And I found out that all those virtues that I believed in: honor, self sacrifice, patriotism, hard work, and charity were alive and well in the USA. I don't agree with everything that Bill says, only maybe 95 percent! And every night when I watched him attack the destruction of American values and the media, I rejoiced. I then read Bill's books: *Culture Warrior, No Spin Zone*, and *Who's Looking Out for You*, and I felt terrific relief that those virtues I hold dear are still alive and well. I don't know what Bill will be like or what he will do in the future, but, as of today he is my hero.

Then Bill introduced me to the guy who explained how things got this way and it all suddenly made sense. Bernie Goldberg. Bernie's book *Bias* explained the incredible extent of the liberal bias of the media. Here is a seven-time Emmy Award winning liberal broadcaster with integrity who had liberal views. But he knew as a professional broadcaster that he had a professional obligation to present the truth and the facts. The fact that he was appalled by the extent that the liberal media distorted the news and then proved it with incredible facts and details knocked me over. The liberal media is poisoning our nation just like the Nazi or Soviet propaganda machine did in Germany and Russia. Every American must read

Bias to understand the wide-spread danger we are facing (his other books like *Arrogance, 100 People Who Are Screwing Up America,* and *Crazies to the Left of Me and Wimps to the Right* are all great reads). Bernard, you are also a hero!

I got to see first hand the media bias that Bernie brought to our attention. I was lucky enough to see President Bush speak to an audience of roughly five thousand people. He spoke for an hour and a half and he was great. The audience gave him several standing ovations. He was clear, concise, funny, and inspirational. The only negative event was when one woman stood up for ten seconds and yelled to bring the troops home from Iraq. She was immediately hauled out and the president never broke stride. After the speech, I noticed one of the news organizations recording the event with their local newscaster and wondered how they would report it. Sure enough, the newscast that night focused on the ten-second incident and the fact that there were apparently a few protestors outside the building. They did not report on the president's excellent hour-and-a-half speech or the fact that five thousand people gave him several standing ovations. It was biased and dishonest reporting in my opinion, and I saw it with my own eyes.

Today, I watch *Fox News* and Bill, Brit and Hannidy to get the straight scoop. And then I watch the *McNeil Lehrer Report* to get the liberal view of the world (but at least they are rational and generally accurate) just to understand the other side and to keep *Fox News* honest. I also now watch Glenn Beck who has an excellent perspective as well. ABC, CBS, CNN, and NBC are just too far off in the ozone to be taken seriously on most issues in my opinion.

Bill has done a great job on raising the illegal alien issue, the war on terror, the bias against Christians and faith, crimes against children, and the media's relentless assault on the very values that made our country great. The most exciting thing I saw was when Bill targeted Pepsi and France as boycott targets. When Pepsi hired the rapper Ludicrous as a spokesman, Bill said he would never buy another Pepsi product until they dropped him because of his destructive impact on kids. The **next day** Pepsi dropped Ludicrous. Bill, why don't you do that every week on some targeted bad influence! What a relief to see that we could have an impact. While the boycott on France did not have the same rapid degree of impact, it did hurt France. I supported both boycotts (I am glad that France changed governments because they do have some nice stuff) and I would support more. Take the lead Bill! Let's go after these folks in the only way that will have an impact—their wallets!

While I don't normally watch CNN, they do have one very effective broadcaster, Lou Dobbs. Lou is a Peabody Award winner and has done a marvelous job on raising the illegal immigrant issue like Bill has. But Lou has absolutely led the charge on how American corporations and executive management are shipping American jobs and technology to China and other countries, which will put our country and our way of life in peril. Lou's book, *Exporting America*, is a must-read illustration of the damage that outright corporate greed and government complicity are causing our nation as our leaders work feverishly to ship our jobs to China, India, and Mexico. Bill O'Reilly, this is one subject that you have not jumped on. It is urgent that you lend your great impact to this critical issue before it is too late. If we can get both Bill and Lou hitting this issue, we can make a difference.

The American media is the greatest danger our nation faces. No enemy can beat us if we are united and American virtues remain strong. But the American media is doing everything it can to destroy those American virtues. Hollywood is a cesspool of immorality in my opinion. It is a collection of immoral, unpatriotic, uneducated (in general), prima donnas, spoiled brats who live in another world. The movies and television programs that they produce are destroying our culture and our children.

The proof of the devastation is overwhelming. Divorce has grown from roughly five percent in 1960 to roughly 50 percent today. Children born out of wedlock have grown from roughly 5 percent in 1960 to 40 percent overall and as much as 70 percent in the African American community today. Data shows that children born to single mothers have a 70 percent probability of remaining in poverty for the rest of their lives. Drug use, alcoholism, violence, and the high school drop-out rate have skyrocketed since the 1960's and the baby boom generation. Most recently, we were informed that 25 percent of all teenagers and 50 percent of African American teenagers have sexually-transmitted diseases. What a tragedy and what an illustration of the destruction of our culture and the damage that it is bringing to those we love most, our children.

The primary goal of civilization and culture over the last 100,000 plus years has been to strengthen the family unit so that children can succeed, and to pass on the values and cultural attributes that will result in strong families and cultures. We have made steady progress as a species for thousands of years until 1960. But I read recently in a sociology publication that the American culture has caused more damage to the family unit in just forty years than has been seen anywhere else in the last 100,000 years. And it is the result of our media. And folks, if you read Osama Bin Ladin's manifesto (or the 9/11 Commission Report), that is why they hate us and call us the Great Satan! It's our media's attack on family values.

Think about it. Television and movies today relentlessly glamorize and glorify senseless murder, irresponsible sex, divorce and bad behavior, and humiliate anyone who believes in

God, family, and country. Over a week, keep track of the number of murders, incidents of immoral behavior, and criticisms of American values that you see on TV, the movies, and on your children's computer games. Our kids are being overwhelmed. And even if you are giving them the right direction, that is for maybe a few hours a day. For the other eight to ten hours the media is relentlessly telling your children that you are a fool and your values are silly.

How can this be? How did we get here? It's very simple: money. Listen carefully and I will describe the enemy and how they threaten who we are. It starts with advertising agencies. They have determined that anyone over twenty has already made their brand decisions. The older age group knows what kind of car they want, what shirts they like, which fast food restaurant they want to go to, and so forth. So the ad agencies have told their clients not to waste their money on the older age groups. The ad target is children and teenagers who have not formed their brand loyalties yet.

Sounds innocent enough so far, but if you want to target this young audience, what kind of entertainment will appeal to them and draw them in? Will this audience want to see what is good for them or hear something that tells them that they need to follow society's rules and values, work hard, be patient, and occasionally experience self sacrifice? Or do kids want to hear that there are no rules; they can have whatever they want right now, indiscriminant sex is good, hard work is boring, and that self sacrifice, patience, and patriotism are for losers? While the ad agencies started the problem, Hollywood and the media are the agents destroying our culture as they create ever worsening immoral trash to infect our children with.

It started slowly, but once the trend was established, TV, movies, radio, and games kept getting worse and worse to draw that audience—much like the gladiator games had to get more and more decadent to pacify the masses in Rome until the culture collapsed. It is in this environment that Hollywood and the media raises its immoral head and feeds on this illness and destroys our children, our values, and if we don't stop it, our nation. And all so that businessmen can reach the young target audience that the ad agencies have identified so they can sell more product to make more money. The media is the decadent vessel that allows it all to happen. In early Rome, actors were considered to be below prostitutes in the social pecking order. Like so much else about Rome, they were right, and ahead of their time!

Wake up America before our children and our culture are destroyed. Our children now live in two worlds and they are desperately confused. On the one hand, they have parents who are trying to teach them the values that made this nation great. On the other hand, the media and Hollywood are telling them that their parents are fools and they can and should have everything that they want as soon as they want it with no work. Folks, just like the grouse population cycles that I talked about or the sudden die-off of the deer herd in hard times, there will be a day of reckoning. And those who don't understand the timeless rules of nature and society will be thinned from the herd. It's nothing personal. It is just the way it is—natural selection.

Bill O'Reilly, please target the worst of the media each week and organize a boycott for the "folks" every week. Let's identify the companies that sponsor the worst offenders and target them for action. Once we hit their profits, behavior will change. It can make a difference and the folks are looking for a leader. Hit the bad guys in the only place that they care about, their profits. You can do it! We just need a leader.

Chapter Eleven

The Ecstasy of Sailing and Diving

You cannot allow yourself to be dominated by the unpleasant things in life and I think that is why God created sailing and diving. Surely sailing and diving were gifts from God because they are both so exquisite. Both can be quietly beautiful, colorful, peaceful, and inspirational. And both can be terrifying, life threatening, and out of control. Just like life. But they will always take your mind off the mundane and sometimes depressing aspects of everyday life!

Sailing

Picture bright blue skies with puffy white clouds and beautiful deep blue waters; the temperature is a pleasant eighty degrees and you are with the love of your life and your best friends. The wind is a pleasant ten knots and you are at the helm of your thirty-six-foot sloop heading to your favorite port and restaurant for dinner. The sails are trimmed perfectly and your boat is heeling gently with the wind and smoothly cutting through the modest rolling waves. You are in total control, on course, and you are the master of your domain. Life is as good as it gets. That is sailing!

Or sailing is grey skies and grey water with thirty-knot winds howling through the rigging. You are cold and the boat is heeling twenty degrees. You are slamming through ten-foot waves at hull speed and every shroud, sail, and sheet is straining with the incredible forces. While in control, you are being tested by nature and adrenalin is surging through your body. You are exhilarated and you are totally alive. That is sailing!

And sailing is the story I told earlier in the book of battling hurricane-force winds, water spouts, fifteen-foot breaking seas, and listening to other sailors over the radio perish in the very same storm that you are struggling to survive in, and wondering if you will live to see the next day. Sailing is all of these things, but no matter what, it always makes you feel more alive and glad that you are here on earth.

Here's an experience that had a major impact on how I view sailing. I was on the racing crew of an Etchells which is a very fast thirty-foot racing sloop. We raced every Wednesday afternoon in a very competitive fleet out of Chicago. Racing is intense and anybody who races is just a little nuts. One day we were racing a few miles offshore when we were suddenly hit by gale-force winds, rain, and eight-to-ten-foot seas. Normally one would shorten sail under these conditions, but not racers! We had full sails up and we were driving so hard that we (three of us) were all on the windward side of the boat to keep her from blowing over. Since I was the biggest and strongest guy, I had the tiller to keep her on course. It was a very wild ride!

I told the skipper that I could not see the leeward side because of the main sail and the fact that we were heeling twenty-five degrees, and he told me that he would keep an eye out and let me know if we had to take evasive action. We screamed down a ten-foot wave and just as our bow got buried in the trough, the skipper yelled "hard a lee" which means turn the boat and cross the wind right now! Only we weren't going anywhere until the bow pulled out of the trough and we got steerage back. Suddenly, at the top of the wave above us (ten feet high) is a Soling class boat (a little smaller than us) headed right to us amidships. There is clearly going to be one massive collision and I cannot do anything about it.

Coming from above us, the bow of the Soling did hit us amidships but on top of our deck, knocking us all into the cockpit deck. We are now looking up at the Soling's bow and then amazingly, the Soling slid down across our deck and dropped off the stern. For a moment, we thought we had avoided a catastrophe, but what we did not notice was that our back stay (one of the cables supporting the mast) sawed itself into the Soling's bow and as the Soling fell off, it brought our mast down with it. Looking up we saw the mast collapsing on top of us! Needless to say, that was not good.

We were now in gale-force winds, eight-to-ten-foot seas, our mast down and threatening to puncture our hull, and the Soling still connected to us by our back stay and slamming into us. All of this is not good! Time stopped and we were all frozen for what seemed an eternity. Because I was at the tiller, I felt responsible for this mess and jumped out of the cockpit onto the stern, and with all of my might I pushed the Soling away and we separated. That is the good news.

The bad news is that I fell overboard from the push and the motion of the high and choppy seas and I was between the two boats. Wow! Well the good news is that I had a PFD (personal flotation device) on so I didn't drown, and somehow I didn't get crushed between the boats and I eventually got back into the boat. We then secured the mast to avoid sinking and rigged a sail on the stump of the mast. Thank goodness the sheriff saw us and towed us back to the harbor.

You would think that everyone would be overwhelmed by the experience because we could have been crushed, we could have sunk, I might have drowned or been crushed, and the Soling was taking on water and she could have sunk. If you thought that, you don't know racers! To them it was no big deal—just one of the hazards of racing—and they could not wait to get back out on the water as soon as the damage was repaired.

I took away a different experience. It changed how I sail. From then on, safety became number one. I carry backups for everything, and I don't trust anyone's judgment but mine, and I carry gear to cut away the mast as well as a life raft and EBIRB (emergency satellite beacon which allows the coast guard to find you and save your butt!). If you sail on my boat, you wear a PFD or you don't go. And I walk everyone through safety procedures before we shove off. Shit happens (don't I know it!) and I want to be prepared.

This leads to a funny story that Ev hates but I love to tell (all's fair in love and war and marriage). We were sailing with non-boating friends one day in light fog with visibility of maybe four hundred yards about five miles from shore. My wife calmly said, "I can see Milwaukee." Now I know that Milwaukee is twenty-five miles away and we can only see four hundred yards so I decide to check it out. It is the SS Milwaukee (large freighter) and it is bearing right down on us and fast! After our own fast action and an abrupt course change (I called on the radio and the freighter said he saw me), we watched as the freighter slid by a lot closer than I would ever like. Bottom line, after that racing experience, I now have to check out everything myself although Ev has always said that right after she said it was Milwaukee, she knew it could not be. But I am not going to cut her any slack!

Most of the time sailing is peaceful and under control. Usually you can avoid heavy weather and choose to sail in the best of it, although nature always has a way of surprising you and you had better always be prepared. But some of us like heavy weather and the test and the excitement that it provides.

Ev and I love to cruise and go to new ports. There is something really cool about leaving your home port just as the sun is starting to rise and heading your bow out to blue water with no land in sight. Even after years of experience, I still get a kick out of plugging a latitude and longitude in to my GPS and fourteen hours later arriving right at the mouth of the harbor that was our destination. Amazing!

I really love night cruising. We program our destination into our GPS and head out as the sun goes down. It is exciting and just a little bit scary to head into the darkness of open water. But later that night when you are at least twenty-five miles off shore, magic occurs. Without the distraction of the lights from shore, the moon and the stars simply explode out of the sky. The sky is absolutely cluttered with light! If you are in the ocean, you may get the added attraction of seeing your wake glow in the dark as your hull disturbs the plankton. It is beautiful.

But if a storm hits at night, it is scary as hell. At night, all of the threats and your fears are multiplied by ten. Surely at night there are sea monsters lurking to take ship and crew! There is no sight as beautiful as the sun rising in the east after you have battled heavy seas all night. It is like being reborn. You get a similar feeling if you have been battling heavy seas and storms for hours and/or days and you start to see the first dim outlines of land for the first time. Salvation!

We had a terrifying night sail during the same trip in which we battled hurricane winds around the Bahamas. Here's the story: As we shoved off, the owner of the boat told us two things to keep in mind. First, when we cross the Gulf Stream, remember that the sharks are migrating and they are all over the place. And second, if the automatic bilge pump kicks on, you are sinking because it is set high. Good things to know!

We left West Palm at sundown and headed to our destination, West End Bahamas, which is ninety miles away. Hours later, it was pitch black and we were approaching the Gulf Stream. A storm hit and the wind blew the opposite direction of the Gulf Stream building the waves anywhere from ten to fifteen feet. It is a bumpy ride and the wind was coming right off our bow. We tacked for a while until some gear fell down from the rigging above. Fearing a rigging failure and tired of tacking, we pulled the sails down and started the engine. We motored for some time and suddenly the motor stopped. And then the automatic bilge pump kicked on!

Holy shit! It is pitch dark, we can't sail because of the broken rigging (we thought), the motor is dead, we are in ten-foot waves in the middle of the Gulf Stream packed with migrating sharks, and we are sinking. This is not good!

Well we checked the bilge and we were not sinking. We decided to try the sails again since we had no other choice, and they stayed up. It looked like we would live after all. Finally the sun came up and there has never been a more beautiful sight. We had made it.

But our ordeal is not quite done. These are the days before GPS and all we had was a radio direction finder and dead reckoning for navigation. We were way off course from the storm and the constant tacking. We didn't have a clue where we were. And then, way off to starboard, we saw a tiny pile of rocks no larger than a car with a flashing beacon light. Checking the flashing sequence in the chart, we found that we were looking at the very last point in the Bahamas. If we had missed that tiny pile of rocks, we would have ended up in Africa or some place like that! Well, after hours and hours, we found our way back to the West End (bumping in to a few reefs) but the sun was going down and we decided not to chance the tricky course between the reefs into the harbor and we dropped anchor.

Anchoring is another challenge. All night we worried that our anchor would slip and we would drift out to sea. The Viking slept on deck, and with his glasses off, he could not see the landmarks that would have confirmed that we were still at anchor. So he started yelling that we had drifted out to sea. I ran up from below, tripped on a cleat, and almost ended up in the ocean. We had not gone anywhere; he just had his glasses off! When I got home from that trip, my wife had a funny story to share with whoever would listen (kind of like my SS Milwaukee story). I sleep naked (sorry but it is relevant) and for a full week after I got home, I would get out of bed in the middle of the night (I was sleep walking), throw open the drapes of our townhouse and stand there for anybody in the parking lot to see, apparently checking to see if the anchor was holding in my nightmare. Finally after a week of this, as I was getting up for my nightly exhibition, Ev told me that she had already checked and the anchor was solid. For whatever reason, that ended it. I am sure that our neighbors were greatly relieved!

Heavy fog is another real challenge. I remember one cruise in which Ev and my son Ben and I crossed Lake Michigan from Ludington, Michigan to Sheboygan, Wisconsin with sailing friends Tom and Helen in another boat. It is normally about a ten-hour trip. We were surrounded by fog so thick that you could not see more than ten yards in front of the boat and the fog stayed with us the whole trip. The scariest part was crossing the freighter lanes and hoping and praying that the Badger (large car ferry) or some freighter did not run us over because we would never see them coming (we did not have radar at the time).

I had just purchased my first GPS for navigation and I had not yet had the time to build my confidence with it. Here is a device for about $500 that supposedly talks to satellites hundreds of miles in the heavens and calculates within thirty yards where you are on earth. Yea, right! Well I had no choice but to trust it in the fog and I followed the heading it told me to take. Ten hours later we were very close to the harbor according to the GPS and the depth is exactly what the chart says it should be if the GPS is right. Suddenly the coast guard announces a tornado warning and tells everyone to get off the lake. Great.

We are already nervous and now we have to deal with a potential tornado plus the fog. In addition, there is suppose to be a harbor fog horn which I should hear now but I don't hear a fog horn. According to the chart there is a reef near by so it is important that we choose the right course.

Of course I told Ev and Ben that everything was under control and I knew exactly where we were (I wish). I sent Ben to the bow to look for the harbor entrance and suddenly, quite calmly and totally trusting me he says, "There it is dad." It was ten yards away and we were about to hit it. Amazing! A miracle! We were saved! We got to the dock and tied up two minutes before the storm hit and the wind started screaming. We made it. It wasn't until we got to the restaurant that we found out that the city turned off the fog horn because it was disturbing the folks in town. You have got to love it. By the way, the next day I bought a back-up GPS and today I have three of them on board (who says I am anal?). I still think that it is magic, but they do work!

I have sailed in Lake Michigan, the Atlantic Ocean, Pacific Ocean, Chesapeake Bay, and all over the Caribbean; from Nantucket to the British Virgin Islands and from Hawaii to Annapolis. I love to explore the ocean and I particularly love diving the endless reefs around the world. But I do love sailing Lake Michigan out of my home port of Racine which is a great harbor. I like the fact that there are no sharks and there is no salt! Some people say that Lake Michigan is not enough of a challenge but I think that issue has been settled forever by Ted Turner. Before he raced the Mac (the longest fresh water sailing race in the world [333 miles] from Chicago to Mackinac Island), he said the same thing. But racing in the Mac he got hit by gale-force winds and heavy seas. After the race, Ted got on the TV and apologized to all Great Lakes sailors! I have sailed plenty of times on Lake Michigan in ten-foot seas, I have seen twenty-foot seas, and theoretically you can get thirty-foot seas in Lake Michigan. That is exciting enough for me!

But if I had to pick one perfect sail, it was off Maui. We wanted to sail on America2, the boat that finished second in the America's Cup race in the 1980's or 1990's. The first day we tried, the wind was over fifty mph and their insurance wouldn't let them go. We would have gone! The second day the wind died down to a paltry forty-five mph with ten-foot seas. They told us we were a go and Ev and I were stoked.

Arriving at the dock, we saw America2 in all her glory. She was a machine. Titanium hull with a huge rig (mast) made for racing (forty feet was taken off to make her more manageable and I cannot imagine the full rig when I looked at her). Our skipper is in his twenty's and he was born and raised on a working schooner. And then we headed out. When we got to the open ocean, they let her go and suddenly we were going fifteen knots through ten-foot seas. For you non-sailors, that is roughly eighteen mph through high seas, which is warp speed for a sailboat. It feels like two hundred mph in a race car. It seemed to me that 50 percent of the time we were under water as we smashed through the waves. It was incredible. I turned around and looked at the skipper and he was comfortably seated and steering with his feet!

We sail a lot and we love it. Most of the sailing is on beautiful days with blue skies, a cold beer, Jimmy Buffet on the stereo, and friends nearby on their boats. We love cruising and discovering new ports. An important part of sailing is the great friends that you make on the dock and sharing meals, drinks, dessert, and tall tales. Friends like Tom and Karen with whom we have cruised most of Southern Lake Michigan and the BVI over the years and shared lots of exciting sails. Each year we look forward to choosing exciting new ports and restaurants to explore or revisiting past favorites with Tom and Karen. And friends like Tom and Helen, Chris and Terry, Ken and Kathy and a host of others with whom we share sailing, meals, or just lots of laughs all summer on the dock. Sometimes sailing is dropping anchor on a calm day and diving into the shallow aqua marine blue waters to cool down. When you're sailing, the world slows down, your cares drift away and life is good.

Another aspect of sailing that is probably hard for non-sailors to understand is the love you have for your boat. Mine is a thirty-six-foot (okay, thirty-five-foot, six-inch) Beneteau and she is beautiful. Your boat is a lady and you love her. After all, you have to trust that she will keep you safe and get you home in thirty-knot winds and ten-foot seas. After a while you don't have to look at your instruments when you are sailing because you become one with your boat. You feel her moves and when everything is tuned just right, she actually hums through the water.

Sailing takes constant attention because there are a million adjustments that you can make to the sails to get the max out of her. And just when you have it right, the wind or the waves make a minor change and you have to do it all again. But you see, it is not work, it is love. And because of that constant attention and becoming one with the boat, your troubles blow away with the wind!

If you are the captain, there is one more dimension to sailing. For centuries, the captain of the boat has carried the deep responsibility of the safety of the boat and all of the souls on board. You are responsible for the lives of your crew and anybody else that you might put in harms way. Knowing what Mother Nature can do, you take that responsibility very, very seriously. You consider every possibility and you prepare for it. In addition to PFDs, a life raft, EBIRB, flares, and jack lines and harnesses, I carry cable cutters and a hacksaw in case we lose the mast (remember the Etchells race). One of the benefits of having been through most of the worst-case scenarios is that you take them seriously and you prepare for them. So as much as sailing is beautiful and relaxing (most of the time), as the captain, the responsibility that is yours is always top of mind. But for me, I enjoy that responsibility because I have the confidence to know that I can handle it and I am prepared for it. That adds a strong satisfaction to sailing that those who have not been the captain will never know.

And then again, of course, there is the excitement. I will share one more story to try to give you a feel for it. Ev and I decided to sail from Racine to Chicago to meet our son for dinner and enjoy the city. The forecast was good with no severe weather so we were anticipating a pleasant ten-hour sail. All is good as we cast off and set sail heading south in fair winds.

About twenty-five miles or three and a half hours from Chicago, our radio blasted a severe weather alert. Fifty-mile per-hour-winds, lightning, and hail are going to hit in thirty minutes. Our top speed was 7.6 knots so we were not going to beat the storm. So we battened down the hatches, got our foul weather gear, harnesses, and jack lines (to keep us on the boat if we get knocked down) and made ready. There was not much else to do. And then we saw it coming.

We could see Chicago twenty miles in the distance when suddenly a huge black cloud appeared to open its jaws and devour the entire city. We have a great picture of it! Suddenly all is black, Chicago is gone, and we are hit with fifty-mile-per-hour wind and driving rain. That we can handle, although it is, to say the least, exciting. It is the lightning that is striking all over the place that really captures our full attention. Watching repeated lightning strikes drawing closer to your boat is not a good feeling when you are sitting next to a fifty-foot metal mast! We were waiting for the hail, but fortunately we missed that. The next hour was exciting, but we got through it okay; we are spared a lightning strike, and with great relief we pulled into port and met our son at the restaurant. You cannot imagine how good that first beer tasted. That is sailing!

Diving

Picture gin-clear waters at a pleasant eighty degrees in the Cayman Islands; you are a hundred feet below the surface and you can still see blue skies and the boat above. Although the boat is a hundred feet away you almost feel like you can touch it. You are weightless at neutral buoyancy and you hear the reassuring sound of your breathing through your regulator and you can see the bubbles dance around your head as they work their way to the surface. You are at the "Wall" where the reef suddenly drops straight down 5,000 feet. In front of you, there is a splash of colors from the coral reef itself to the hundreds of brightly colored tropical fish that busily squirt all around you. An incredible mixture of bright reds, oranges, blues, yellows, and every other color in the rainbow. Below you lay the abyss; you follow the wall down with your eyes until all turns black and your imagination anticipates what lurks in the darkness. But all is calm, serene, and beautiful. That is diving!

But diving can also be the exhilaration of jumping off a perfectly good boat at night in to the dark sea for a night dive. I don't mind saying that night dives scare the hell out of me and I love them. First, I know that there is a twenty-foot great white shark just beyond the beam of my flashlight. You can spot me on a night dive because my flashlight is the one that is waving madly as I look for that shark! But then as you approach the reef, it is so beautiful that you forget to be afraid. The colors of the coral really come out at night and you see life forms that you don't see during the day. Like the six-foot moray eel that leaves his den for a nighttime stretch. Bright yellow-green and massive, they are beautiful! And no, they won't bother you if you don't bother them. Or the sleeping fish that are all around, like colorful parrotfish that are motionless and do, in fact, seem to be sleeping. Octopus come out at night and they are really cool as they change colors right before you eyes.

My best night dive was at Maui over the snake pit. The day before the dive, someone at the dive shop asked if I was going on a night dive and I told him the name of the reef we were going to. "Ah, the snake pit," he said. "You won't ever forget that." He was right! First we had to swim through a four-knot current which was impossible. We dragged ourselves hand over hand along the sand bottom. Getting past the current, we were in the coral and eels of every kind surrounded us. They were swimming to my left, to my right, and between my legs—all kinds of them, from moray eels to leopard eels. Hundreds of them and they never caused a problem. But they sure had my attention!

I have dived all over the place from the Cayman Islands, Hawaii, the Florida Keys, St. Marten, Aruba, etc., but my best diving was at Maui. I dove day after day with five-foot turtles that were so close I could touch them. As I said, the snake pit was also at Maui.

My best day dive was when we dove on an ancient Hawaiian village site seventy feet below the surface. I don't know if it sunk or if the ocean rose but there were intricate steps carved into the rock by the ancient natives that lead down to what used to be the water's edge. Great reef fish were everywhere and it was beautiful. From there we swam to some caves which held three six-foot, white-tipped reef sharks. White tipped reef sharks are man-eaters but they are on the friendlier side of man-eaters and they are not overtly hostile. Apparently they will only eat you if they are pissed at you or very hungry. Anyway I was in the cave with them and they were less than six feet away. I kept one eye on the sharks to make sure that they were not pissed or hungry and one eye on the dive master to see if he is cool. Everybody seemed to be having a good time and finally the sharks got bored and headed out of the cave.

I didn't mention that on that dive my wife and about twenty people were above us snorkeling at the surface. The three white-tip reef sharks started motoring all around and headed toward the snorkelers. Getting closer to the snorkelers than I would like, the sharks finally peeled off and went away. Getting back to the surface, I asked my wife if she saw the three sharks that zoomed by her. Nope. Morale to the story: as a diver you are part of the action. As a swimmer or snorkeler, you are bait!

Generally, diving is very safe if you follow the rules.

But the rules are unforgiving, which is why you have to be certified by PADI or some other agency. Don't dive without the instruction, because this is a case of "what you don't know can kill you." As an example, I got my certification over thirty-six years ago when I was twenty-one. Being way too cool, I didn't think the rules applied to me. So on one dive where I did not stick with my buddy (cardinal rule), I was having a good time at seventy feet and decided to stay down after I started to run out of air and pop my reserve once I was out of air and go up on my reserve. Now this is stupid for several reasons. The rule is you go up when you have 500 pounds of air or less, and you don't count on your reserve. I was invincible so I waited until I was completely out of air and pulled my reserve, but I found that the reserve had already been pulled. I was seventy feet down and completely out of air!

This is another of the times that my life flashed before my eyes (all twenty-one years!). I am going to die. I only get to choose how. If I hold my breath and speed to the surface (which is what my body is screaming at me to do right now), I will die instantly as my lungs explode with the decreasing pressure of the water and the increasing pressure in my lungs. My lungs will explode within five feet of starting up. On the other hand, if I follow the rules and go up slowly and only as fast as my bubbles while exhaling all the way up, I will certainly run out of air and drown. I decided that if I was going to die, I was going to do it according to the rules. I did not want it to be said that I panicked. Amazingly I found out that as I rose and the water pressure on my lungs decreased, the air pressure in my lungs and in my tank were enough to keep me alive even though I exhaled all the way up (I should have figured that out, but I don't remember them telling us that in class). I was totally amazed to get to the surface alive.

The morale of this story is to do exactly what they tell

you in your certification class and you will certainly be alright. I have been diving for thirty-six years and 99 percent of my dives were beautiful and uneventful. You can make diving as exciting as you want to or as safe and uneventful as you want to. All of my close calls have been because I was not following the rules. Like the time that I mentioned that I ran out of air. Or the time I was with a group of divers who dove in ten-foot seas. Because we were veterans, the dive master thought it would be okay so we all went in. However I would recommend in the future that hanging on to a dive ladder and looking up at a ten-ton boat that is several feet above you and heading down on you is a bad idea. Now that I have finally grown up (it took fifty years) and follow the rules, all diving is good!

Chapter Twelve

Books that Will Rock Your World

Reading is one of life's simple but incredible joys and in my view, a civic responsibility so that you can participate in the decisions of life in an informed way. It is a shame that it is a skill that is rapidly disappearing in our new culture (read *The Dumbest Generation* by Mark Bauerlein). All the knowledge that you could desire about our planet, galaxy, history, philosophy, religion or any other possible subject is available for anyone who is simply willing to go to the library.

I wanted to use this chapter to share some incredible books that I have read over the years that have had a major impact on me and my outlook on the world. Books provide the critical knowledge that each of us must have to be responsible citizens and make good decisions. In my view, the books that I will be sharing are like gifts of knowledge and they will change your view of the world. I have expressed some very strong opinions throughout this book and the knowledge found in some of the following books is part of the supporting proof of my positions.

First are five books that several experts say have had the greatest impact on western knowledge and philosophy and that everyone should read if they want to understand our world today. I will start with those and share what I learned from them:

Decline and Fall of the Roman Empire written by Edward Gibbon in 1776. This is an incredible but massive work. Historians today still call it the best book ever written on history. Reading it is work, but well, well, worth it. It is the story of the Roman Empire and how it collapsed, but the lessons to be learned are timeless and for any great society of any age. Just change the names and you could be reading today's papers. Some of the debates that he describes in the Senate of Rome are happening in our Senate today. It is amazing that history just keeps repeating itself and we never seem to learn the lessons of the past. The same arguments that we are having today about morals and values, outsourcing, welfare, the military, and immigration were being debated 2,000 years ago and are covered in detail by Gibbons. Amazing! And it tells you how the story can end if you don't get it right. In the case of Rome, the result was the destruction of the dominant and most powerful world power and leader in technology with the highest standard of living in the world resulting in 1,000 years of dark ages and suffering! Rome was lost through the decline of its values and morals, and the "will" of the Roman people to stand strong in a dangerous world and abandoning the traits that made them great. Those same morals and values and our own national will are being tested today in a dangerous world.

Battle Cry of Freedom by James McPherson is a great and very readable book about the American Civil War. Winning the Pulitzer Prize, this book makes the Civil War come alive. Reading it is like reading today's headlines on the war in Iraq. Forty percent of Americans in the North did not think it was worth American lives to free the slaves. There were riots against the war and President Lincoln was called stupid, an ape, incompetent, and every name that President Bush has been called during the Iraq war. The Union lost most of the big battles in the first two years and the press labeled Lincoln and his generals incompetent (sound familiar?). Six hundred thousand Americans died, and in the South 50 percent of military-age men were wounded or killed during the war. After reading this book I bought some actual newspapers from the time and I swear it is like reading the *New York Times* about the Iraq war today. They called President Lincoln a war criminal and the destroyer of American civil liberties when he suspended the writ of habeas corpus. Amazing. The more things change, the more they stay the same! But the primary take-away of this book for me was the incredible power of resolute leadership, the greatness of Lincoln, the toughness of the American people at that time, and the incredible sacrifice made by Americans in the name of freedom and our country. I wonder if we would be willing to make those sacrifices today for those same principles.

Rise and Fall of the Third Reich by William L. Shirer. This is a horrifying story about Hitler and the Third Reich and why 60 million people did not have to die. It outlines the cost of international cowardice and why peace through strength, not appeasement, can prevent massive war and loss of life. Hitler himself said that had Britain and France "sent one soldier" to stop him in Austria, Alsace Lorraine, or Czechoslovakia, he would have turned around and gone home and there would have been no war. But the cowardice of politicians in Britain (Neville Chamberlain and "peace in our time"), France, and the world as he grabbed power convinced him that they would never try to stop him. And finally when the world stood up to him, he had all but conquered Europe and 60 million people had to die around the world to end the war that could have been avoided. Do we ever learn? It is a great but terrifying book. How one of the most sophisticated and civilized nations on earth could resort to the horrible inhumanities that Germany did should be a wake-up call to all of us and forever.

Freedom from Fear by David Kennedy is a great book which explains what the United States went through from the Roaring Twenties to the end of World War II. It is a very readable and riveting book. It outlines how the Roaring Twenties were very similar to what we are seeing today with immoral behavior, irresponsible spending by the public, a stock market that lost its grasp on reality, and then the economic crash which originated with land and housing price collapses in Florida. Sound familiar? It graphically outlines the impact of the crash, how hard it hit regular folks, and how close we came to chaos and communism. And then it covers World War II and how 88 percent of Americans did not want to help France, Britain, and the rest of Europe fight Hitler. Only the attack on Pearl Harbor changed their minds. It shows the continuous trend that most Americans generally don't support wars as in the Revolutionary War, the Civil War, and then World War II. It takes a brave and determined leader to stay the course, take the heat from the press, and persevere to win as Roosevelt did. Just like today in Iraq. It clearly shows how the United Sates with its manufacturing might and technology, and Russia with the blood of twenty million dead led the way to final victory in World War II. And the book shows that Britain and Winston Churchill will forever earn honor for their courage in standing alone against Hitler until America and Russia joined the war.

The Iliad. Homer's timeless classic will forever describe the best and the worst traits of man. *The Iliad* was the bible for ancient Greece and Alexander the Great and created those great societies. It shows that what drives man has not changed in 3,500 years. Positive attributes such as honor, sacrifice, and pride are offset by brutality, jealously, and arrogance—just like today. It's a tough but beautiful read. You can't consider yourself literate until you have read it. If you read it in high school it doesn't count. Reread it as an adult when you have some idea what life is all about.

Those are the five must-read classics according to some and they are incredibly powerful (and I agree that they are the basics). There are a million more great books out there. Here are a few that I think have high impact and will change your view of the world.

The 9/11 Commission Report formally named **Final Report of the National Commission on Terrorist Attacks Upon the United States**, is the official report of the events leading up to the September 11, 2001 attack. It was prepared at the request of President Bush and Congress by the bipartisan National Commission on Terrorist Attacks Upon the United States (informally known as the "9/11 Commission." This is absolutely a must read. It never ceases to amaze me when I debate the Iraq war and our war on terrorism with people, how few have any facts whatsoever on something as critical as our war on terror and the deadliest attack on the soil of America. They have no facts, they are totally ignorant, yet they get to vote and they have strong opinions. This is a powerful book. The second chapter, The Foundation of the New Terrorism, tells in just twenty-four pages why the militant Islamists want to kill us all. Their view of the world has been around for over 1,300 years and they have attacked the West repeatedly for that long. They conquered the Middle East by the sword, converted Constantinople (Turkey) by the sword, and invaded Spain, France, and Eastern Europe repeatedly. If you want to participate in the debate, then you have to read this. If you don't read this, shut up and please don't vote.

The Koran and the Hadith. After 9/11, I wanted learn more about our new enemy so I read the Koran and much of the Hadith. I found out first, why they are an old enemy, and second why there are two Islams; one good and one that is very bad. Ninety-five percent of the Koran is peaceful, respectful, and quite honestly, beautiful. But there are some passages that are simply unacceptable to our culture regarding the treatment of "non-believers" that will always be a source of potential violence between Islam and any other religion. But you will not find the horrible treatment of women and others in the Koran that you see in some Islamic cultures today. The Koran is the word of God told to Muhammad by an angel, and in many ways it is a similar message as that found in the Christian Bible. The Hadith is Islam's interpretation of God's word which has been continuously modified over time. And that is where things get nasty. When you learn about Islam's history of violence and its view of a Muslim's obligations to spread Islam at any cost, you will understand why we have been at war with Islam for 1,300 years. Add to that, according to the Koran and Muhammad, the only certain way a Muslim can get to heaven is to die a martyr (they also get seventy-two virgins and lamb in paradise for being a martyr), and you then have an appreciation of the irrational danger that the rest of the world faces.

A majority of the 1.5 billion Muslims in the world are good

people and just want to live their lives in peace. Unfortunately that leaves millions of Muslims who want to kill us all; who will not compromise one iota, will use the most heinous means to kill our children and our wives, and would be happy to die as a martyr doing it. I am not sure how you negotiate with that thought process. The conflict between militant Islam and all other beliefs will be a life-and-death problem for the world for a very long time!

The Bible is easy to take for granted because we are a Judeo-Christian nation and we have heard about the Bible throughout our lives in church; it is the foundation of our culture. It is a magnificent book, and we are finding out that much of the Old Testament is grounded in history although there is an incredible amount of important disagreement about critical facts in both the Old and New Testament within the Bible itself. I must admit I do not understand the sudden change in God's views from the Old Testament to the New Testament, but I will talk about that in a later chapter. Even if you are not a Christian, the Bible tells you the common-sense rules of life for a civilized nation. Like the Koran, there are passages that will permanently cause problems between Christians and other religions that are tough to justify.

Bias by Bernard Goldberg. I have already talked about this book, but it proves without a doubt the incredible bias of our media and why the media is the single greatest danger our nation faces. You have got to read it and it is a great read.

Team of Rivals written by Doris Kearns Goodwin is about Abraham Lincoln, the Civil War, and how Lincoln put his political rivals on his cabinet to build cross-party cooperation and to build a highly functional team. This is an incredible book for several reasons. First, it is a great management tool that shows the importance of teams and that a team with divergent views is a stronger team. It shows the importance of a strong leader and what he/she can get from a good team. And it shows with incredible intensity what a great man Lincoln was, how he suffered, and how strong he was even when the press crucified him and many in the country wanted to give up. These are lessons that will be true forever!

Almost a Miracle by John Ferling is amazing. It is the story about how close we as a nation came to losing the Revolutionary War and what a miracle it is that we won. When you read this book you realize that we have turned in to a nation of spoiled brats! It documents the incredible and unbelievable hardship that a generation of American patriots endured to be free. They refused to give up. It proves again that 50 percent or more of Americans at the time wanted to give up, they did not want to sacrifice, and they did not think it was worth it. But it shows that a group of determined, stubborn, and relentless men and women can overcome impossible odds to accomplish incredible things. The book also shows what an incredible man Washington was. He was a gift to our country and a one-in-a-billion man in history that was here at the right time and place.

The Crucible. Fred Anderson does a great job of bringing alive America's unknown war, the French and Indian War (otherwise known as The Seven Years War). You will be fascinated to learn that the French and Indian War was really the First World War which had a tremendous and long-lasting impact on Europe and America. Like all of our wars, many in America wanted to give up and were unwilling to make the sacrifices that were required. But as is so often the case in history, a few brave and determined men stood their ground and did not give up and they prevailed. The shocking thing is the extent of suffering and death experienced in the colonies in this war. And the incredible violence and brutality between the whites and the Indians is simply unbelievable. Both were horrible to each other. Today in our politically correct culture, the Indian is portrayed as this innocent victim of the horrible white man. Read this and you will find that the Indians were so brutal and cruel that many French and British officers did not want to use them in their armies because they broke all of the rules of civilized behavior and humanity. A great read that you will not be able to put down (at 850 pages, plan your time wisely).

Naked Ape. Desmond Morris has written a book that completely explains why men are men and women are women and why we act the way we do. He shows that our core behaviors have been developed over a million years of evolution and they have rational and common-sense reasons to exist. For instance, the primary roles of the male of the species were to mate with as many females as possible to spread its genetics, to hunt and kill for food, and defend the family. That is why men produce a million sperm a day, are physically bigger and stronger, and more aggressive. Women, on the other hand ,were designed to produce a limited number of eggs, nurture and raise the young, and gather food in a hunter-gatherer society. Because females can only produce a limited number of eggs and must support the child for years until it can support itself, females are very selective of mates. To keep the male around to provide food and defend the family as the children mature, the female human is the only species in the animal world that enjoys sex and is willing to have sex even when she cannot conceive. That keeps the male around. The female has different (but equally important) critical skills that center on nurturing and communication which are critical to her role. These characteristics have been developed over a million years and they still influence how men and women act today. It is an epiphany! Of course it is all politically incorrect!

The Coming China Wars by Peter Navarro. I have

already talked about this book earlier. Our national security, our culture, and our children's futures are at stake. Read this book!

I could write about another hundred great books that I have loved, but I guess I had better stop here. I promise that if you read these books, they will dramatically change your view of the world!

Chapter Thirteen

From Angels to Demons

I simply do not understand why I have been so lucky. I have been blessed to have shared life with some incredibly good people. And I have also been blessed to be with some truly horrible people. Some folks would be astonished to hear me say that I was blessed to be with murderers, rapists, thieves, and creeps. But I will share a cosmic rule. You cannot truly appreciate the best things in life without experiencing the worst. Maybe that is a sad statement, but I think that it is a core human reality. We need comparisons and contrast to understand the important things in life.

Almost everybody feels that their mother is the best person on earth (tragically, that is not always true and must cause inconceivable pain when it is not). You have read about my mom and surely her bravery, intelligence, and values have given me the foundation of who I am. And my dad had a major impact on me as well. Both were brave, stood their ground, sacrificed for what they believed in, and did it every day. I was incredibly lucky.

Added to that is my wife Evelyn. She took up where my parents left off. She is the rock who has always known what is right and she has done it. She is one of the lucky people who have always known what she wanted to do with her life. Driven to be a nurse and help people, she has reinforced in me the joy of helping others that my mom started. Together, they introduced me to a world of disadvantaged people who remind me how lucky I have been in life. But the wonderful surprise that I learned is how much joy you get when you work with these folks and help them out. You get far more than you give! Ev is also one of those very lucky people who have no doubt about the purpose of life and what it is all about as a devout Lutheran. And she lives her life that way. By the way, trust me on this, you can still have a lot of fun and be a good Christian.

I have been blessed in that many members of my family are great people like my brother and sister, and my mother's family back at the farm. They are the salt of the earth and all that is good about people. And we have been blessed by good friends who I admire. Like our very close friends Keith and Carol. Besides being a lot of fun to be with (they are as crazy as Ev and I are), they have the highest integrity of anyone I know. But to fully appreciate these good people, it took being exposed to the other side of humanity.

I have looked into the eyes of a fourteen-year-old who committed murder simply because someone "dissed him," No remorse or regret. It is like looking in to the gates of hell or the eyes of a shark—pure evil!. The sad thing is that the kid has probably never known love and he simply cannot feel compassion because he never it experienced growing up. In my criminology days, I saw far too many kids who have never known love or experienced compassion, and because of that, are capable of the most horrible crimes. That does not excuse their behavior or excuse them from punishment, but it is tragic for them and society. In my view, the destruction of our culture and the family by today's media will only make this worse.

I told you the story of the red necks when I was wild boar hunting. I don't know if they really did murder black folks, but they seemed nasty and evil and horribly prejudiced against anyone that did not fit their view of the world, including me! And while I consider myself a basically good man, I was fully prepared to kill them for what they said to me. Let me build on that with another series of experiences involving prejudices that are more complex and are hard to label as completely good or evil.

It involves several experiences that I have had involving American Indians. As I indicated earlier, I am part American Indian on my mother's side and quite proud of it. Anyone who hunts or spends time in the wilderness fully understands that American Indians were the best there was in the wilderness and you have to admire them and their skills. Growing up, I never saw prejudice to Indians or from them. And then I started hunting in northern Wisconsin and Canada.

There was intense prejudice against American Indians up there which I just was not aware of before hand—prejudice that led to bloodshed and intense hatred in some cases. It starts from the non-Indian perspective in that Indians don't have to follow the same hunting and fishing laws that everyone else has to follow (at least that is what I was told). Because of that, the Indians are said to devastate the fishing and hunting for everyone else. They fish during closed spawning season and at night with lights and nets killing the millions of future game fish that should be protected during spawning. They don't have to honor property lines because of treaties and can fish anywhere they want—even on other people's property (again, so I am told).

We deer hunted on a bird game farm run by a friend which was closed for us deer hunters during deer season. It happened to be next to an Indian reservation and I was told that the Indians regularly trespassed and shot deer out of season which reduced the herd for everybody else (again, that is what I was told).

When bear hunting in Manitoba, the guides talked about how at the end of each season, they had to dig ten-foot deep pits to bury all of the gear of the camp and leave the cabin doors unlocked because the local Indians stole everything of value during the winter, broke the locks, and totally trashed the interior of the cabins every year.

I was surprised to see the intensity of the dislike for Indians as a result of these issues in that part of the country from people who in every other way were very reasonable. There have been shootings and other kinds of violence as a result that I just can't relate to. Indians are painted in a very bad way because these are very important issues up there.

That was one side of the story. As we were driving through Manitoba toward our bear hunt, I got to personally see the other side of the story. We stopped to get something to eat, and to get to the restaurant, we had to walk through a bar in which there were about twenty Indians sitting around and drinking. They glared at the five of us and began muttering nasty and derogatory names as we walked by and you could see things getting ugly and violent in a hurry. Fortunately we had the smarts to move on since there could be no good outcome if there was conflict (and we were outnumbered four to one), but the intensity of what felt like obvious hatred toward us really stuck with me. From their perspective, we stole their land, their culture, and their pride. Their hatred was real, and in some ways, understandable.

Bottom line, both sides had legitimate issues with each other. After witnessing the intense emotions from both sides, I can see how easily violence results. Tragically, part of the reason for the devils and demons in the human condition are the result of long-standing historical experiences and it is hard to see how they will be resolved. As someone who understands both positions and harbors no ill will toward either side in this case, it is a heart breaker.

I have witnessed utter human helplessness that broke my heart. When Ev and I volunteered at Dixon State Mental Hospital, we worked with people who could not speak, understand what was being said them, walk, eat without assistance, or do anything for themselves. I have also worked as a lifeguard with great kids with Down's syndrome (Mom's students) who loved life and made the most out of what they had every day despite their handicap.

I have worked with multi-millionaires who are incredibly selfish and self centered and have no appreciation for what they have. And I have worked with lots and lots of good, hard-working regular folks at our plant in South Carolina who didn't have much but enthusiastically donated to our cancer drives and their friends whenever they could.

Here's a quick story about a good multi-millionaire. I had a chance to work with a major guy in our industry who obviously fit that good category. He invited me to fly out on his personal jet to meet him in Nantucket to spend a weekend with him on his very large yacht to discuss a potential business relationship (yes I got approval from the boss!). This is a guy who has tons of money but was a very approachable and nice guy. The clincher was when I got up in the morning and found him alone in the engine room of his yacht, full of grease and oil, doing some maintenance on his engine! I knew from that minute that this is a regular guy and we ended up having a very good business relationship. And by the way, Nantucket is beautiful!

I have worked with self-centered business executives who had no problem firing good people to make more personal bonus, and I have worked with illegal aliens on a road crew who sent their entire earnings home to their family. They had nothing but were willing to share what little they had with a college student who they knew was headed for the good life (me).

I have been with men and watched them risk their lives to protect others and/or me, and I have seen people refuse to help someone who desperately needed it simply because it was inconvenient or would reduce their personal income.

I have worked with drug addicts who would kill their mothers to get their next fix, and I have worked with ex drug addicts who approached the abyss, got control, got their PhD, and then dedicated their lives to helping other addicts find their way home through rehab.

I have been incredibly impressed with the people who volunteer at charities. I have volunteered my time at Dixon, PADS, United Way, Habitat for Humanity, Love INC, and a bunch of other charities. I have seen people who are poor or disadvantaged give their time and what little resources they have to help others who were worse off. There are an incredible number of these great folks. Maybe that is why I am so hard on many of my fellow business executives who have everything and give nothing back to society. The contrast is amazing.

When volunteering, you see all kinds. You see homeless people who don't have anything but their dignity helping others at the shelter. On the other hand, I have seen some folks on welfare who don't accept any responsibility for themselves and expect to be taken care of by society. We are seeing the growth of the "nanny state" in which we are all "victims." Society must find the right balance of providing help when it is needed but also holding people accountable for their own actions and welfare.

Speaking of the plight of the homeless, it is like an invisible disaster. People would be shocked to know that right in our well-to-do communities there are people living in tents (if they are lucky) in the freezing winter with nothing. In many cases, these are people who are either just down on their luck, mentally ill, addicted to drugs or alcohol, or just socially maladjusted. It is a tragedy. It is a worthwhile cause if you would like one to get behind and give back to society. Again, we need to find the right balance between help and accountability.

And then I talked about my great team at Scotsman and the moral courage of Cary and Anmarie. There are plenty of good folks in business, just not enough at the higher levels that make policy!

As I close this chapter, I guess I can make a few conclusions from the breadth of my experience with people. First, you can't make any total generalizations about any group of people. There are good white people and bad white people; the same is true for African Americans, Hispanics, Asians, etc. There are good wealthy people and bad wealthy people. Hell, there are probably even good liberals (just kidding)! You just have to take the time to figure each one out individually as you meet them and deal with them. But I also know that you cannot possibly know that until and unless you have seen a wide cut of all kinds. It took me some time to figure that out and I am not proud of some of the opinions that I have had in the past or the things that I have said and done in the past. And I am sure that I will say some things in the future in the heat of the moment that I will regret.

Clearly there are a lot of incredibly good people out there, but unfortunately, there are also an awful lot of bad ones too. You need to know which is which and what to do with both!

Chapter Fourteen

You Can't Appreciate the Good Old USA Until You Have Seen the Rest of the World

Having been to a fair bit of the world and having passionately studied history, I can tell you without hesitation that this is the best country in the history of the world. Don't worry, I will back that up with some facts. Unfortunately, most Americans have never been outside of this country, they don't know history, and they simply don't know how good we have it and how lucky we are. And that is scary as hell because they get to vote!

In business I have had the privilege of working with people from all over the world who shared riveting experiences with me that we Americans simply cannot relate to. Let me share a few of those experiences with you in this chapter. I met the manager of a Chinese plant from another industry while he was in the US. He was a very nice guy and I really liked him. Let's call him John Doe since he continues to go to China occasionally. He was a Chinese national who came to live in the US for many years. He represented the best of both worlds in that he was Chinese, from China, he spoke English, and was very comfortable in the US and China.

I went to China on business a few years ago and met him while I was there. I was shocked when he told me that he was resigning his position and moving back to the US. Over dinner I asked him why. From my perspective he had a great job. He was home in China, he was making a great income, and he was living like an emperor in the nation of his birth. Why on earth would he resign?

He said that he would try to explain, but he felt that as an American, I would probably not understand. He was born in China and was on the fast track. He joined the Chinese army and rose rapidly. He was then sent to college and because Mao wanted China to become powerful in business, he learned business. After college, he was made a manager of a Chinese business. He and his family reached very high status in the communist party and enjoyed the best houses, privileges, and honor in the community. Life was very, very good.

Then one night, soldiers broke his door down, arrested him, and brought him to prison. Apparently Mao had a change of heart and decided that business was bad. Mao started the Cultural Revolution and many businessmen and intellectuals were sent to prison and hundreds of thousands were killed. Suddenly, John was a criminal. His parents were humiliated, and he was mocked and imprisoned for an extensive period of time in a "re-education camp." He had gone from the top of society to being thrown in prison and humiliated for no reason. From hero to bum just because Chairman Mao changed his mind. Eventually he got out of prison and somehow he got to the Unites States.

John summed things up this way: "It is true that I am back at home in my country. And it is true that I have a great job, with high prestige, I am very wealthy, and I live very well. But every night I worry that this is the night the government changes its mind and my door will be broken down again, and I will have to go back to prison. Every night!"

He tells me that as an American, I cannot even conceive of the fear that he is talking about. And the reason he is quitting is because he wants to go back to the only country in the world in which he knows for sure that he can go to sleep at night in peace and never have to worry about his door being broken down by soldiers. And that country is the United States of America!

His story had a shocking impact on me and I did have a small understanding of what he was talking about. After all, I was with him at that time in China. While preparing for the trip, the US State Department warned me that all visitors needed to exercise caution in China. First, you were warned not to have any political or religious conversations with anyone in China or you put yourself at risk. In addition, I was warned that it was not unheard of to have rooms or phones bugged in China and I should exercise caution about what I said. As an American, the reality that I had to be careful of these things was a huge wake-up call.

Don't get me wrong, China is not all bad. I went there prepared to not like the country or the people because I feel that they have a national strategy of stealing our jobs and technology by extensive cheating. I do feel that in the long term, China will be a strategic threat to our country. But in fact, to my surprise, I found that I liked the people. They are hard working, take responsibility for their lives, are optimistic, and are willing to roll their sleeves up to make progress. They are like Americans a hundred years ago. But you never forget for a moment that it is a communist country with an all-powerful, autocratic, dictatorial government. While China (at least what

I saw of it) is not very pretty, it is a nation with a grim purpose to improve itself.

You have to see China to believe it. Side by side you will see the most modern technology right next to a donkey pulling a cart down a major road. You will see more modern skyscrapers and houses being built than you can possibly believe. But drive through at night and you will find that at least half of the buildings are empty. China is building all of this in accordance with their state-run hundred-year plan. It is scary. We don't have a hundred-year plan.

In China you will see opulence at the Ritz Carlton and in the city shopping centers surrounded by overwhelming poverty. Work conditions are prehistoric compared to America. The air is so polluted that you are afraid to breath. China is running out of water and polluting what is left. They are sacrificing their people's health and safety for industrial progress. I felt like I was in eighteenth-century industrial revolution England with polluted air, child labor, and unsafe working conditions right next to the most modern luxuries that you will find here in America.

China is the Wild West where cheating, stealing, industrial theft, employee abuse, fraud, and destruction of the environment are all apparently acceptable to the government as long as it leads to the growth of Chinese power in compliance to the hundred-year plan to dominate Asia and maybe the world.

We need to wake up, America, and understand the threat that China represents to our country and our way of life. While China cheats and steals our technology and jobs (actually we are dumb enough to give them away), they are increasing their military spending by at least 17 percent a year (that is what they report; experts believe that it is actually double that), shooting down their satellites for practice (what do you think that they are practicing for?), enabling the slaughter of innocent people by Sudan in return for access to oil from the Sudanese government (because they have not exerted maximum pressure on the Sudanese government to stop), and forming alliances with our lethal enemies.

Here is another quick story that shows that you need to be from somewhere else to appreciate America. I was hailing a cab from downtown L.A. to the airport right after the Islamic terrorists tried to blow up those flights in London. I got picked up by a huge six-foot-five African American Muslim and I must admit I was a little nervous that I was about to be kidnapped (I know, my weakness). But the guy was great, made record time, and he had Beethoven and Mozart playing on the radio. Getting me to the airport on record time, I told him that it was a great ride and that life was good riding with him. Suddenly he turned around and with great intensity he said, "Life is good in America! Life is not so good in Nigeria. You Americans don't know how good you have it!"

Wow! He then told me the countless ways that America is good and how glad he is to be here. I gave him an extra $20 tip and asked him to tell every American that gets in his cab that story. He is right. Most of us don't know how good we have it.

Why is it that those people who come to America from somewhere else constantly talk about how good America is and how spoiled we are, yet on our media and at our universities, all you hear about is how bad the US is? If we are so bad, why are millions of people from around the world trying to move here to live?

Go to Thailand and that will make you appreciate home. Thailand is very beautiful in some ways, but scary as hell in others and you feel that you have walked back in time by centuries. Before my trip, the State Department again cautioned watching what you say in Thailand. You will go to prison for ten years if you say anything negative about the King of Thailand. If you are found with drugs, you are executed. And if you are sick and dumb enough to visit one of the sex shops for child sex, you will likely be drugged and you might wake up robbed of your wallet and without one your kidneys which are sold on the black market (besides surely going to hell right after you go to prison in the US).

The contrast in Thailand is amazing. The people are physically beautiful and incredibly gentle. That is unless they are selling their children into slavery or cutting out your kidneys! There are magnificent and beautiful temples that are centuries old, but there is also unimaginable poverty. Driving from Bangkok to our plant thirty minutes from the border of what is now Kampuchea (Cambodia) I felt that I was going five hundred years back in time. There were endless villages on stilts in the river where people were washing their clothes in the very same river that they went to the bathroom in. The poverty was unimaginable. Just miles from our plant were the communists in Kampuchea who had murdered 2 million people, or 17 percent of their population under Pol Pot (man, did I feel naked without a weapon). While the trip was magnificent, it once again reminded me of how incredibly lucky we are here in the US.

Even if you spend time in thoroughly modern London, Milan, Paris, Tokyo, or Venice, you will find that we Americans have it better on average based on my observations. Our houses are bigger, our average income is higher, and we have more choices in virtually everything. Step a notch down in modernity to cities like Barcelona, Athens, Istanbul, or Naples and you will see a clear difference in the standard of living from America. These are vibrant and interesting cities with lots going for them, but the standard of living clearly does not match the lifestyle of the average American.

If you need a starker comparison, go to Mexico City. I will never forget flying over Mexico City as we approached the airport. It seemed like there were miles and miles of tiny little tar-paper shacks surrounding the city. Poverty is overwhelming for the majority of people. The contrast between the overwhelming poverty of the majority of the population and the wealth and opulence of the minority is incredible. I don't understand why there has not been a revolution there when you look at the high percentage of the poor.

Unlike here in the US were anybody with skill and the will to work can succeed (like an immigrant from Italy that came with nothing), the poverty in Mexico is crushing and it is due to the corruption and the control of the economy by the few at the expense of the many. I can't confirm it, but I have read that 75 percent of the wealth in Mexico is controlled by fifty families. While I truly feel sorry for the majority of poor Mexicans, they need to throw the bums out of their government and fix their country.

It is when I come back home to America with the fresh images of the rest of the world and hear our media talk about how awful our country is that I get angry. And many of the people who I know and like accept this because they simply do not know the truth. Do we have problems? You bet. Are we perfect? No way. But we had better not throw the baby out with the bath water because when you are on top, it is easier to fall down than to climb up. That doesn't mean you don't try, but you need to build on the strengths that you have, not throw them away out of ignorance.

While I have shared some of my experiences and observations of the outside world to support the proposition that this is a pretty damn good country, I'll provide some facts and data as well. One of the things that drives me crazy is ignorant Americans (fueled by the media) that talk about how bad our country is and how we have damaged the world instead of being proud of the incredible things our country has brought the world and continues to bring it.

Let me throw out a few minor contributions that we have made to the world. First, we have saved freedom and democracy in Europe—four times. Let's review the history. First, in World War I, Germany was at the brink of victory over the rest of Europe. Russia had just surrendered to Germany allowing Germany to take all of its troops from the Eastern front and send them to finish off France, Britain, and their allies on the Western front. The French army had suffered several major defeats and was in the middle of a national mutiny of its army. The end was in sight, and then Germany sank the Lusitania. Finally Americans were convinced to help join the battle and we sent three million doughboys to save the day and lead the defeat of Germany. We secured the freedom of Western Europe, and then we went home!

France and Britain didn't listen to Woodrow Wilson but instead put onerous surrender conditions on Germany which created Hitler and World War II. Instead of standing up to Hitler after they created the conditions for war, France and Britain gave away part of Czechoslovakia (without asking them) and other territories in an attempt to appease Hitler. It didn't work (appeasement never does); the World was again at war and all of Western Europe (except Britain) fell to Hitler in just a few months after the fighting started. Despicably and to its everlasting shame, France surrendered its country and freedom to Germany after just six weeks of fighting. While France had the largest army in Europe, their political leadership was so weak, so poor, and so timid that they lost their nation, their freedom, and their honor. Are there any lessons to be learned from that?

Fortunately for the world, Hitler attacked Russia (former ally of Germany) and Japan attacked the US. Russia and the US saved the free world and rescued Britain in its valiant stand against Hitler. Russia contributed to the rescue by the blood of twenty million of its people as they destroyed the German army in Russia in some of the largest land battles in the history of the world, and the US contributed to the rescue by the incredible manufacturing power of America which became the arsenal of democracy. The infusion of millions of American soldiers that invaded and re-conquered the countries taken by Germany and Japan with their allies did not hurt either. And then we went home—the second time!

Unfortunately, sensing weakness in Western Europe because of the destruction and wide-spread poverty caused by the war, Russia started to prepare itself to conquer a weakened Europe through the appeal of communism. Once again America stepped in and rebuilt much of Europe and Japan with the Marshall Plan. Taking US taxpayer money, the US poured billions of dollars into Europe and Japan to raise the standard of living which defeated communism in those countries. America ended up investing about 4-5 percent of its GDP (far more than we are spending in Iraq) to rebuild Europe and Japan. We also rescued two and a half million West Berliners through the Berlin airlift who Russia had tried to starve to death by its blockade. Then we went home. That was our third save of Western Europe and we introduced democracy to Japan which then blossomed to be a positive world power and ally. We also converted Germany from an enemy to an ally with that investment. History says that nation building can, in fact, work!

Never in the history of the world has a country dominated the world militarily as the US has and instead of occupying the world for its own interests, invested its own resources to improve the world, introduce freedom and democracy, and then go home. Most of our kids don't know any of this. They hear in school and from the media that their country is a horrible place that has done terrible things to people all across the world.

But we were not done yet. Russia began to expand its military to conquer all of Europe through force, and the cold war started in earnest. Eastern Europe was enslaved by Russia and most of Western Europe wanted to give up and submit (again). They wanted to "make nice" with Russia and the Soviet Union. But thanks to brave and relentless leaders like President Truman and Reagan and billions of American taxpayer dollars, the US fought for Europe's freedom (even though they wouldn't fight for their own). Despite millions of protestors in Western Europe, America armed Western Europe with Pershing missiles to block the Soviet's threat of SS20s. And President Reagan raised the stakes and introduced "Star Wars" (and was ridiculed for it).

Finally the Soviet Union conceded that it did not have the resources to compete against American technology and "Star Wars" (the world does owe thanks to Gorbachev for having the courage to recognize that) and they collapsed and disbanded. The United States saved Western Europe for the fourth time and also freed Eastern Europe from Soviet domination. Never in the history of the world has there been such an investment of national wealth by one county for the benefit of others with no direct return. Do our kids know this?

Because of my global business connections, I got to talk to people from all around the world. Nothing is so moving to me than to have someone from Poland, East Germany, Rumania, Kosovo, or somewhere else in Eastern Europe describe what their life was like under communism and how miraculous freedom is. I have actually had people from these countries thank me as an American for bringing them freedom. It makes you proud and almost brings tears to your eyes. But invariably they will tell you that while they love Americans and America, they are stunned by how naïve and ignorant we are as a people about the cruelty and danger of the world. And they fear for us in our ignorance because they have seen the dark side of the world.

Do our kids know any of this? Are they being taught this in school? Do they even remember that the US lead the world in freeing Kuwait and securing 60 percent of the world's oil supply in Saudi Arabia and the rest of the middle East from the fourth largest army in the world (Iraq)? Does anybody tell our kids what a historical miracle it is that the US had 500,000 troops and an invincible army sitting on 60 percent of the world's oil and we secured it, gave it back to those countries and the world, and then went home! Does the majority of adults in America know and appreciate this? I am afraid not. The Europeans keep screwing things up and we keep saving their butts while they criticize us. Amazing!

And it is happening again as we try to combat world terrorism and introduce democracy to Iraq.

The world and the media like to criticize America for not doing enough. They like to complain that America's government does not contribute enough charity to the world. But of course they have that wrong too. Unlike Western European citizens who like their government to run their lives, we like to allow our citizens to make choices. While the US government makes massive contributions to the world, the real charitable contributions come from American citizens, and it is staggering. Check out the facts from *Who Really Cares* by Arthur Brooks. Americans volunteer more than any other people on earth and Americans donate more money per capita or as a percentage of GDP than any other country on earth. The closest European country gives less than 50 percent of the GDP charity percentage as the average American. Americans are the most generous people on earth. Why isn't that on the six o'clock news? Why is the fact that President Bush has directed the US to spend far more money on AIDS help to Africa than the rest of the world combined not on the news?

I have seen a lot of the world and I have intensely studied world history. For what it is worth, this guy knows that the United States of America is the best and most generous nation on earth. It is just too bad that our media and our schools are keeping it a secret from our kids as they try to subvert what made us great.

I will close this chapter with a great incident and quote which involved Colin Powell:

When in England at a fairly large conference at the start of the war in Iraq, Colin Powell was asked by the Archbishop of Canterbury if our plans for Iraq were just an example of empire building by George Bush.

Powell answered by saying, "Over the years, the United States has sent many of its fine men and women into great peril to fight for freedom beyond our borders. The only amount of land we have ever asked for in return is enough to bury those that did not return." It became very quiet in the room.

Chapter Fifteen

Cosmic Rules Learned the Hard Way

There are clearly some unchangeable rules of the universe. In our technology-cushioned culture, we sometimes forget those rules and then we get smacked upside the head with a reminder. Occasionally that smack will kill you and it should be avoided if possible! I have covered a few of those rules already, but let me reinforce a few that have been learned the hard way by mankind (including me) to help others avoid the pain.

You don't know what you've got until it's gone. (Joni Mitchell, "Big Yellow Taxi")

We humans often take good things for granted, right up until they are gone. The moral of the story is to make sure that you appreciate what you have got and say thanks before it is too late and gone. Especially to loved ones!

That which does not kill you makes you stronger. (Nietzsche)

Nietzsche had a pretty rough view of the world and I disagree with much of what he said. But on this issue, he has captured one of the most important rules of life. Like steel, we must be hardened by fire to be strong. If your life is too easy, you will be weak. But just like surviving the hurricane-force winds made me a better sailor and surviving my scary calls at the White House and Pentagon made me a stronger executive, surviving hard times make us all stronger. I wish there was an easier way, there just isn't. "No pain, no gain" is a more modern version of this cosmic rule! I am concerned that today in our quest to make life easy for our children, we are shielding them from failure and they do not get the strength-building experience that failure or adversity can bring. They will not be prepared for the dangerous world that is always out there.

Only the dead have seen the end of war. (Plato)

Forever true as long as man is man. There will always be evil men who will take anything of value that they can from the weak if they believe that they can get away with it. Anyone who has studied the 10,000-year history of modern man knows that this is a relentless truth. The only unanswered questions of the future are when the next war will be, what the fight will be over, and who will prevail.

Never, never jump a hill on a motorcycle unless you know what is on the other side. (Rossi)

While racing in the desert I did, and in mid-air at fifty-miles-per-hour, I realized that I was about to get cut in half by a barbed wire fence. Choosing instead to lay the bike down and use it as the cushion to absorb the collision with the fence, I left most of the skin of my right leg on the desert floor. Hospitals, crutches, intense pain, and months of ruined pants as desert rocks oozed from my wounds, have all served to remind me of the truth of this cosmic rule.

Peace through strength. (Reagan)

This is as true between humans and animals as it is between nations. I know it works. In the Arctic, those bears absolutely wanted to kill me and eat me. I would have provided them with all of the calories that they would have needed to survive the winter and hibernation. Why didn't they? Because I stood up to them, was very aggressive, and was prepared to kill them. They knew that and backed off to look for easier prey. Such is the law of nature and of men forever. Never be the easy prey!

Walk softly and carry a big stick. (Teddy Roosevelt)

This works well in business and in life. Start out calmly and reasonably and hopefully your partner, customer, or competitor is reasonable as well. If so, all goes well. But if things go south, let it be known (subtly, but absolutely) that you carry a big stick that you can and will use if required so that those who are inclined to cause trouble will decide to seek weaker prey! Works well for nations and is closely aligned with peace through strength!

The world is a dangerous place. (Reagan)

This dovetails nicely with my Chapter 6 about Mother Nature. If you understand that the world is a dangerous place, you will prepare for it and be successful; those who don't become the casualties of nature, bad men, or other nations.

Never touch your front brake when you are going down a ski slope on a motorcycle at fifty-miles-per-hour. (Rossi)

Especially if you are dumb enough to be going through moguls. When, or if, you regain consciousness after flipping over your handle bars, you will regret it. Trust me on this.

Success is more likely when failure is not an option. (Rossi)

It creates a critical sense of urgency that increases the odds of success. When Cortes and his 500 men landed in Mexico with a goal of defeating 500,000 Aztecs, one might say that he had set lofty goals. To insure success, Cortes burned his ships upon landing. Failure was not an option to his men and they beat impossible odds and succeeded. Life is like that. Drug counselors will tell you that addicts don't beat their addiction until they have hit bottom. Failure is not an option at that point and success is the only alternative to death. And so it is in other aspects of life.

Trust but verify. (Reagan)

Truer words have never been said. If you accept the fact that this is a dangerous world, then this is only common sense. You want to build trust to build alliances, but because it is a dangerous world, you must verify before you bet the farm!

He who knows the enemy and himself will never in a hundred battles be at risk. (Sun-Tzu)

Studying bear behavior before my hunt is what allowed me to survive those bear attacks on my subarctic hunt. I knew what they would do and I knew that I could handle it.

It didn't hurt that I also studied bear anatomy, possessed a high-powered rifle, and knew where to put the bullet when it counted! So it should be with any enemy or competitor. This is very important in business. A good SWOT analysis that honestly identifies your company's and your competitor's strengths and weaknesses is the most important strategic tool that you can develop. Those who can not acknowledge their competitor's strengths or their own weaknesses are doomed to surprise and failure.

No good-looking babe in a bikini is worth crashing into the car in front of you when you are on a motorcycle. (Rossi)

If you are getting the sense that motorcycles and I are a bad combination, you're right. This happened in Daytona on the beach during spring break when I was in college. Fortunately the guy in front of me was a student as well with a rental car and completely understood when I pointed out the babe.

Death is nothing, but to live defeated is to die every day. (Napoleon Bonaparte)

I hate to lose at anything. Those who are okay with losing get good at it.

For what the leaders are, that, as a rule, will the men below them be. (Xenephon)

Said almost 2,500 years ago, no truer words on the importance of leadership have been spoken. Just as I said in my business chapters, business values always start at the top. Leaders, walk the talk; the men are watching!

Every kingdom divided against itself is laid waste, and a divided household falls. (Luke 11:17)

We as a nation had better get our act together because the world is a dangerous place and time is running out.

Those who don't learn history are doomed to repeat it. (Edmund Burke)

I find it shocking how our culture is rejecting or rewriting history to fit into the preconceived "politically correct" agenda driven by the media and universities. We are creating an incredibly ignorant and ill-equipped generation that will be at great risk in the real world. I am afraid that there will be a whuppin'.

A man reaps what he sows. (Paul in Galatians 6:7)

The modern version of this is "What goes around comes around." Ask Elliot Spitzer!

You cannot truly appreciate the best things in life until you have also experienced the hard things in life. (Rossi)

A tragic truth of the human condition. You cannot fully appreciate having money unless you have been broke. You take good health for granted until you have been very ill. You take love for granted until you have lost it. The bad news is that we have to go through the hard times. The good news is that when we experience hard times, it sets us up to truly appreciate with total joy the good times.

All that is required for evil to triumph is for good men to do nothing. (Edmund Burke)

There is a lot of pressure from the media and liberals not to pass judgment on others and to avoid having our country take strong stands against evil nations which may result in violence. But Edmund Burke is so right. If we do not stand prepared to defend the innocent against evil using whatever force is required, evil will triumph. And evil has no conscience. Ask the hundreds of millions of people who died as a result of Hitler, Stalin, Mao, and others throughout history. If you want good to prevail, then you must be prepared to defend her. And each of us from time to time has the opportunity to stand up to evil, but it does involve personal risk. In the end, each of us has to determine what we stand for in the timeless battle between good and evil.

Chapter Sixteen

Pure Love

Pure love is something that cannot be adequately described to someone who has not experienced it. And I suspect that the reverse is also true. If you have experienced pure love, I am sure that it is impossible to imagine life without that experience or how people who have not experienced pure love look at life. I can't.

I do not know why I have been so lucky in life. I have been (and continue to be) given pure, unconditional love. And I give unconditional love in return. It is impossible for me to imagine what life would be like without it. There is simply no more powerful feeling than to give and receive unconditional love.

Pure love, in my view, is unconditional and complete love for someone for no reason other than to be loved in return—no expectation of material gain, status, or any other tangible benefit. It is a love so great that you would be willing to trade your life to protect the one you love. A love that greatly changes your life as you are incredibly motivated to do everything possible to please the one you love.

I have talked to people who did not have warm and loving parents and I know that shaped them and made it hard for them to share intense love later in life whether it was with their spouses or their children. I simply cannot imagine that. I cannot imagine a greater emptiness than not knowing pure love.

I talked at length about my mom and dad in earlier chapters. They were great people. But I did not mention the unconditional love that I received from them. No matter what I did, there was never any doubt in my mind that they loved me unconditionally. Don't get me wrong. When I was young and misbehaved, there was hell to pay. But I knew why and it was because they loved me. It really was for my own good. I knew that no matter what I did, they would love me and support me. There was just never any doubt. And I realize now, that I would have done anything for them. My greatest fear was disappointing them. My greatest reward was making them proud of me.

As I said, I know that many people have never received that kind of love from their parents and because of that, they never were able to find it later in life. The two are clearly connected. But I was lucky twice. I experienced that pure love from my parents, and then I found it again with Evelyn. We have been together since we were sixteen and, putting it simply, we are soul mates.

I am a lunatic and never really cared about myself. If it were just me, I would be in the military, the wilderness, or anywhere there is action and an adrenaline rush. I did not care about a career, nice houses, nice anything. I just did not care. Because of that, I did lousy in high school. In fact my counselor told me not to bother going to college; I would never hack it. I was about to join the Navy with a buddy to either be in the Seabees to drive bulldozers or join the Seals to dive, shoot, and blow up stuff (all passions of mine at the time). We were ready to go in together the summer after we graduated.

And then I fell in love. And suddenly I wanted to give Evelyn the best of everything. And the way to do that was to go to college and get a degree and build a career. That is what motivated me and changed my life. My mom was thrilled and loved Evelyn. I am sure that Mom felt that Evelyn saved my life. Maybe she did—she certainly changed it. Suddenly I went from being a lousy student in high school to an honor student in college. The difference was that I now had the incentive of providing for the one I loved. It changed everything for me.

I cannot imagine living life without her. She is my wife and my lover for sure, and that would be enough, but she is also my best friend, confidant, buddy, and partner. We love to sail together, travel and explore new countries together, read together, and on and on. About the only thing we did not share is my love for hunting, but she supported my love of it even though it took me away from her and occasionally put my life in danger. She knew that was part of me and is who I am.

As my career advanced and I started to get fancy titles, big paychecks, options, and all that stuff, Ev said that her role was to keep me humble. She was never pretentious or phony and she simply would not put up with that from me. She was my rock and kept me grounded in the values that I knew really mattered.

We have been together now for forty years. While you might think that we are bored with each other, nothing could be further from the truth. We love being together and treasure each hour, each new day that we are granted. Being physically close and intimate is a big deal to us and we still act like teenagers when we're alone (we're not dead yet)! Often late at night or early in the morning, when it is quiet and just the two of us, we hold each other and talk about how lucky we are to freely express our deepest feelings and fears. How strange we agree it would be to share the intimacy of sleeping with a spouse and not be able to openly and candidly talk with them about anything and everything.

Ev continues to shape my life. Mom and Dad built the foundation for a good and honorable man. But I got lost for a while and did some things that I am not proud of (statues of limitations, Officer). And then Evelyn found me, and brought me back to the values that I know are right. Sometimes in my younger years, even when we were together, I was a jerk and forgot the right path. I can be overly aggressive, self centered, driven for results at any cost, overly emotional, and insensitive. But Evelyn always reminded me of what was right, and my love for Evelyn always brought me back. They say that behind every successful man, there is the love of a good and supportive woman. I don't know how true that is in general, but it is 100 percent true in my case. Now that I am older (okay, old) and finally just starting to grow up, I work hard at being a good guy. But I admit that there were plenty of times in the past when I have just been a jerk and deserved to get my butt kicked. Thank goodness Ev hung in there and did the ass-kicking when necessary!

And pure love is what I feel for my son Ben. Ben is adopted, but that makes no difference with pure love. We could not have children and Ev desperately wanted a child. I was okay with the idea but more importantly, I wanted her to be happy. I was not as motivated as she was, primarily because I was concerned that I was too immature and not ready. But there was no doubt in Ev's mind and we pursued it hard.

Finally after months and months of waiting on pins and needles, the day came that we got to meet Ben when he was just one week old. There is a movie out now *(Juno)* that says that adoptive mothers bond with the idea of the baby but fathers don't bond until they see the baby. They are absolutely right. When I saw Ben for the first time, I fell totally and instantly in love with him. He was a beautiful baby in a yellow sleeper and he was ours. Under adoption law, the mother has six months to change her mind. As I was holding Ben for the first time, I told Ev that they will have to bring a gun to take him back (Ev says that I said that they would have to find us. I like my version better)!

Over the years my love for Ben grew stronger and stronger. He is very bright, handsome, and a good man. Like many kids today he went through tough times that stressed all of us. But he is on track now and he is a good man with a good heart. I think that Ben made me a better man too. He taught me an important lesson in that I cannot control everything, and sometimes you need to trust in God that things will work out. He taught me humility. Ben is making his own way in the world and that is as it should be.

In addition to my Mom, Dad, Ev, and Ben, I am very lucky that I am very close to my sister Laura and her family and my brother Mark and his family. And it seems as we get older, and maybe less consumed by careers, we are getting closer and the love has grown. After watching what happened between my dad and his sister, we have all worked very hard at staying close. And writing this book has even made things better!

I guess that I will close this chapter as I opened it. I don't know why I have been so lucky. And I simply could not understand what life is like without knowing pure love. And I have been blessed both to receive it and give it.

Chapter Seventeen

Life and Death and What It Is All About

As Jimmy Buffet said, "there is a fine line between Saturday night and Sunday morning." We can kid about it, but any introspective person spends a lot of time wondering why we are here on this earth and what, if anything is after this life. If you are serious about life, you want to make sure that you get all there is out of it and fulfill your destiny.

You may have noticed that I have some opinions on a few things and don't shrink from expressing them. I don't much care what people say about my opinions. I have had many extreme experiences in my life which most people have not experienced, and with extreme experiences come strong opinions. But religion, now that is a sensitive subject with no provable data-based right or wrong positions on the subject. So first, let me say that I think that anybody who has faith is lucky and I respect them as long as they do not force their faith on anyone else, don't cause harm to people, and as long as they respect other points of view.

I have spent a lot of time pondering what I think are the three most important questions in life. What is the purpose of life, does God exist, and is there life after death? The power of culture and environment is immense. I was raised as a Christian in a strong Christian home. I was also raised in a country in which 85 percent of the people say that they are Christian. Three of the people I love and trust most in the world are devout Christians. Therefore the conclusion for me should have been obvious. Unfortunately, I don't work that way. And I do mean unfortunately because if you are a devout Christian (or Muslim, or Jew, or whatever), I do believe that you are a lucky and a very happy person.

So I have spent a lot of time researching these questions in the only way that I can deal with things: facts, data, and logic. Starting in college and continuing to this day, I have studied the following to find the answers; the Bible, Koran and Hadith, the Torah, St. Augustine, Socrates, Plato, Aristotle, Buddha, Confucius, Bhagavad-Gita, Gilgamesh, the Druids, Baal, the faith of American Indians, Mithras, Zoroaster, and Greek and Roman mythology.

And then like a thunderbolt, it hit me. All of these religions are trying to do the same thing and answer the same age-old questions—what is the purpose of life, is there a god, and how does God want us to live our lives. Eighty-five percent or more of what they were saying was the same. They just used different names for a god and a faith that they all pretty much agree on! For at least 4,000 years these religions have been building on each other to describe God and the purpose of life. The more I learned, the more I realized how much each new religion borrowed from the previous religions right up to one of the newest of the great religions, Islam, which is clearly built on top of all of these religions and particularly on the Jewish and the Christian religions.

These religions could have approached their differences in a warm and cooperative way as it was in the Greek and Roman times. In those cultures, all religions were respected and given credibility as long as that religion offered reciprocal respect (Christians did have a few tough decades in Rome under a few of the emperors). But today, many religions have drawn hateful lines against each other and declared that anybody that does not believe exactly in their version will surely go to hell. In some cases, the belief is that the faithful are required to kill all non-believers. For instance, over the last 1,400 years, both Christians and Muslims have murdered tens if not hundreds of millions of people in the name of God. Even within the Muslim and Christian faiths, the faithful have murdered each other over which variation of that faith was the true way of God.

The problem with religion is not God, but man. As is true in all things regarding man, the root cause of the problem is centered on power and money. For power, many religions foster the belief that if you do not believe exactly as the religious leaders tell you to believe, you will go to hell. The religious leaders say that only they are empowered by God to interpret His wishes and there is no room for any other interpretation. That is absolute and total power. And absolute power corrupts absolutely. That is why the Catholic Church held services in Latin and forbid the printing of the Bible. They did not want people to interpret and challenge their leader's interpretation of God's will. That is why some Islamic leaders tolerate absolutely no challenge to their interpretation of the Koran. It is absolute power enforced by the ultimate threat of death and eternal damnation. The fact that this threat must be used is the ultimate confirmation of the weakness of these religions. They should win the hearts of people on the beauty of their religion, not the threat of death and eternal damnation.

So here is my conclusion after studying all of these perspectives. If there is a god (I will address my belief on that in a second), then I believe that he is in heaven weeping over the fact that his children are killing each other over miniscule differences such as what his name is. If there is a god, he is Jesus Christ, Yahweh, Allah, Buddha, the Great Spirit, and Mithras (for example). Eighty-five percent of the content of these religions describes the same God and the same core beliefs. In many cases there are just minor differences that religious leaders control for power and domination over their "flock."

If you can pull yourself out of your ingrained faith and look objectively at other religions (pretty damn tough when the penalty is death, hell, and ostracism from your culture!), you will see so many more of the similarities between religions instead of the differences. In my view, Socrates said it best (I wish I could remember the exact words), "I am simply a mortal man and cannot possibly understand all of the wishes of the gods. I can only live my life well and treat my fellow man as I wish to be treated and hope that the gods will be satisfied with that."

I ask all Christians, Muslims, and Jews (or any other religion) these fundamental questions; do you believe that Gandhi went to hell just because he followed a different faith than you? Do you believe that this man who lived an incredibly brave and peaceful life for the benefit of his people and died so that they could be free went to hell? Do you believe that a person who prays to God every day, follows the Ten Commandments to the letter, and dedicates his/her life to helping other people will go to hell just because they happen to call their God Jesus Christ, Allah, or Yahweh contrary to the name that you call God? I refuse to believe that God, if He exists, would send someone to eternal damnation just because of the name they chose to call Him which was determined primarily by which culture that person was born into.

I had another epiphany on a recent trip with my wife around the Mediterranean which really confirmed my belief that the major religions are more alike than different. One of the cities that we went to was Istanbul in Turkey and while there, we went to the Blue Mosque which is one of the largest and most famous mosques in the world. It is beautiful and people of all faiths are welcomed inside. As my wife and I approached the entrance, people were sitting at fountains carefully and tenderly washing their feet, faces, and hands in preparation for prayer. You see, they wanted to be clean and pure when they address God.

When they entered the mosque, they not only kneeled, but fully prostrated themselves on the carpeted floor as they prayed to God; the reverence, love, and deep passion that they exhibited for God was overwhelming to me. I have never seen such passion in churches in the US as we sit comfortably in our pews and occasionally kneel on our padded kneelers. Knowing that they follow the same Ten Commandments as Christians and/or Jews and pray with as much or more love and passion as Christians and/or Jews, I simply can not see how Christians, Jews, and Muslims can condemn each other to hell as nonbelievers. If everyone could see what I saw and be open minded about it, they would realize that Christians, Jews, and Muslims are all brothers worshipping the same God. How could God love any of these people less than the other just because they address Him with different names? Surely God does weep at the hate and violence that His name has caused here on earth.

Does God exist? As I wrestled with this critical issue for myself, I have come to the conclusion that the rational proof and the logic are 50/50 for and against. There is a strong rational case to be made that there is not a god, and that the universe and all that it is, is simply the result of scientifically driven laws of nature. But I also believe that there is an equally strong case that there is a god. Because of the fact that we exist, the fact there is a universe, and the fact that there are so many experiences in the history of mankind that only make sense if there is a god, then the case can be made that there is a god. Sort of, "I think, therefore I am," proof of the existence of God.

Pure facts, data, and logic didn't get me all the way there. I then had to reach down into my emotions, guts, and feelings. I have described some of my life experiences and they have had a strong impact. Sitting in my tree stand at 4:30 a.m. deep in the woods, looking at a star-filled sky, feeling the frost in the air, hearing the sounds of the forest, and feeling the ten thousand sensations that go through my mind, I feel His presence. Looking out over the Rockies at 12,000 feet at the setting sun and the majesty of the mountains, I feel His presence. Sailing at night, many miles from shore and looking at the incredible beauty and complexity of the heavens, I feel His presence. When I see the complexity of DNA or the universe, I feel His presence. Science cannot explain it all.

In my view, something had to be the beginning of the universe—Alpha and Omega. There are so many experiences that millions of people have had over the millennium that are unexplainable but for the presence of God or something beyond what science can explain. And I have witnessed one miracle myself. In college, Evelyn died and then came back and described things that she saw and heard that were impossible to explain without something beyond science. She tripped running up some stairs and she fell in such a way that the point of the steps paralyzed her diaphragm and she stopped breathing. I had dropped her off and happened to look in my rear view mirror and saw it happen. By the time I got to her she was unconscious, not breathing, and starting to turn blue. She was dead.

Having taken first aid and CPR, I knew what to do. Positioning her for CPR, and as soon as I started mouth-to-mouth resuscitation, she immediately started breathing so I suspect that all she needed was a kick start to get the diaphragm working again. But what she told me when she came to astounded me.

She told me that she tried to scream at first but could not breathe. And then suddenly she was at peace and left her body. She told me how she walked through the crowd and tried to tell us there was no need for an ambulance as I asked the crowd to call for one. She told me where people were standing and what they were saying. She told me how she tried to tell us it was okay and not to worry—that all was well. She was in total peace and felt no fear or pain. She felt that she saw it all as if she was in the audience and it was happening on a stage. And then she came to with my lips on hers as I was giving her mouth-to-mouth resuscitation. On top of the incredible things that she was telling me, was the impossibility of what she saw and heard. She was describing things that she could not have possibly seen and heard from her position. It was physically impossible. But her descriptions were 100 percent accurate. If I had not been there and seen and heard it all with my own eyes and ears, I would not have believed it. How do you explain all that? After the ambulance ride to the hospital, and in response to my question, the emergency room doctor said that Evelyn may or may not have started breathing again without help. What made me look in my rear view mirror at that moment so that I could rush back to help?

In the end, I have chosen to believe in God and I feel very good with that decision. I feel His presence in so many ways and there is so much that is simply unexplainable but for the presence of God, I believe. Combined with the strong (but not overwhelming) rational case for God plus my feelings, experiences, and the millions of unexplainable of events over the millennium, I believe. Rationally, I figure it this way: the scientific data says that people who believe in God live happier and healthier lives. Therefore if you don't believe in God you could be right, but you would be a two-time loser because you will be less happy in life and there is no Heaven. If you do believe in God, you can only be a one-time loser. Because if there is no God you will be happier in life because you believed in Him, but there will be no Heaven, thus, a one-time loser. But if you are a believer and you are right, then you are a two-time winner and you will be in Heaven with God. Believing in God is therefore the rational choice!

What kind of God do I believe in? Well a combination of the Old Testament, New Testament, Buddha, and the Koran. However I believe that God is too great to feel jealousy, revenge, or rage. Those are human weaknesses and a God that created the universe or DNA does not get jealous over which name you call Him. That is far beneath the dignity of my God. Much of what is in those holy books and beliefs describes common sense rules of society and successful human relations. I also feel that believing in something greater than ourselves is healthy and encourages good human behavior (taken the right way). Knowing that there is an ultimate judge of our actions encourages good behavior in life.

I believe that God gives us the freedom of choice. He does not want to tell us the precise path, but to let us make our choices and learn from the experience. I believe that the Bible, Koran, Jesus, Mohamed, and all other religions and prophets are gifts from God to help shape those choices. And God gave us our brains and logic to sort things out and to learn from the process. If He bluntly told us the way with His unlimited power, we would simply be robots and how boring would that be to us and to Him!

I believe in God, and I do believe in some kind of life after death, and I choose to believe in Heaven. From a rational perspective, nature wastes nothing. That is science. Therefore, I believe that all of the billions of experiences and feelings that make up who each of us are cannot be wasted in death. In addition, there are just too many documented afterlife experiences of mankind that are unexplainable by anything other than some form of life after death. I have shared my own after-death experience with Evelyn.

I choose to believe that after we have been here on earth and had the breadth of experience of joy and suffering in life, God brings us to Heaven with Him. In every person there is some good, even the most heinous. I believe that God takes the good part of each of us to be with Him in heaven. Only after the suffering here on Earth can we appreciate the joy of heaven. And even those that are evil have contributed in helping us to appreciate what Heaven is (as a contrast). As I said, humans can only truly know joy after they have suffered. It takes the bad things in life to help us appreciate the good things in life and Heaven. It is my choice to believe this and it makes as much sense to me as anything else.

I believe that we should try to live life exactly as I remember Socrates saying that he lived his life. We should treat our fellow brothers and sisters as we should like to be treated. The books of the Bible, Koran, and other great religions in many ways spell that out, but I also believe that we have to be prepared to fight to the death to protect the innocent and defend ourselves against evil. It is simply the law of nature which God created and it is a part of life. Peace through strength. All creatures have the right to defend themselves. But we should not impose our religious beliefs on others or condemn them for theirs. That to me is a golden rule.

There is a difference between religious beliefs and the laws of society. Society has the right to regulate behavior that endangers the greater good of society. Thus we would all agree that society has the right to punish rape, murder, and theft. The problem in society gets to be in defining the line between religious beliefs, personal freedom, the realities of life, and destructive antisocial behavior. What is murder and what is self defense? Is having ten children out of wedlock and putting the burden for their support on society something that society has the right to weigh in on (put aside the morality question of having children out of wedlock)? Does society have the right to control the media if they endanger our children with immoral messages? How far should free speech go? Where is the line between yelling fire in a theater when there is none (clearly against the law and all would agree is wrong) with true free speech? Where is it that the line should be drawn?

Our problem in society is defining which things society has the right to weigh in on, and which things society has no right to weigh in on. Where is the appropriate line for personal religion or personal freedom and where is the line for society's right to establish rules for the greater good? That will be the debate that mankind will have forever, even if we can get past the current downsides of religion as it is practiced today and keep the good parts of religion which describe appropriate human behavior and a relationship with God.

So in the end, what is the purpose of life and what to do? As I have said, I choose to agree with Socrates. I am a mere mortal. I believe in God, but I surely cannot understand Him in His entirety. Therefore, all I can do is live my life as well as I can with the gifts that I have been given, in the realities of the world, and treat my fellow man as I would expect him to treat me. On top of this, and above all else, is to live honorably. The best definition I have heard of honor was said by Rob Roy as he explained it to his sons in the movie, "Honor is a gift that a man gives to himself which can be taken by no man, and can only be lost by that man himself."

Each of us has to find his or her path in life. This is mine and I believe that God will be satisfied.

Chapter Eighteen

Post Script: Life After "Retirement"

I think that Socrates was right when he said, "The more that I learn the more I realize that I don't know," or words to that effect. I thought that life would slow down after I "retired." Yes, I had my bucket list to keep me busy, but I thought the pace would throttle back. Wrong!

In the following chapters I will share some extreme experiences that I had after I retired which most folks will never get to experience:

• Post script: Life After retirement: In this chapter I will summarize a whole bunch of cool stuff that I learned and got to do now that I am "retired" and have the freedom to do what I like and want to do.

• Israel—Where the Timeless Lessons of History Come to Life Every Day: I will share in detail our incredible trip to Israel and Jordan and the extreme things we saw and experienced there.

• Elk Hunting Heaven: I finally got that world class elk at 10,000 feet! You will feel like you were there with me!

• Shark Diving Senior: Discover what it is like to scuba dive surrounded by thirty, five to seven foot long, hungry sharks with no safety cage!

• Timeless Words of Wisdom: One of the benefits of reading thousands of books on history and philosophy over a lifetime is that you discover incredible wisdom from great people. Over the years, I recorded the best of the best from our Founding Fathers, Plato, Winston Churchill, and even Johnny Cash and Mark Twain. Everything you need to know in life is here.

• The Greatest Nation in the History of the World Is in Trouble: I will share my four years as an elected official working with politicians. We are in deep trouble!

I wrote these next chapters five years after I had "retired' and after this book was first published. Who could have known those five years would have been as exciting or as busy—maybe more so—than what you have already read about in the previous chapters. By the way, I was thrilled that my book did get published (only 1.5% do) and my book got a Five Star Rating from the Midwest Book Review. It doesn't get better than that!

I found out that the old saying, "God laughs at Man's plans," is absolutely true. Instead of focusing on my bucket list once I finished my book, my focus went back to business as a consultant, politics, travel, charity work, and sailing, all of which kept me busy twenty-four seven.

But first, let me talk about the most important thing in retirement: Family. So many people cannot adjust to retirement because they just don't know how to fill the time previously occupied by traditional work. In addition, sometimes husbands and wives cannot adapt to spending so much time together, and they drive each other nuts. I am blessed in that retirement has made my family life even better. I am incredibly lucky that my wife, Evelyn, and I enjoy many of the same things including sailing, traveling, volunteering, and reading. We are having a riot and I would rather be with her than anybody else! Now instead of working sixty to eighty hours a week away from her, we can spend tons of time together doing what we both love. How great is that? Plus we have enough differing interests that we have time to focus on those as well.

And talk about improving the quality of life! I have diabetes and I go in for check-ups every three months. I didn't tell my doctor that I was retiring, and my next appointment was three months after I had retired. I was very concerned as he walked into the room reading the results of my blood work. He looked like something was very, very wrong. I assumed that I was about to die like so many of my friends who had died within months of retiring.

He looked at me and said, "Have you made any major changes in your life?" "Well—I did retire three months ago."

"Why the hell didn't you tell me that? Your blood work has never been so good and it didn't make any sense. When executives like you retire, they always have a dramatic improvement because their job stress was killing them."

Who knew?

The other nice thing about retirement is watching your children and grandchildren grow. My son, Ben, has really blossomed. He married a great gal named Amanda, and they have two wonderful kids. It is great watching Ben move into business management and deal with the mature issues of life, with his family, and with life itself. I am incredibly proud of Ben, and I tell Amanda that she saved Ben's life just like Evelyn saved mine. Once you fall in love with a good woman, you drop the crazy stuff—most of it anyway—and focus on making sure your family has what it needs. And it is great playing with the grandkids and watching them grow!

Now, back to business. My old hunting buddy—previously mentioned in the book—connected me to another hunter in our industry, Steve Maahs, whose family owned a very successful business. Steve's dad had recently passed away, leaving Steve in charge. While a young guy—anybody under forty-five is young when you are an old fart like me!—Steve was very business savvy with mature judgment and he knew his business very well. He also knew that he needed to bring world class practices to his business in order to take it to the next level and to stay competitive. Steve had heard what I had accomplished at my company with my team, and he asked me to help him bring those same world class practices to his company. That sounded interesting and soon I was a member of Steve's board of directors, and I became his consultant.

This relationship exceeded all of my expectations, and I think Steve's as well. For me, not only did Steve provide a very fair financial arrangement, but I was overcome with the satisfaction that I got helping a very good group of people dramatically improve their business. I won't go into detail, but together as a team, we saw Steve's company dramatically improve in sales, EBITA, ROI, cash flow, quality, and in virtually every aspect of their business. In many areas, they are approaching world class status and in some cases, they have achieved it! And it all happened even faster than I would have predicted based on my prior experience.

Steve is a very ethical guy and as the owner, he made sure that his company treated employees and customers like professional businessmen are supposed to treat them. He also showed courage, in that he was willing to take the risk of introducing change in order to achieve dramatic improvement. It was fantastic watching the combination of world class practices and high business ethics, unencumbered by external short term profit pressure from external sources, achieve spectacular results. And to add to the pleasure, as a consultant, I got to stay at the high "strategic level" of issues. I kind of compare that to being a grandfather. You get to play with the kids and when they poop in their diapers, you get to hand them back to their parents—in this case to the business owner!

I had several offers to go back as a president in several other companies. but I just wasn't into that. But I really enjoyed consulting, so I have been involved in helping other companies. In each case, they were family owned businesses without external profit pressure. That is the only way to fly!

I really get a kick out of seeing the very same world class business practices that made it possible for my past company to be named one of the Top Ten Plants in North America (Industry Week Magazine award) and a finalist in the Shingo Award (the Nobel Prize of lean manufacturing according to Business Week Magazine) help other companies experience dramatic improvements in their businesses too. I am going to keep consulting for as long as it continues to be fun, although, I will choose my clients carefully to make sure that they hold the same ethical business values that I do.

I also got involved in politics. Holy crap are we in trouble! After living "The American Dream," I felt that I owed it to my son, my grandchildren and my ancestors to try and help preserve the greatest nation on Earth and the values that made it so great. I started writing millions of letters to the editor sticking up for traditional American values and trying to share my global experience with "uninformed readers." (Okay, two a day times five years equals 3,650 letters!) So far, I have had 200 of those letters printed in the Wall Street Journal,

Chicago Tribune, and The Daily Herald in Lake County, Illinois. Pretty soon I was asked to join the Tea Party and to be a writer for a conservative group called "The Freedom Writers." I really enjoyed that, although it is a wake-up call when you see hundreds of hate "attack letters" online in response to your letters and get nasty calls and letters at home. More than once I slept with my 9 mm next to the bed! But after a while, you just get used to the harassment. As Voltaire said, "It is lamentable that to be a good patriot, one must become the enemy of the rest of mankind." Today every one of my letters goes to hundreds of people as they are circulated to other "Freedom Writers" or concerned citizens who share my values, and several times a month hundreds of thousands or even millions of people see these values when the various papers print them.

Pretty soon, I was contacted by the Republican Party and asked to run as a Committeeman. Kind of like a Precinct Captain. I agreed and I was elected. What an experience! No wonder our country is in such trouble. I remember when I was taken to the county capital building to file for the election. The local Republican guys are very nice people and they walked me through the process. I got to meet and observe all the politicians of Lake County (both parties) which is a very prosperous county in Northern Illinois. On the way home, the very nice person who took me for my observation asked, "Now that you've seen it firsthand, what do you think?"

"After seeing it first hand, I don't know how democracy has lasted this long!" I said.

Here is the short version of my observation. For anybody who has been trained in psychological profiling or behavior interviewing, here is how I would identify the politicians I saw (and I bet this would be universal): thirty-three percent were good people just trying to do their duty and serve the people.

Thirty-three percent were people with massive egos and they were simply there to feed their egos. And the last thirty-three percent were folks who were simply there for the buck or for the connection that could get them their next buck. The heck with the "people"! During the political process, I worked with the local Republican Party and tried to introduce them to the same world class business practices that allowed my company to achieve greatness. Processes like strategic planning, modern communications tools, team prioritization and motivation, etc. But I think the current local Republican political process is stuck on "that is how we have always done it" mode and the "good old boy" network, instead of a results-oriented meritocracy. You can't win with that outlook! Change is scary and the attitude shown by the Republican Party which resisted change is the same attitude that dooms so many businesses that resist change.

In my first two years, I did have the pleasure of being asked by a new Republican candidate for Congress, Joe Walsh, to help him on his campaign. Mainly, I served as a sounding board, provided some strategic options, and did some writing for him. The general thinking was that Joe didn't have a chance but the Freedom Writers and other Tea Party folks got behind Joe, and darn if he didn't win by something like 300 votes! That pumped me up because I could see how the Freedom Writers and I certainly could have made the difference in getting those 300 votes! And I must admit, it is a kick to get a call from a Congressman actually on the floor in Congress asking my opinion on how I thought he should vote on a particular issue. While Congressman Walsh and I did not always agree, I never doubted that he always voted for what he thought were his constituents' best interests. His intent was always pure, in my opinion.

As a side note, my wife and I went to visit our good

friends Keith and Carolann in Washington, D.C. with the goal of spending time in one of our favorite places, Williamsburg, Virginia. While we were there, we asked Congressman Walsh for tickets to visit Congress and the White House (standard procedure for all Congressmen). He was able to get us tickets to Congress and it was a interesting to visit Congressman Walsh's office and then visit Congress in session! Unfortunately, Republican Congressman Walsh was unable to get us tickets to visit Democrat President Obama's office at the White House. Congressman Walsh's staff told us that he has never been able to get tickets to the White House despite asking hundreds of times. But I am sure that politics had nothing to do with it!

I won't dwell on it, but my involvement with politics went downhill after that. The frustration of trying to get the Republican Party to join the 21st century was maddening. They usually had the philosophy right, but they were incredibly ineffective. But even worse, was the general public. I worked my precinct hard in the primaries for the 2012 presidential election. I was astonished by the apathy, ignorance, and cowardice of the average voter. Our country was approaching $16 trillion in debt, unemployment was 8% and underemployment was 17%, and we were spending 40% more than our revenue. But the folks just didn't care. They were more interested in "Dancing with the Stars" than keeping up with the news. Seventy-five percent of the voters in Lake County (and the US) did not bother to vote in the primary. Simply disgusting! As Plato said, "The price of apathy in public affairs is to be ruled by evil men." And so we are!

After a while, I was asked by the Republican Party to run for higher office. I politely declined saying, "I won't run for higher office until they legalize dueling again!" After watching the distortions, dishonesty, and slanderous lies that are accepted and unchallenged by the media, I don't know why anybody would run for office. I am sure it would not be helpful to punch your opponent in the nose every time he slandered you, so I thought it best I stay on the sidelines and help as a writer and as a precinct committeeman.

I knew the presidential election would be close for several reasons. First, the biased media would continue to be Obama's co-conspirator, hiding his failures and his dishonesty. Second, Romney and the Republicans decided to use the "Nice Guy" strategy. Instead of attacking Obama's failures, dishonesty, and "class warfare" and "nanny state" strategy, Republicans hoped that by being nice, the American people would figure out that Obama was a failure. My big concern was that America was approaching an abyss in which 51% of Americans were in favor of the "Nanny State" and that the only way to win was to make it darn clear for America why Obama was a failure and leading us to be Greece. In either case, this was my last election as a political player. If Romney won, we would be back on course and headed in the right direction. I could then kick back, drink lots of wine, and enjoy the last years of my life. If we lost, our country was going off the cliff and would only change direction because of intense pain. My strategy if we lost was to kick back, drink heavily, and enjoy the last years of my life! We lost and I am drinking wine as I write this Postscript! I will cover more of my political experience, what dangers our nation faces, and how we could launch "The Great American Renaissance" just by getting back to our traditional American values, in the last chapter.

Just a quick couple of notes on more fun stuff since retirement. First, since I first wrote the book and had it published, I did get more input about my family as relatives read the book and contacted me with more data. For instance, I found out some very cool stuff about Grandpa Augusto. You will remember him from the beginning, so I won't rehash what you already read. I found out that he was a Lieutenant in the Italian Alpine Corps. He fought in the horrible battles of the mountains around Trieste where about 700,000 Italians were killed in battle. He was at the monastery in Austria featured in The Sound of Music. You already know that he was wounded three times and gassed. But then I found out that he was also court-martialed! He was ordered to make an attack a certain way that would have annihilated his platoon. He disobeyed orders and attacked by a different route which succeeded. During the court-martial, his men enthusiastically and unanimously supported him and said his decision to attack differently is why the mission was successful. He was not only found innocent, he received the Italian Medal of Honor. He also received a Chevalier, the French Medal of Honor.

He almost died from his wounds and being gassed, and he spent months in a Swiss hospital where he also got tuberculosis. He received permanent injuries to his feet after spending months in trenches with freezing water. After the war, he went back to Bologna as a war hero and worked as an executive with the railroad, as the Rossi family was wealthy and a major investor in the railroad. And then Mussolini came to power. Mussolini was a fascist and my grandfather was probably a socialist and they didn't get along. In addition, Mussolini's mother worked for the Rossi family years ago as a maid, which probably didn't help the relationship—at least that is the story. And then to add to the conflict, Augusto worked with a group dedicated to kicking Mussolini out of power or assassinating him. Ooops!

Suddenly, Augusto got a warning that Mussolini's "Black-shirts" were marching to Augusto's home to arrest him and then to execute him, and they were just thirty minutes away! Friends and family put him in a potato sack, which was then put in a wheel barrow, which was rolled down the street right past the "Black-shirts," and he escaped to America leaving his family at the mercy of Mussolini and his men!

The terror for my grandmother, aunt, and my baby dad began immediately. One of the members of Augusto's gang—who was my aunt's Godfather—was captured shortly thereafter. He was executed and then decapitated. His head was sent home to his family. The man's son was there and swore he would kill Mussolini. Supposedly, he was there when Mussolini and his mistress were murdered. Revenge is best served cold!

For five years, Mussolini's men came to Augusto's house every day to harass and terrify Grandma, my aunt, and my dad. They would lock the door at 7 PM every night so they could not leave and then open it in the morning. In the mean-time, my grandfather was in Chicago working as a carpenter (vs. railroad executive back home!) and saved his money to bring his family to America. He finally saved $5,000 (today easily worth over $100,000) and gave it to Al Capone at the same hotel that was featured in a TV show when they discovered his safe there and opened it on live TV. Suddenly, Senator Adlai Stevenson got involved and both Italy and the US allowed my father, aunt, and grandmother to leave Italy and enter the US legally. You don't suppose that Senator Stevenson got a piece of the action do you? There is nothing new under the sun!

Just another post script. I mentioned our proud Italian heritage in earlier chapters. My father, Rome, was named after Rome. My grandfather was named after Emperor Augustus, the most powerful and successful emperor in Italy's history (my opinion), and I just found out my great-grandfather was named Caesar. Naturally!

One other cool thing was on my mom's side of the family. Ev and I got to visit Robert Morris senior's home in Oxford, Maryland. Robert Morris Jr. lived there for a year with his dad. It has been converted to an inn which was awarded for having the best crab cake sandwiches in Maryland! It was very cool to walk through the bedrooms, dining rooms, living rooms, and other rooms that my ancestors lived in back in the 1700's. Oxford had a Robert Morris museum, and when I told them I was related to Robert Morris, the attendant told me how much the town still loves Robert Morris Sr. She spent an hour going over the history of his impact on the town. Robert was responsible for all trade between Britain and the Pennsylvania Colony. All that ended when a British ship came to port and the captain invited Morris on board for dinner. As he left the dinner in his honor on the ship, he was accidentally killed when they fired an honorary salute with their cannons. Unfortunately, he was still close to the ship and the wadding from the blank charges hit him and ended up killing him! The town then went through a hundred years of economic decline as trade shifted to Philadelphia with Robert Morris' demise.

A final note on Robert Morris. I read a great new book about him, written by Charles Rappleye who did a wonderful job of identifying the incredible contributions Grandpa Morris made to the United States risking his life by signing the Declaration of Independence, funding the military, and later signing the Articles of Confederation and the Constitution. Without him, the army would not have been paid, the navy would not have been built, and the weapons needed to fight the war would have never been acquired. Bottom line, without Robert Morris, the "Financier of the American Revolution," there would be no America.

But, the best part of the book is a description of the final meeting between President George Washington and Robert Morris. They were extremely good friends, and Morris even gave Washington his home in Philadelphia to use while he was president. Then Robert Morris went bankrupt after his multi-million dollar land investment failed, and President Washington visited him in debtor's prison. As they discussed the massive risks that they both took over the years, President Washington asked him if it was worth it. Morris' reply should go down into history forever, "I would rather die like a lion than live like a lamb!" Amen!

My family at the farm loved the family history and took me on a tour of the family graves throughout the county. Those graves went back to the early 1800's. I found out that another member of our family died fighting Indians. Instead of seven, number eight died in Texas as a member of the US Calvary fighting the Comanches. I also found out that Uncle Lowell served with General Douglas MacArthur during the occupation of Japan. Fascinating! Uncle Lowell joined Mom and Dad in Heaven shortly after that trip.

Back to post retirement! Ev and I have done some fantastic travelling which has been a real eye opener despite the fact that I have been to dozens of countries for business and pleasure before retirement. First, we did a three week cruise in the Mediterranean from Barcelona (interesting), Rome (I love Rome even after four trips there), Naples (Capri is spectacular), Venice (love it even after ten business trips there), Athens (disappointing except the Acropolis), Dubrovnik (gorgeous!), Ephesus (fantastic!) and finally, Istanbul (exceeded all my expectations!). Other trips included Israel and Jordan, a river cruise in France, and a river cruise which covered Prague, Budapest, and Germany and many, many trips in the US. Our visit to Israel and Jordan was so inspirational that I wrote a chapter on it which follows.

Another benefit of working with Steve as a consultant was that he was a fellow hunter who convinced me to go on one more hunt to get that world class elk. When I told him that I was done sleeping in tents at 12,000 feet with no toilet or shower, he showed me another way to hunt! It was so much fun I did a chapter on it as well. I finally did get that world class elk! Finally, now that I am old and on the downhill slide of life, I thought I would do a few more crazy things as well. You will find a chapter on my crazy shark dive, in which I spent a few hours surrounded by six and seven-foot sharks that were all looking for something to eat—no cage!

After that physical excitement, I want to get back to a cerebral exercise. The next chapter is entitled, "Timeless Words of Wisdom." I have been fortunate to have read thousands of books on history and philosophy over the years and have taken over sixty post graduate courses from fantastic professors from the best universities in America through the Teaching Company. In this chapter, you will find famous quotes that I discovered when I read these books and took these courses. This chapter is a priceless and timeless gold mine and tells anybody everything they need to know about life!

And finally, I want to share what really scares me to death—the direction of our nation! When I wrote my book five years ago and predicted the direction our country was headed, I was hoping I was wrong. I was hoping that I am not "The Last Man to Live the Real American Dream." I was wrong. Things are much worse than I imagined. I will close this post script with an update of why I love this country so much, and why I am scared to death for my son and grandkids. I wrote that chapter including a letter I sent to the Republican Party after Romney's loss to Obama. It explains what is wrong with our country and how dangerous it will be if we don't quickly turn things around. It also explains from my view what it will take to turn things around.

Chapter Nineteen

Israel: Where the Timeless Lesson of History Come to Life Every Day

Having just returned from my first visit to Israel, I am still decompressing from the powerful experience. There is nowhere else on earth that features the same intense and incredible intersection of history, religion, extremes of nature, and the reality of life on a daily basis. I decided to write down my impressions of our trip while they are still intense in my memory. Not only do I want to describe what I saw in Israel and Jordan, I want to document what I learned while I was there and what I felt. There are a thousand impressions that I could share from my visit, but me let first focus on three intense experiences that I think will justify my view of the special nature of Israel and will also establish a sense of being there.

Our first official stop in Israel was Megiddo, also called Armageddon in the Bible, and supposedly the site of the last battle between Good and Evil at the End of Days. First fortified over 5,000 years ago, Megiddo has been destroyed and rebuilt over twenty-five times as various cultures fought over the land. Built on a high hill or "tel" overlooking vast plains, it is a perfect defensive site with miles of visibility. It is situated at a critical transportation route to the sea (Via Maris in Roman times) and to the trading centers of Babylon and Persia.

Whether it was the Egyptian Pharaoh Thutmose destroying the Canaanites in 1468 BC or British General Allenby defeating the Turks in 1918 AD, Megiddo has proved Plato correct when he said, "Only the dead have seen the end of war." Megiddo has been conquered by Cannnites, Egyptians, Ancient Jews, Assyrians, and on and on. Megiddo oozes history wherever you look, like when you walk through King Solomon's stables. As you walk down the incredible water tunnel hand dug through solid rock thousands of years ago, so that defenders would not have to leave protective walls to get their water, you are reminded that the world is a dangerous place. This experience at Megiddo set the stage for my next epiphany days later, as we crossed from Israel to Jordan and a border which featured masses of barbed wire, a 200-hundred-yard "no man's land", and many armed soldiers on the Jordanian side. As we were walking through "no man's land" I thought back about Megiddo and realized that nothing has changed in 5,000 years! The world remains a dangerous place and all that changes is the name of the enemies and their weapons. Seeing it first hand was an emotional epiphany, despite the fact that I have read about this history of conflict for years. Rational knowledge obtained by reading is very different from the emotional experience of seeing it firsthand.

The third experience that reinforced the intense intersection of history, religion, and the reality of life occurred in Jerusalem. We were by the Western Wall or "Wailing Wall." It is the retaining wall of the Temple Mount and it is Judaism's holiest site. Built by Herod the Great over 2,000 years ago, the Temple and walls were destroyed by the Romans in 70 AD. Walking in the same places as Herod the Great, Jesus Christ, Emperor Vespasian, and Saladin, you are overwhelmed by the history of Jerusalem. Looking at the Wailing Wall, the Dome of the Rock, and Church of the Holy Sepulchre, you realize that you are at the holiest spot on earth based on Christianity, Islam, and Judaism and the billions of those people who believe in those religions. And that is special, no matter your religious beliefs.

What made this experience intensely relevant to how the world continues to be a dangerous place, involves what happened at that site while we were there and how our guide reacted. Charlie was our guide. He came to Israel from France as a child, as his Jewish family wanted to "come home to Jerusalem." He served in the Israeli army and then became a professional guide with an intense background in history. Charlie was always upbeat, happy, and carefree, and he loved to share the beauty of Jerusalem with his clients. We never saw a negative emotion from Charlie until "it" happened.

Overlooking the Wailing Wall surrounded by people and fresh new Israeli army recruits being "reintroduced" to their Jewish heritage, Charlie was his usual enthusiastic and passionate self, explaining everything to Ev, Dan, and me. Suddenly he stopped. His eyes riveted on something. He had an intense look on his face that those of us that have been confronted by a life and death experience immediately recognize. Following his eyes, I saw a bag that contained two large bottles of liquid along with what looked like a small box in the bag. I immediately understood that Charlie thought that this could be a bomb. It was in a perfect place to kill hundreds of Jewish people at any time.

Charlie, this normally upbeat and passionate man, then

quietly apologized for the interruption and told us to move away immediately from where we were and to move below the site and behind a large stone wall, while he went to talk to the authorities. He never said it was a bomb, but he looked into my eyes, knew that I understood, and we immediately moved behind the stone wall as he left us.

You see, Jerusalem has been attacked and destroyed many, many times for thousands of years by Canaanites, Jews, Assyrians, Babylonians, Romans, Greeks, Muslims, Crusaders, the English, and many others have been killing each other in horrible ways for 5,000 years in Jerusalem. Today, it is Islamic terrorists trying to kill Jews and innocent tourists. It was a stark reminder that the world is and will always be a dangerous place.

But, what immediately followed was the good news we experienced in Israel and another critical lesson. After he reported the threat and we had moved to safety, Charlie immediately reverted back to his carefree and passionate self, the incident long gone and forgotten. This fit with my general observation of Israelis in that they certainly understand the danger they face, but they also seem to enjoy life with more passion than we do. The lesson? Yes, life is dangerous, and we must be alert and prepared, but life is also dear and we should enjoy every good moment that we have to its fullest and with passion.

While those incidents give you a feel for the intensity of Israel, let me continue to describe the diversity of the Israel we saw. First, we were lucky in that our tour guides were Jewish friends of the family who fought in several of the Israeli conflicts, one as a tank commander and one as a paratrooper and military intelligence officer, who then retired and became a professional guide. I assure you that we saw a side and perspective of Israel that folks who go on those church tours will never see!

We left Megiddo for our second stop on that first day, Mount Tabor. Famous as the sight where Jesus Christ was transfigured, while in the presence of Moses and Abraham, it was also the site of a major battle between the Romans and rebelling Jews in 66 AD. In the church built on the site, you can see the rock that Jesus was standing on when he was transfigured. Muslims and Crusaders also built forts during the Crusades here 800 years ago. From Mount Tabor you can see for many miles and Nazareth, where Jesus grew up, is clearly in view on the next hill.

From Mount Tabor we went to Beth Shean which is simply fascinating. It features the best preserved Roman ruins in Israel, and it has been inhabited for 5,000 years starting with the Canaanites. It has been conquered by Egyptians, Jews, Philistines, Greeks, Romans, Muslims, and Crusaders. Today, you see the magnificent and orderly Roman ruins that are 2,000 years old. The ruins still clearly illustrate a high standard of living not seen even today in much of the world: magnificent marble public baths with centrally heated pools, changing rooms, magnificent and still beautiful mosaic floors, a 3,000 seat theater, and public restrooms which had flowing water and underground sewers. Straight and orderly paved streets with markets and public buildings and temples demonstrate how modern the Romans were 2,000 years ago. Yet, just at the top of an adjacent hill, we are reminded of the breadth of history because we can see where King Saul and his sons were killed by the Philistines 1,500 years before the Romans arrived here 2,000 years ago!

Coming home that night (we were exhausted because we must have walked ten miles, all uphill) we returned to our hotel in Tel Aviv, The David Intercontinental. As a reminder of the reality of Israel, right across the street from our hotel was a mosque and a deserted bar and night spot in which twenty-four teenagers were killed by a terrorist a few years ago. But life goes on, and we went to a terrific Italian restaurant for dinner and then returned to our hotel where we collapsed.

The question we always get about our trip is, Were you nervous because of the Arab/Israeli conflict? One thing is certain. You do not forget for one second that danger is possible. Every eighteen-year-old Israeli is in the Israeli army, and they are required to carry their weapons wherever they go so that they can be ready to instantly respond to violence. It is very strange to see a gorgeous eighteen-year-old gal with a M-16 over her shoulder! So, weapons are everywhere. All police vehicles are required to have their emergency lights on all of the time to reinforce their presence to the bad guys. There were always huge army tanks on the road when we were around Jerusalem. In the Golan Heights there are signs all over the place warning of land mines in English, Hebrew, and Arabic. Huge walls separate the West Bank from Jerusalem so that terrorists can't shoot innocent civilians. And while eating breakfast one morning in Tel Aviv, I read in the newspaper that Hamas just got access to rockets that can now reach Tel Aviv. Great. So, you cannot forget for one second that the possibility of danger is real. On the other hand, people go about their business and their lives and you soon take it all in stride. It adds to the excitement. Very strange!

That was our first day! Next we headed off to Northern Israel and the Sea of Galilee just a few miles from Syria and Lebanon. Green, hilly, and full of agriculture, it was not the desert that I expected. Simon explained that it used to be a desert, but Jews arriving in the early 1900s introduced drip irrigation agriculture and replanted all the trees the Arabs had cut down over the centuries all over the nation. They made a desert into a garden. We stopped for breakfast in Tiberius, on the edge of the Sea of Galilee. Built during the reign of Emperor Tiberius and named in his honor, it is a resort town today on the shores of Galilee.

We then went to Capernaum and saw the ruins of Saint Peter's house and the town where he lived. Capernaum is also where Christ was said to join the Apostles as they fished in the Sea of Galilee, and you can go to the shore to see where they probably kept their boats. In addition, you can walk through the well-kept ruins of a large synagogue where Jesus is said to have preached. The Sea of Galilee is actually a large fresh water lake that used to separate Syria and Israel. Simon told us as a kid his parents warned him not to spend too much time on the beach, as the Syrians might try to take a shot at him across the lake. That is not a problem now because Israel controls all of the Sea of Galilee up to the Golan Heights.

Next we went to the Mount of the Beatitudes where Jesus held his Sermon on the Mount, a beautiful site on a hill overlooking the Sea of Galilee. From there we went to the Church of the Multiplication of the Loaves and Fishes where the Bible says Jesus fed 5,000 followers with five loaves of bread and two fish. The Church was built over the rock that was used to serve the meals and features some beautiful mosaics from the Byzantine period. It was interesting to see the area where Jesus and the Apostles spent so much of their time and to walk in their footsteps.

We drove around much of the Sea of Galilee and came to the Golan Heights, the scene of vicious fighting in 1967 and where Simon was stationed as a tank commander. As I said earlier, it was a beautiful, green, and hilly site but warning signs about land mines are posted all over the terrain, a contrast that reminds you of the war the Israelis fought there. On the top of one hill stands a Roman fort that is 2,000 years old next to another hill that holds a Syrian Fort from 1967.

Nothing is new under the sun!

Our final stop that day was at Caesarea. Built 2,000 years ago by Herod the Great on the shores of the Mediterranean over an ancient Phoenician port, it was named to honor Emperor Augustus Caesar. It is another example of how incredibly modern the Romans were. It features a manmade harbor, huge Hippodrome (race track) for chariot races, elaborate heated baths and pools, and a very large theater that seats 4,000 people that is still used today for concerts. Beautiful, intricate, multi-colored mosaics on many of the floors of the buildings testify to the lavish lifestyle of the Romans. A huge aqueduct that still stands brought millions of gallons of fresh water from the hills twenty-five miles away. From Caesarea, Emperors Vespasian, Titus, and Hadrian launched their wars against the rebelling Jews and the Crusaders fought Saladin. As the sun went down, we sat in a restaurant in the ruins looking out at the sea having a traditional Jewish meal and wine, just as Herod the Great and the Romans no doubt did 2,000 years ago!

The next day we headed south deep into the desert and to the lowest spot on earth, the Dead Sea. Deep canyons and high cliffs mark the desert and surely nothing can live here. We stopped at a place that points the way to Sodom—where God destroyed Sodom and Gomorra—and turned Lot's wife into a pillar of salt. Looking around at the desolation, you believe it! We drove by the Dead Sea and could see why it is dead. Salt and minerals line the shore and make up thirty-three percent of the water content. There is no life in the water and around the shoreline, and if someone drank the water, he would die. The Dead Sea is huge and desolate except for the resorts that feature spa treatments with the water and mud. Just on the other side one can see Jordan.

Next we stopped at Masada which is the mountain top

fortress in the middle of the desert 1,300 feet above the Dead Sea. Built 2,200 years ago, it was where the last 1,000 Jewish rebels fought the 10th Roman Legion in 66 AD. It is stark and surrounded by desert mountains. Herod the Great built a grand palace there with baths, pools, and storage facilities to arm and support 10,000 troops. Huge water cisterns provided enough water to last years. Beautiful mosaics illustrate the past splendor. Hoping to hold off the Romans, the Jews felt that Masada was unconquerable. But the tenacious Romans built multiple forts in the desert around Masada (they are still there) and then built a ramp up the mountain (still clearly visible) for their gigantic siege machines. The Jewish rebels knew that they were doomed as the ramp came up the mountain and they prepared for the end. Just as the Romans were about to enter Masada, the Jews decided to commit suicide rather than submit and they drew lots to determine who would do the killing. The lots they used are still there to see in the museum at Masada. The Romans entered to silence and gave the dead Jews their respect as worthy foes. Being at Masada and looking at the harsh desert, one cannot believe that men would live there, fight there, and die there for honor. Today graduating Israeli army recruits walk the 1,300 foot path up to Masada in the desert and swear to never again be defeated. This is done to make sure each generation of soldiers understands that they are fighting for the very existence of Israel and that what happened to the Jews at Masada can happen again.

We then left Masada to visit Ein Gedi, an ancient Oasis in the desert. On the way we crossed the river Jordan. River is the wrong word. Creek is more appropriate! Suddenly we were in Ein Gedi where the desert blooms with trees and green vegetation. Walking up in the cliffs there are water falls, Ibex (we actually saw these magnificent desert gazelles with their huge curved horns), lyraxes (very large rodents which we also saw), and occasional leopards (that we didn't see!). King David—before he was king—hid in Ein Gedi when King Saul was trying to kill him. The Jewish rebels of Masada killed 800 fellow Jews in Ein Gedi who had inhabited the site since 500 BC to take their food. The Dead Sea scrolls were found right next to Ein Gedi in local caves. Life moves on. On the way home we passed Bethlehem but because it is a Muslim city, tensions were high, and because we had two Jewish people with us, we could not enter. But I did get to ride on a camel when we stopped to fill up with gas nearby! The ride on a camel is not pleasant, and by the way, they stink.

I suppose this is as good as any place to talk about the conflict between Arab Muslims and Israeli Jews. Everyone reads about it in the news, but believe me, until one is there and sees it with his eyes and hears the facts from the folks who are there, one can have no idea of what is going on. Let me start with a true fact that illustrates the intense hatred that has existed for centuries.

Standing at the Mount of Olives in Jerusalem and looking toward the Temple Mount, one notices a huge Jewish grave yard that has been there for centuries. It is the most popular grave site in Jerusalem because it is near the Golden Gate of the Temple Mount where Jews believe God lives, and it is through this gate that Jews will enter heaven when the Messiah comes. The Jews want to be buried near the gate so that they can be the first to enter Heaven. Knowing the importance of this to Jews, the Muslims put a Muslim grave yard between the Jewish graveyard and the Golden Gate when they had control of Jerusalem. The reason they did this is that they thought that the leader of the dead Jews would not be able to step over the Muslim graves to go to Heaven through the Golden Gate when the Messiah came, because it would be unclean to do so according to Jewish law. The bottom line: the Muslims hated the Jews so much that they want to stop them from going to Heaven! You won't hear this on PBS or CNN. By the way, the joke is on the Muslims in this case. The leader of the dead Jews is permitted to step over the graves of the Muslims according to Jewish law and when the time comes, he will be able to lead his people to Heaven.

When the Muslims took control of Jerusalem from 1948 until the Six Day War of 1967, they took all of the marble grave markers off the Jewish graves and used them to pave their roads or as toilet seats. Once Israel was declared a state by the United Nations, Muslims kicked all Jews out of Jerusalem, even if they had been citizens and their family owned their property in Jerusalem for hundreds of years. They forbade the Jews from visiting their holiest sites on earth. And finally, while the Muslims controlled the land of Israel for more than 1,000 years, it remained an empty desert. When the United Nations made tiny Israel an independent state in 1948 with less than 2 million Jews, hundreds of millions of Arab Muslims vowed to annihilate Israel and tried three times to do so. Somehow these facts always get lost in the world's vicious attacks on Israel.

Contrast how the Muslims behaved toward the Israeli Jews while in control of Jerusalem with how Israeli Jews have acted toward the Muslims when they had control of Jerusalem and what they have done in the fifty years while they have controlled the land. Jews began legally buying empty land in Israel from local Arabs and Turks in the early 1900's to legitimately start a new homeland under the Jewish National Fund. They legally created Tel Aviv from the empty desert. When the United Nations proposed an independent Israeli nation in 1947, Israel agreed to honor every condition proposed by the UN, but the Muslims agreed to none. The Muslims then united and tried to kill all Jews in Israel. Once the Jews miraculously defended themselves and got control of Israel, they turned the desert into a garden in less than fifty years. They allowed Muslims access and control of all their holy sites in Jerusalem and continue to do so today. They have created more wealth in the tiny state of Israel in fifity years than the combined wealth created by Muslims in Jordan, Syria, and Lebanon in 1,000 years with more than twenty times the population. Arab Muslims living in Israel have a much higher standard of living than their Muslim brothers in Syria, Jordan, and every other Muslim state that does not have oil. All I can say is that the Jews have been more tolerant of the Muslims than I would have been had they tried to kill me every day.

Despite the fact that Muslims have tried to annihilate the Jews three different times, there is a lot of pressure from the naïve Western world pushing the Jews to give back the land they won in the Six Day War. Recently, Israel tried appeasement and gave back the Gaza strip in exchange for a promise of peace. In return, the Palestinians have launched 5,000 rockets into Israel from the newly acquired Gaza Strip. If I were an Israeli, I would not give back one inch of the land that was won after being invaded three times by Muslims trying to annihilate me. Israel has more right to the land that it now occupies than the US has to California, which we won after invading Mexico. Today, six million Jews are surrounded by hundreds of millions of Muslims that continue to refuse to even agree to the right of the Jews to exist. And they continue to try to kill the Jews every day. There is no room for compromise under these circumstances. There can only be the will to stand strong and defend their ancestral homeland which they have bought with money and won again with blood after 2,000 years of losing their homeland. Never again!

On day four we headed to Jerusalem with Charlie. Jerusalem is beautiful. It is hilly, green, filled with trees, and all the buildings are built with gorgeous Jerusalem stone according to the law since the Jews took Jerusalem in the Six Day War. Viewing the old city from the Mount of Olives takes one back at least 4,000 years. We then went into the walled city through the gates that Herod the Great built 2,000 years ago. The fortress walls are still magnificent and majestic. Charlie showed us two large grave markers just past the gates. Apparently, Herod the Great hired two contractors to build the walls and they cheated him. There is nothing new under the sun! Herod executed them and put their graves by the gate as a warning to all who enter the city—too bad we can't do that today. We walked through the Arab markets which offered everything for sale that one can imagine. It was lively and spirited as any Mediterranean market is. And then we entered the special space where Jesus was crucified, the Church of the Holy Sepulcher.

Charlie had a special surprise for us as we entered the church and introduced us to the "Gate Keeper" of the Church of the Sepulcher. Eight hundred years ago when Saladin conquered Jerusalem, he wanted to protect the Christian Church for posterity. Saladin was a very honorable Muslim. He assigned a Gate Keeper who locked the church, opened it for the faithful Christians, and protected it at all times. For 800 years, the gate keeper's responsibility was passed down in the same family and the "Gate Keeper" who we met was the great, great, great, great, great, great, (forty greats!) grandson of the original gate keeper chosen by Saladin. He still took his responsibility to protect the Christian church very seriously even though he was a devout Muslim. The gate keeper told us that his greatest challenge today was to protect the Church from various Christian Sects who dispute each other's "turf" within the Church. I suspect that most tourists have no idea who the "gate keeper" is as they pass him.

We then entered the Church and walked the same steps that Jesus walked as he was crucified. One sees where Jesus was nailed to the cross and where the cross was placed in the stone at Golgotha. The stone is still there under an altar. One then sees where Jesus' body was laid on the Stone of Unction to be washed and anointed with oil after his death. Unfortunately, the stone that is there now was placed in 1810. Finally, one walks to the tomb where Mary Magdalene discovered Jesus had disappeared and risen from the dead. It is certainly a very special place. Unfortunately for me, it is all covered under an elaborate church with intense Byzantine artwork surrounding everything. To me it takes away from the true history of the place and makes it impossible to imagine it as it was when Jesus was there. But it is still a very special place.

We then went to the Lutheran Church and walked up the 180 steps of the bell tower to get the best view of Jerusalem. From there we took magnificent pictures of all of the old city and the Temple Mount. Next we went to the Western Wall, or Wailing Wall, which is the holiest site for the Jews and the only remaining vestige of the Temple Mount built by Herod the Great. Both Ev and I had taken written prayers of friends from home who asked us to place them in the wall, which we did. It is also a very special place. Orthodox Jews practically live at the wall talking to God and constantly bowing as they do so. I was cornered by one of the Orthodox Jews who wanted to vigorously debate the superior nature of his religion versus mine right at the wall. That is Israel!

Unfortunately, we could not visit the Dome on the Rock because of our Jewish friends. The Muslims control the site and they will not allow any Jews and sometimes no Christians to enter. Even though the Jews now control Jerusalem, they allow the Muslims to control their holy sites and even allow them to forbid Jews from going in to see their own sacred places. That is a powerful example of the difference between the Muslim and Jewish mentalities. But the Dome on the Rock is beautiful, and covers the stone where God asked Abraham to sacrifice Isaac. Jerusalem has thousands of magnificent sites which we saw, too many to cover here. But it was time to go home for the night and we had walked another ten miles, all uphill!

The next day we returned to Jerusalem to visit the Israel Museum. First we saw the Dead Sea scrolls that are over 2,000 years old. They were discovered in a cave near the Oasis of Ein Gedi which I talked about earlier. In addition to the scrolls, the museum showed how the people lived in those days. Next we went into the great Archaeology Museum that shows what life was like in Jerusalem over the millennium with Paleolithic, Canaanite, Egyptian, ancient Jewish, Babylonian, Persian, Greek, Roman, Muslim, Crusader, and Turkish weapons, art, treasure, and everyday items used in life.

From there we went to Yad Vashem, or the Holocaust museum which graphically documents the murder of six million Jews in World War Two by the Germans and many other nations that cooperated with them. There is simply nothing one can say that can explain the experience. One observes as many people weeping as they had family members who were lost in the Holocaust. Simon's mother and father suffered in the holocaust and they lost their parents and many family members to the Nazis. As an example of the intensity of the emotion the Holocaust Museum elicits, I'd like to share something with my readers which Charlie, our guide, told us about. One day he was leading a group of tourists in the museum, when suddenly an older woman screamed and fainted. When she came to, she pointed to a large photograph of a train releasing prisoners doomed to go into the concentration camp. She pointed at a women holding the hand of a small girl. She explained, "That is my mother and me. My mother was killed."

I felt angry at thought of the cowardice of the world that let this happen and at those people who assisted the Nazis.

We headed home to our hotel deep in thought. For those of us who study history, we know that this kind of slaughter has happened many, many times before. The world is a dangerous place and the forces of good must always be prepared to stop the forces of evil who will commit any heinous crime to seize power.

The next day began our new adventure to Eilat, Jordan, and Petra. We caaught a morning flight to Eilat which flew south over the Dead Sea and Masada to Eilat. Eilat is at the northern edge of the Red Sea and is basically a very nice seaside resort city. Our hotel was, naturally, the Herod which is very nice and next to the new water park (Herod would have been proud)! Ev and Dan joined me in a cab ride to my scuba "date" and then they headed back to relax at the Herod pool and get some sun. My plan involved a little more physical activity!

At the dive center I met Enosh who was a master diver and he would be taking me diving in the Red Sea. I was stoked because the Red Sea is famous for diving. I was a little surprised and disappointed when he said that we would dive right off the beach. I was used to a dive boat ride taking me out to a spectacular reef as in other dives I had experienced, and from the boat just hopping into the water with my gear on. You should have seen me crossing the busy road on the way to the beach wearing my wet suit and 100 pounds of diving gear while dodging cars. Not pretty!

Well, my fears were unfounded as soon as I submerged. True to the reputation, the Red Sea is teeming with life. I did a two tank dive and I saw more numbers and varieties of fish than I have seen in Florida or the Cayman Islands. In addition to the thousands of colorful groupers, parrot fish, angel fish, butterfly fish, clown fish, and every type of colorful reef fish one would normally see, I saw spectacularly colorful sting rays, moray eels, and lion fish. Lion fish are very poisonous and it is the first time that I have seen them in person. It is a little strange maneuvering within one foot of them to get a close up picture knowing that if you accidentally touch them you will pay dearly—stings are normally not fatal, but mighty painful. But, I took the pictures!

Well, the sun was going down and it was time to head to the hotel and have a great Italian dinner at the beach overlooking the Red Sea. Dan loves Italian and Ev and I can be talked into it!

In the morning, our guides came to take us across the Jordanian border to Petra. First, we had to cross the border, and I have described the surreal experience of about one hundred security checks every ten feet—okay that's a slight exaggeration, barbed wire everywhere, a 200-hundred-yard open "no man's land" between the borders, so that they can easily shoot you down if they need to, and armed soldiers everywhere. It is not quite like crossing from Illinois to Wisconsin! But the guides did a great job and everything went smoothly and we were on our way.

For two hours, we traveled through the desert and clawed our way up into the mountains, going from sea level to over the mountain top. The scenery is magnificent and one sees the stone trails, markers, and campsites used for three thousand years to guide caravans along the Silk Road connecting the Middle East to Europe and the Far East. Our guide told us that a small caravan back then had 500 camels in it. Believe me, having been around four or five camels at one time on this trip, 500 would stink to high heaven!

As we approached the summit of our mountain and the road down to Petra, we saw a small white stone hut at the top of the highest peak in the mountain range across the valley. Our guide told us that it is where Aaron, Moses' brother, was buried. Apparently, it is a very special holy spot and the guidebook says that people take a three-hour horse ride plus another three-hour climb to pray at it. Looking up at the mountain top, I believe it. Then we started our decline into the valley that holds Petra.

If one has seen the movie, "Indiana Jones and the Lost Crusaders", one has seen Petra. There is nothing like it in the world. It was built 2,400 years ago by the Nabateans. They carved a massive city in a stone river bed surrounded by 100-foot cliffs. It is a perfect defensive setting and they were one of the few peoples in history who were actually able to defend themselves against Roman sieges until they reached a peaceful alliance. One will see many massive temples carved into the stone along the two-mile walk in the narrow valley. Hundreds of caves carved into the stone served as homes for the people. Our guide lived in one of those caves until he went to school. Falling in love with his history, he got his Bachelor's and Masters degrees and worked for the King of Jordan giving high profile tours (Hillary Clinton, President Ford, etc.).

It is hard to describe the magnificence and scale of Petra. In addition to the massive temples carved into the hills by the Nabateans (the treasury building is the most famous), the Romans built their usual 600-seat theater in the rock and a "Cardo" (main street with columns). All I can tell you is that we walked about two miles downhill surrounded by massive temples and cliffs. That means when it was time to go home, we walked two miles uphill! The camels, horses, and carts that the Arabs offered for rides back up started to look pretty darn good but we toughed it out! There is nothing on earth like Petra!

Another two-hour drive through the desert—we almost hit a donkey in the middle of the road in the dark!—and a flight back to Tel Aviv and we were back to our hotel at roughly 10 PM. We were exhausted and collapsed into our beds for a long night's sleep.

We woke up to our last day in Israel. It was our first cloudy day. We had a traditional Israeli breakfast, which always includes salad, cheese, and great rolls, plus omelettes sitting at the beach looking out over the Mediterranean. And then we were off to the ruins of a crusader fort originally called Apollonia, in honor of the god Apollo when the Greeks occupied it. It is in a beautiful location on the coast of the Mediterranean and features a manmade port and a view of Tel Aviv to the south and Caesarea to the north. First settled 2,500 years ago, it was conquered by King Baldwin of the Crusaders in 1101 but fell to the Marmeluke Turks in 1265, who then destroyed the fort.

Later that day Ev and I walked through the ancient and hilly Arab seaside town of Jaffa to unwind and prepare for our trip home. Leaving at midnight after another twenty-five security checks, we were headed home and we arrived there after fourteen hours in the air. Just to add a little spice, I had to worry about a beautiful antique Arab dagger that I bought in Jordan making it through US customs. About a hundred years old, it is a magnificent work of art with a delicately curved blade and handle. The handle features a beautiful horse's head at the end. The entire external surface of the knife is inlaid with silver and the blade is magnificent Damascus handmade steel. It must have taken hundreds of hours of an expert craftsman's time to make. But it is the handle itself which is made of camel bone that is the problem. Although legal and declared, if a customs agent thought that the handle was made of ivory (it looks like ivory but is not), they would have seized it. Thankfully all went well.

Safely home, and going through the 500 pictures we took, it occurred to me that pictures don't tell the whole story. So I decided to write down my impressions now before Alzheimer's takes the memories away!

My conclusions about my trip to Israel and Jordan are obvious. Nowhere on earth is there such an intense intersection between ancient history, religion, magnificent extremes of nature, and the everlasting realities of life. Israel reminds you that life is and will always be dangerous, but it is also beautiful and fun and you have to enjoy the good times with passion, while always being prepared for the tough times. The Israelis are living that life every day.

Chapter Twenty

Elk Hunting Heaven

Sometimes you need to experience Hell to appreciate Heaven. And I just got back from Elk Hunting Heaven at Chama Land and Cattle Company.

I have been hunting for fifty years from the Arctic Circle, to the desert, swamps, fields, and mountains. But my last elk hunt four years ago was so disappointing that I decided to retire from hunting all together. After getting food poisoning from the camp food (my assumption), I spent a full day seeing no elk while having severe diarrhea, which forced me to have my pants off in the rain, sleet, and snow. I suddenly had an epiphany. I was fifty-six years old, freezing my butt off (literally), and not having any fun. Instead, I could be sailing comfortably in the British Virgin Islands with my wife while having a rum and coke. And at the end of that elk hunt, that is exactly what I did!

But then my buddy, Steve Maahs, asked me to consider hunting with him at Chama. He was a retired hunter as well. His best hunting buddy was his dad, and when he passed, Steve lost interest in hunting for several years. But he got the urge again and told me about Chama. He said that I shouldn't retire from hunting on a low note after all these years, and elk hunting at Chama Land and Cattle Company was as good as it gets and we would see a ton of elk. In my younger days I would have said no. I knew Chama was first class, but hunting while staying at a first class lodge with plush surroundings just didn't sound "manly." But after decades of sleeping in tents and shacks and going for a week without a shower, the idea of plush surroundings appealed to me. After all, I still had not gotten my elk despite two elk hunts, and I felt that my work was not done. Plus Steve would be great company on a hunt. So I got approval from the "boss" (my wife) and the hunt was on!

Let me point out the three major differences between Chama Land and Cattle Company and my other two elk hunting experiences. As a start, there were the first class accommodations, which included gourmet meals, a great room, and a warm shower. Second, was the absolute professionalism of the entire staff, from guides to cleaning staff. And finally, the place was crawling with massive elk which were in the rut over thousands of acres of land in a beautiful mountain setting at ten thousand feet!

Driving from Albuquerque where we landed, we headed north and left the desert heading uphill to the southern end of the Rocky Mountains. We went from the dry drab desert to beautiful mountains capped with pines and aspens. Arriving at Chama Land and Cattle Company, I was struck by the large, handsome, and "masculine" hunting lodge. We were greeted by the guides and General Manager, Frank Simms, as we stepped out of our car. They immediately made us feel welcome. Frank must have been cast from a Hollywood western. Tall, thin, with a huge cowboy hat, denim jeans and denim shirt, Frank was the new civilized image of a "cowboy." That pleasant "howdy" masked a smart business manager and promoter of Chama through intense customer service.

Steve and I were introduced to our guides, quickly threw our stuff into our rooms, and immediately headed to the 100-yard rifle range with our guides, to make sure our rifles were still on target. The guides paid close attention to our marksmanship and made suggestions on where to place our sights at 100 yards to insure the best odds at 200 and 300 yards based on our ballistics. We then gathered for drinks and moved to the conference room to cover safety rules and how the hunt would be conducted. Very professional. Next was a great gourmet dinner (four choices) and then off to bed. Four-thirty in the morning comes early!

After a great breakfast, each of us left with our guides to our section of the mountains. Walking in the starlight on the mountain at 10,000 feet, you could smell the pines and then suddenly the elk bugling started. Unbelievable! We were surrounded by bulls, and the bugling was loud, haunting, echoing across the mountain, and came from every point of the compass. You could hear the elk moving in the trees, smacking their lips, and the cow elk were calling back to the bulls. And the unique and strong musky smell of elk was everywhere. I have never experienced anything like it before! As the sun rose, we could then look down the valley and watch the elk start to gradually move up the mountain.

They were everywhere. We glassed the elk and chose which ones we wanted to position ourselves to shoot. That first day we saw at least one hundred bulls and cows within our shooting range. Of those one hundred, at least twenty were bulls in the 5X5 or 6X6 category. (For anyone who doesn't understand elk hunter language, this means ten-point or twelve-point racks). I would have been thrilled with any of them but my guide told me to be patient and wait for a monster because they were out there.

Because we were in full cammo, we had bulls walk within thrity yards of us providing me with a clear and easy shot. Sometimes we were in heavy cover and while we could not see them, we could hear and smell bulls that were within twenty yards of us bugling, smacking their lips, and scraping their antlers. That was our first morning, and I could have taken many great bulls. But my guide said, "Patience, there is a monster out there for you."

Let me step back for a moment and share my frame of mind at that time. Although I have been hunting for close to fifty years all over North America, it had been four years since I had hunted. I was once a good shot with a lot of confidence, but the years and lack of practice had reduced my skill and confidence. I told my guide that I would trade bull size for a good, clean, high probability shot. My worst nightmare was wounding a bull with a bad shot and losing him. I would be very happy with a nice, symmetrical 6X6. I did not need a massive 350 point bull.

For the next two days we covered hundreds of acres of mountain side by truck after glassing the elk that we wanted. Then we walked miles to position ourselves for a shot (always uphill!) and spent time in blinds near water holes or obvious trails. We saw tons of elk, and many great bulls within shooting range. But always my guide said, "Patience." There were one or two giant bulls that my guide said were worth taking, but they were long shots beyond 300 yards and beyond my comfort level. After seeing so many good bulls within easy shooting range, I did not want to take a low probability shot.

During those two days, we saw elk fighting, swimming, and rolling in the mud just fifty to 150 yards away. We saw hundreds of elk cows and calves playing and prancing all around. We saw a 400-pound black bear, eagles, hawks, and coyotes. And all of this in beautiful pine forests at 10,000 feet.

Once while tracking a bull elk in heavy cover, we stumbled into a clearing within twenty yards of a huge 1,500 pound buffalo that spun to face us and defensively dropped its head and "hunkered down" as it prepared to charge us. We had surprised it, we were a potential threat, and it was getting ready to charge us to defend itself. No one can imagine how huge and intimidating a 1,500 pound buffalo is just twenty yards away as it prepares to charge! And that head and those horns are just massive.

I immediately jacked a shell into the chamber of my rifle and froze just as my wilderness survival training said to do. There was no doubt in my mind that one step forward toward the monster would trigger a charge as a defensive reaction. That training said to prepare to fire but freeze until the situation stabilizes and then very gently back away from the threat. My guide was urgently yelling at me to get ready to fire with a lot of "energy" which surprised me since he was a former federal SWOT officer, who was used to handling traumatic situations. I knew we were in serious danger, but my training said to be as calm and unthreatening as possible. I found out later why he was so excited!

I didn't want to shoot for two reasons. First, we were only twenty yards away, and even if I blew the bull's heart out, he could still kill me at that range before he died. I learned that after shooting a 220 pound white tailed buck through the heart and he still ran 100 yards before collapsing. And a shot to the brain, which would immediately drop him, would be difficult because bison's heads are so enormous and their brains are very small. Not good odds at twenty yards (one or two seconds away)! The second reason was, if I lived, shooting him would cost me $5,000! Evelyn would kill me for spending another $5,000 on top of the cost of the trip!

Well, everybody stayed calm and while the bison stayed poised for an attack, he let us gently back away, and at about fifty to seventy-five yards, he went back to grazing and we walked away. When I asked my guide why he was so "excited," he explained that buffalos are just nuts, dumb, and unpredictable. One had attacked his pick-up truck on one hunt, almost turned it over, and caused a significant amount of damage to his truck. Bottom line, he doesn't like them or trust them. Good to know!

Putting that unforgettable moment aside, every morning and late afternoon the mountain side was booming with bulls bugling all around us. There were elk everywhere. It was awesome!

And then it happened. It was the end of the third day, and we were at a blind where I had just let a nice 6X6 go, even though it was an easy shot, because my guide said, "Patience." Then over the radio, Frank, who was a mile away and glassing the mountain, said that he saw a great bull at a small lake about a mile away from us. It was dusk and we only had another hour of daylight, so we moved out in a hurry. While I walked three and half miles a day to get back in shape for the hunt, I was exhausted from all the walking (always uphill at 10,000 feet!). Not only did we have to hurry, we also had to use stealth as we approached the lake. I was huffing and puffing and then we saw the bull. He was massive and 175 yards away. I dropped down to take a sitting shot using my bipod for stability. And time freezes.

We had maybe twenty minutes of good daylight left and just as I got a good sight picture, the bull moved behind a bush. I had to move quickly to reposition. But it was a poor head on shot this time and I waited. Then he moved again and I had to reposition again. I was really winded now but I had a great broadside shot. The range was reasonable at 175 yards and I had a good target. I was breathing hard, which is not good for a stable shot, but the sun was going down and I probably wouldn't have another chance. So, I took the shot.

After the recoil I tried to find my target for a second shot but he was gone. The guide pointed the way he took off and he then asked me if I hit him. He did not hear an impact so we ran to the impact point to look for blood and track him through the brush. No blood. My guide then called Frank (now one half mile away) who was glassing the mountain side and asked if Frank saw the bull. Frank answered that he and Randy (another guide glassing the mountain) saw the bull and he was definitely hit hard. But my guide didn't believe it, because there is absolutely no blood. Frank directed us to where the bull was standing still and we headed that way. But because we found no blood, my guide decided to head up the mountain to cut off the bull from the heavy cover. If he got there, he would be lost.

It was now almost dark and we ran for almost a half an hour straight uphill to cut the bull off. We got within thirty yards of another huge buffalo, but we never gave it a thought and he ran from us! Adrenalin and our focus on the wounded bull sucked up all of our attention, and we didn't have time to worry about a 1,500 pound bison! I was dying (10,000 feet!), but there was no way that I was giving up. Not only for myself, but this was all on the radio and twenty guides were listening to the "play by play" action. Finally, it wass too dark to run anymore.

So, we went back to the truck and drove to the impact site. Using a flashlight we searched for blood but there was none. My guide was sure I missed. But Frank and Randy were sure that the bull is hard hit and went down. They both saw what looked like an exit wound and they saw the bull shaking from side to side. Frank then suggested that we go back to the lodge and start the search in the morning. He didn't want to spook the bull and if he was wounded, he wanted the bull to settle down and bleed out, if he wasn't already dead. My guide and I headed back to the lodge.

It was a long and quite drive. My guide was clearly disappointed, and he clearly thought that I missed the shot because there was no blood. When we got back to the lodge everybody knew that I had taken the shot and knew that we hadn't found the bull. Everybody also knew that my guide thought that I missed the shot. We met with Frank to discuss next steps and had a large audience. The rules of the camp were clear. If you wounded a bull and couldn't find him after two days, your hunt was over. That is fair but the stakes were high.

Then Frank showed why he was such a pro. He said the plan would be to start the search in the morning. First we would go back to the impact site and look for blood. Then we would retrace the bulls path looking for a blood trail right up to the spot where he and Randy last saw the bull as it looked like it was about to collapse. Frank said while it was disappointing that we didn't find blood, he was certain the bull was hit. It only ran 100 yards and then stopped cold even when we were within twenty-five yards of him. Both he and Randy saw what looked like a wound and they both saw the bull shaking from side to side. Frank calmed me down and said if we didn't find blood or a bull in the morning, my hunt would continue. That is as fair is it gets. I went back to dinner with Steve and the whole camp was watching. Then I went to bed for a very long night. I didn't sleep for one minute!

Well, after breakfast Frank, Randy (another guide), my guide, Frank's dog, and I went back to the impact site to retrace the action. No blood at the impact site. We traced the bulls track. No blood there either, and that's not good. Everybody back at the lodge was listening to the "play by play" over the radio. Great! Well, we decided to split up and look for the bull, but the outlook was not good. I broke from the group and headed for the spot where I remembered Frank telling us the bull stopped, hoping for the best. I walked all around the cover and suddenly I saw a monster bull lying on the ground. What a huge relief! Not taking any chances, I jacked a round into the chamber and touched the muzzle of the gun to his eye. He was dead. Halleluiah! I unloaded my gun and called the others. For the first time I was able to really look the bull over. He was awesome. He was a huge 700-plus pound 7X6 and very symmetrical. And there was not one drop of blood anywhere although I can plainly see the entrance wound.

Well, long story short, Frank was truly excited and shook my hand. He was more excited than I was, and he said in all his years he had never shot as big a bull. My guide was a little sheepish but he was happy too. We also found out why there was no blood. I didn't make a great shot because the bull had started to turn as I pulled the trigger, and there was no exit wound because the bullet went through a lung but angled back through the liver, not through the other lung and out. But it was good enough and it caused the bull to die within minutes of being shot! As my guide started to field dress the bull, gallons of blood spurted from his body. Now it all made sense why we couldn't find a blood trail, the blood was still in his body! Frank and the guides took a million pictures and everybody was happy.

The trip back to the lodge was very different from the night before. Relief and happiness ruled instead of frustration and embarrassment. When we got back to the lodge, every guide, guest, and staff member already knew the story and offered me congratulations. What a difference from the prior night! To top it off, I was told that Steve got a nice 6X6 bull as well. Everybody gathered at the parking lot to look at my bull and I now felt great. The guide that does the scoring for Chama estimated that my bull scored at 340. Big boy and good enough for me!

Looking at it all in hindsight now, I could not have written a better script for a great hunt. My first two elk hunts were very disappointing and I did not get an elk. My Chama Land and Cattle Company experience was great, but the long night of wondering if we would ever find my bull was pure torture. But the relief and excitement when we did find him the next morning was magnificent. I truly went from elk hunting Hell to elk hunting Heaven!

Chapter Twenty-One

Shark-diving Senior Citizen

Well, I am sixty and "retired," but it has been a good ride. But, I am not ready to hang up my spurs yet, so I am always looking for the next thrill since I have less to lose now that the clock is ticking down. Evelyn booked a nice cruise in the Bahamas to get some sun, and as I was checking out the tours, I noticed a two tank shark dive that looked pretty cool in which the divers are fully exposed (no cage) to about twenty to thirty sharks circling around the master diver and the "diving guests". I told Ev, "That looks interesting," and I put it in my "under consideration file."

Before our cruise, I was asked to make a presentation to a very nice "senior" group for a homeless shelter where I volunteer. These are very, very nice people and many folks would refer to them as "cute seniors." But, as I think back on my trips hunting in the Arctic and sailing and diving around the world, I decided that being a "cute senior" is not one of my goals in life. As my ancestor Robert Morris—the one who signed the Declaration of Independence—said, "I would rather die like a lion than live like a lamb,"—or cute senior!. When I got home, I asked Ev to book the shark dive and she did as she reached for my life insurance policy to check out the terms.

Well, we headed to Miami and our ship to enjoy a few very nice and peaceful days sunning on the deck, reading, and drinking fancy "umbrella" drinks. Because Ev had hurt her back a bit and was still recovering, this was the first relaxing vacation we had taken in forty years where we weren't rushing about on tours twelve hours a day and collapsing after dinner.

And then the day of the shark dive arrived. Ev's plan was to get a massage and study my life insurance policy one more time. I departed the ship and met up with my three soon-to-be diving buddies. One was a young thrity-five-year-old guy who had had no intention of doing a shark dive, but his normal dive was cancelled. He was definitely nervous. The other buddies were a husband and wife team who were about forty years old. They were pumped and fun to be with.

After an hour on a small bus driving through the poor parts of Nassau (really tough and poor), we finally arrived at Stewart's Cove, the dive company. They were nice people and our dive master was a very gregarious English fellow who made us feel at home. He took some time to run us through what we were about to experience. First, we would all go on a one tank dive to explore the reef and a wrecked oil tanker at about sixty to eighty feet down. What he didn't tell us was that this was his chance to watch us and make sure we knew what we were doing before the sharks were unleashed on the second dive.

Then he told us about the shark dive. First, he said that we would all go to the bottom and sit on the deck of the oil tanker. He would then join us bringing the bait and about twenty to thirty sharks would be following him.

"Not to worry," he said, "these are grey reef sharks about five to seven feet long and up to about four hundred pounds. They are not normally aggressive and only rarely attack the guests. As long as we are cool and don't freak out, the sharks will almost always be cool and everybody will get along."

Great! Oh, by the way, "Occasionally we will see mako sharks," he said. Mako sharks are known as the most aggressive sharks in the ocean. But he told us that they generally stay away. And oh yeah, then he said, "For the last three weeks we have seen a fourteen-foot hammerhead, but she usually stays above the crowd and hasn't caused any problems to date."

Excellent!

Just a side note. About ten years ago I had a meeting with my President's Council in Nassau, and one of my distributors and I went on a night dive while we were there. I am pretty sure it was with Stewart's Cove. I remember it well for two reasons. First, on the day of our dive, a scuba diver was killed by a mako shark there. Second, in a separate incident, a diver was attacked on a shark dive by one of the feeding sharks that mistook his hand for bait. So, when our dive master was talking about mako sharks and how important it is to stay cool, he had my full attention!

Well, we checked our gear, met the female photographer and diving instructor who would record our trip to the dark side, and our English master diver went to start the boat. Once. Twice. And then three times. But, it didn't start, so he yelled for the mechanic. My confidence was heading down hill fast. The good news is all was well, and with just a minor adjustment we headed out to sea.

We only went out maybe five miles and we dropped anchor over the wreck. We chose our diving buddies, checked and strapped on our gear, and jumped in.

I have been diving now for about forty years so, I have been around. In fact, lately one of the things I get a chuckle out of is when master divers see me now with my grey beard for the first time, you can see them really worrying that I will have a heart attack on their watch. I get special treatment! Anyway, I have seen sharks before and I have even been in a cave with three six-foot black tipped reef sharks which are occasional man eaters. But I wasn't prepared for the first thing I saw when I hit the water. There were five to seven foot sharks all over the place and within twenty to thirty yards of me.

The deal was that Stewart's Cove comes here to feed them every day at the same time. So, the sharks have got the program down. My attention is pretty focused for a few minutes, but everybody is cool, and then our master diver leads us down to the reef and the wreck. The first thing we see on the bottom was a five-foot sting ray lying low and doing his thing. So we headed on over and checked him out. Cool!

Then we explored the reef. We found trumpet fish, yellow snappers, and big old groupers. Looking around we saw lion fish, which I have only seen in the Red Sea in Israel before. Very cool, but don't touch them because they are very poisonous! Next, the group headed down the reef to about eighty feet to check out the view. But my diving buddy—the nervous one—kept heading down and I suddenly realized that he was below one hundred feet, which is a no-no. So, I headed down to get him and bring him back to the group. I got a thumb's up from the master diver. Well, the master diver checked our air and everybody but the wife and I had reached the safe limit of their air supply and headed back up to the boat. The dive master realized that my diving experience and the wife's small size had left us with quite a bit of air, so we explored the wreck until it was time to do our safety stop and head up back to the boat. Stepping up the ladder back in the boat with three foot waves and a hundred pounds of gear on is a lot of fun!

Back on the boat we got briefed again. Only this time it was serious. Our diving master and the photographer put on chain mail to cover their entire bodies and hands to protect them from shark bites. You see, they will actually be feeding the sharks and pushing them away when required. We didn't get any chain mail! This was where the dive master offered to sell us his chain mail suit for $1,000. Very funny! The dive master reminded us how important it was to be cool, keep our hands close because the sharks may think they are bait (remember my night dive?), and he went over emergency signals and actions. It was time to "die like a lion" and we dove in.

There were sharks everywhere! We headed down to the wreck and gathered around where the dive master would feed them. And then the dive master headed down with the bait, followed by twenty to thirty sharks. Holy Mackerel! He then knelt down in the middle of us and we were only separated by five to ten feet as he got ready to feed the sharks. He used an old Renaissance sword "knock off" to put the bait on and suddenly the sharks were going nuts going for the bait and shoving each other around. It was chaos! Sharks were flying by and about every thirty seconds you had to duck or you would get hit by the shark's fins as they screamed on by. But there were no attacks on us because the sharks were focused on the bait and pushing each other around. We were extremely focused for five to ten minutes to make sure that everybody was cool. And they were!

That dive is proof that you can get used to anything! For five to ten minutes, we were riveted with adrenalin pumping through our veins. But after ten minutes with no attacks, one starts to calm down, relax, and take in the view. It was very cool. The sharks are awesome and the perfect killing machine. Sleek, powerful, and ravenous with mouths full of incredibly sharp teeth. What is really funny is that while the sharks are going nuts, groupers and yellow tailed snappers are just lazily floating around as if the sharks are their buddies. The sharks never even look at them.

The photographer was focused on us as she took both still pictures and a video. Sharks were bumping into her left and right, but she was cool as a cucumber and didn't even seem to notice. After a while, sharks flying by and ducking to avoid getting hit by fins was no big deal. The focus was now on looking cool while your picture was being taken. It was now just fun and exciting and the adrenalin was out of our systems.

Soon the hour was up and we headed back to the boat. You could tell that our master diver was relieved that all went well and everybody made it back. The relief from everybody in the was obvious. The sun was shining, we were all still in one piece, and life was good!

How do you explain that experience to anybody?

Chapter Twenty-Two

Famous Quotes: Words of Wisdom Ignored at Man's Peril

This chapter contains brilliant quotes from the past that I discovered as I read great books on history and life. A few of these quotes were mentioned in my previous chapter "Cosmic Rules Learned the Hard Way." But this chapter is a "treasure trove" of wisdom including quotes from the Founding Fathers to Ronald Reagan, the Bible to John Wayne, and Winston Churchill to Johnny Cash! Anything that you need to know in life can be found here. Make sure that you check out George Washington, John Adams, Benjamin Franklin, Thomas Jefferson, James Madison, Winston Churchill, and Ronald Reagan. Mark Twain is pretty darn good too! And finally while short and sweet, Plato captures the critical aspects of life in just a few words.

Basically laid out by subject in historical sequence, you will find the wisdom of the ages and anything you need to know in life organized under the following topics:

- Freedom and Democracy
- 2nd amendment and why it is critical
- The disaster that is debt
- Leadership
- Importance of history
- Capitalism vs. socialism
- Traditional values
- Just for fun!
- Conservative vs. liberals
- Morality
- Government
- God
- Philosophy
- War and competition

Freedom and Democracy

Pericles (430 BC):

"Just because you do not take an interest in politics does not mean that politics won't take an interest in you."
"Any citizen that doesn't pay attention to politics has no right to live in Athens."

Plato (400 BC):

"The price of apathy in public affairs is to be ruled by evil men."

"Democracy passes into despotism."

Edmond Burke:

"All that is required for evil to triumph is for good men to do nothing."

Voltaire:

"The art of government consists of taking as much money as possible from one party of citizens to give to the other."

"Those that can make you believe absurdities can make you commit atrocities."

"It is lamentable that to be a good patriot one must become the enemy to the rest of mankind."

"It is dangerous to be right in matters which the establishment are wrong."

"To learn who rules over you, simply find out who you are not allowed to criticize."

George Washington:

"I did not defeat George III to become George I."

"It is the citizens choice, and depends upon their conduct, whether they will be respectable and prosperous, or contemptible and miserable as a Nation. This is the time of their political probation; this is the moment when the eyes of the World are turned upon them."

John Adams:

"Those who trade liberty for security have neither."

"Remember that democracy never lasts long. It soon wastes, exhausts, and murders itself. There was never a democracy yet they did not commit suicide."

"Men must be ready, they must pride themselves and be happy to sacrifice their private pleasures, passions and interests, nay, their private friendships and dearest connections, when they stand in competition with the rights of society."

Benjamin Franklin:

"The man who trades freedom for security neither deserves nor will ever receive either."

"The Constitution only gives people the right to pursue happiness. You have to catch it yourself."

"Democracy is two wolves and a lamb voting on what to have for lunch. Liberty is a well-armed lamb contesting the vote."

"Only a virtuous people are capable of freedom. As nations become corrupt and vicious, they have more need of masters."

Thomas Jefferson:

"Democracy will cease to exist when you take away from those who are willing to work and give to those that are not."

"My reading of history convinces me that most bad government results from too much government."

"A government that is big enough to give you everything you want is strong enough to take away everything that you have."

"The tree of liberty must be refreshed from time to time with the blood of patriots and tyrants."

"A government that fears the people is a democracy. A government feared by the people is a tyranny."

"All tyranny needs to gain a foothold is for people to remain silent."

"Timid men prefer the calm of despotism to the tempestuous sea of liberty."

"When injustice becomes law, then resistance becomes duty."

"I think we have more machinery of government than is necessary too many parasites living on the labor of the industrious."

"If a nation expects to be ignorant and free then they expect what never was and what never will be."

James Madison:

"Be warned of laws so voluminous that they can not be read, or so incoherent that they can not be understood."

"If men were angels, not government would be necessary. If angels were to govern men, neither external nor internal controls would be necessary."

"An elective despotism was not the government we fought for; but one in which the powers of government should be so divided and balanced among the several bodies of magistracy as that no one could transcend their legal limits without being effectually checked and restrained by the others."

"They can make no law which will not have its full operation on themselves and their friends, as well as on the great mass of society." (referring to Congress in Federalist No. 57)

Patrick Henry:

"Give me liberty or give me death."

Joseph Warren:

"Our country is in danger, but not to be despaired of. Our enemies are numerous and powerful; but we have many friends, determining to be free, and heaven and

Earth will aid the resolution. On you depend the fortunes of America. You are to decide the important question, on which rest the happiness and liberty of millions yet unborn. Act worthy of yourselves." Boston Massacre Oration.

Alex de Tocqueville:

"Democracy can endure up to the point when politicians realize that they can bribe people with their own money."

"The American Republic will endure until the day Congress discovers that can bribe the public with the public's own money."

"A democracy cannot exist as a permanent form of government. It can only exist until the voters discover that they can vote themselves largess from the public treasury with the result that a democracy always collapses over loose policy, always followed by a dictatorship. The average age of the world's greatest civilizations has been 200 years."

Abraham Lincoln:

"A house divided cannot stand."

"America will never be destroyed from the outside. If we falter and lose our freedom, it will be because we destroyed ourselves."

"You can fool all the people some of the time, some of the people all of the time, but you cannot fool all of the people all of the time."

Mark Twain:

"Patriotism is supporting your country all of the time and your government when it deserves it."

Wendell Phillips:

"Eternal vigilance is the price of liberty."

Lord Acton:

"Power tends to corrupt and absolute power corrupts absolutely."

Winston Churchill:

"It has been said that democracy is the worst form of government except for all those other forms that have been tried from time to time."

"The best argument against democracy is a five minute conversation with the average voter."

"An appeaser is one who feeds a crocodile hoping it will eat him last."

"We sleep soundly in our beds, because rough men stand ready to visit violence upon those who would do us harm."

"When the eagles are silent, the parrots begin to chatter."

FDR (1935 State of the Union speech):

"The lessons of history, confirmed by evidence immediately before me show conclusively that continued dependence on relief induces a spiritual and moral disintegration fundamentally destructive to the national fiber. To dole out relief in this way is to administer a narcotic, a subtle destroyer of the human spirit....It is a violation of the tradition of America. Work must be found for the able bodied."

Henry Morgenthau, FDR's Secretary of the Treasury (House Ways and Means 5/1939):

"We are spending more money than we have ever spent before and it does not work. I want to see the country prosperous. I want to see people get a job. We have never made good on our promises. I say after eight years of this administration we have just as much unemployment as when we started and a momentous debt as well."

Edmond R. Murrow:

"A nation of sheep will beget a government of wolves."

Dean Acheson:

"No people in history have ever survived who thought that they could protect their freedom by making themselves inoffensive to their enemies."

Dwight Eisenhower:

"A people that values its privileges above its principals soon loses both."

"History does not long entrust the care of freedom to the weak or timid."

John F. Kennedy:

"Let every nation know, whether it wishes us well or ill, that we shall pay any price, bear any burden, meet any hardship, support any friend, oppose any foe, in order to assure the survival and success of liberty."

"Finally, to those nations who would make themselves our adversary.... We dare not tempt them with weakness. For only when our arms are sufficient beyond doubt can we be certain that they will never be deployed."

"And so my fellow Americans, ask not what America will do for you, ask what you can do for your country."

"It is an unfortunate fact that we can secure peace only by preparing for war."

Ronald Reagan:

"The world is a dangerous place."

"Trust but verify."

"Peace through strength."

"Government's first duty is to protect the people, not run their lives."

"Government is not the solution to our problems, Government is the problem."

"Freedom is never more than one generation from extinction."

"The most terrifying words in the English language are : I am from the government and I am here to help."

"If we ever forget that we're one nation under God, then we will be a nation gone under."

Daniel Patrick Moynihan:

"It is culture, not politics that determines the success of society."

2nd Ammendment and why it is critical

Oliver Cromwell:

"Keep your faith in God but keep your powder dry."

George Washington:

"A free people ought not only to be armed and disciplined, but they should have sufficient arms and ammunition to maintain a status of independence from any who might attempt to abuse them, which would include their own government."

"A free people should be an armed people."

Thomas Jefferson:

"No free man shall ever be debarred the use of arms."

"The strongest reason for the people to retain the right to keep and bear arms is, as a last resort, to protect themselves against tyranny in government."

"Those that hammer their guns into plows will plow for those that do not."

"The beauty of the second Amendment is that it will not be needed until they try to take it."

James Madison:

"Besides the advantage of being armed, which the Americans possess over the people of almost every other nation, the existence of subordinate governments, to which the people are attached and by which the militia officers are appointed, forms a barrier against the enterprises of ambition, more insurmountable than any which a simple government of any form can admit of."Federalist No, 46, 1788.

"I ask you sir, what is the militia? It is the whole people. To disarm the people is the best and most effective way to enslave them." 1788.

Noah Webster (1787):

"Before a standing army can rule, the people must be disarmed; as they are in almost every kingdom in Europe. The supreme power in America cannot enforce unjust laws by the sword,; because the whole body of the people are armed, and constitute a force superior to any band of regular troops that can be, on any pretense, raised in the United States."

Isoruko Yamamoto (in response to Tojo's question):

"You cannot invade mainland America. There would be a rifle behind every blade of grass."

Debt disaster

Proverbs 22:7:

"The borrower is slave to the lender."

Cicero (55 BC):

"The budget should be balanced, the Treasury should be filled, public debt should be reduced, the arrogance of officialdom should be tempered and controlled, and assistance to foreign lands should be curtailed lest Rome become bankrupt. People must again learn to work instead of living on public assistance."

John Adams:

"There are two ways to conquer and enslave a nation. One is by the sword and the other is by debt."

Benjamin Franklin:

"Beware of little expenses. A small leak can sink a great ship."

Thomas Jefferson:

"It is incumbent on every generation to pay its own debts as it goes. A principle which if acted on would save one-half the wars of the world."

"I predict future happiness for Americans if they can prevent the government from wasting the labors of the people under the pretense of taking care of them."

"The fore horse of this frightful team is public debt. Taxation follow that, and in turn wretchedness and oppression."

"The multiplication of public office, increase of expense beyond income, growth and entailment of a public debt are indications soliciting the employment of the pruning knife."

Samuel Adams:

"If you love wealth better than liberty, the tranquility of servitude better than the animating contest of freedom go home from us in peace. We ask not your counsels or your arms. Crouch down and lick the hands which feed you. May your chains set lightly upon you, and may posterity forget that you were our countrymen."

Winston Churchill:

"I contend for a nation to try and tax itself into prosperity is like a man standing in a bucket and trying to lift himself up by the handle."

Albert Einstein:

"Compound interest is the most powerful force in the universe."

Leadership

Xenophon (400 BC):

"For what the leaders are, so shall the men below them be."

Sun Tzu (500 BC):

"Strategy without tactics is the slowest route to victory. Tactics without strategy is the noise before defeat."

Hannibal (200 BC):

"We will either find a way or make one."

Benjamin Franklin:

"By failing to prepare you are preparing to fail."

"Tell me and I forget. Teach me and I remember. Involve me and I learn."

"Those that won't be counseled can't be helped."

"If you think education is expensive, try ignorance."

"It takes many deeds to build a good reputation and only one bad one to lose it."

Will Rogers:

"When you're ridin' ahead of the herd, take a look back every now and then and make sure that they are still there."

Importance of History

Ecclesiastics 1:9:

"What has been done before will be done again; there is nothing new under the sun"

Confucius (550 BC):

"Study the past if you would divine the future."

Cicero (55 BC):

"To be ignorant of what happened before your birth is to remain always a child."

Edmond Burke:

"Those that don't learn from history are doomed to repeat it."

Shakespeare:

"Past is prologue."

Winston Churchill:

"The farther backward you look the farther forward you can see."

Capitalism vs. Socialism

Winston Churchill:

"The inherent vice of capitalism is the unequal sharing of the blessings. The inherent blessing of socialism is the equal sharing of misery."

Socialism is the philosophy of failure, the creed of ignorance, and the gospel of envy. Its inherent virtue is the equal sharing of misery."

Margret Thatcher:

"Socialism always fails because eventually you run out of other people's money."

Frank Borman (NASA astronaut):

"Capitalism without bankruptcy is like Christianity without hell."

Rush Limbaugh:

"The safety net for the needy has become the hammock for the lazy."

Traditional values

Thessalonians 3:10:

"If a man is not willing to work, let him not eat."

Confucius (550 BC):

"Our greatest glory is not in never failing but in rising every time we fail."

Benjamin Franklin:

"God helps those that help themselves."

"He who lives upon hope will die fasting."

"He who rises late must trot all day."

"If passion drives you let reason holds the reins."

"Work as if you were to live to a hundred years. Pray as if you were to die tomorrow."

"When you make poverty too easy you will have more of it."

"He that is good at making excuses is seldom good at anything else."

"Do not bite at the bait of pleasure till you know there is no hook beneath it."

"Never put off until tomorrow what you can do today."

Thomas Jefferson:

"When we get piled upon in large cities as in Europe, we shall become as corrupt as Europe."

Robert Morris:

"I would rather die like a lion than live like a lamb."

Napoleon Bonaparte:

"Death is nothing, but to live defeated is to die every day."

Andrew Jackson:

"One man with courage makes a majority."

Frederich Nietzsche:

"That which does not kill us makes us stronger."

Anonymous:

"Any fool can learn from his own mistakes. A wise man learns from the mistakes of others."

Abraham Lincoln:

"Better to remain silent and be thought a fool than to speak out and remove all doubt."

Admiral Farragut:

"Damn the torpedoes, full speed ahead."

Teddy Roosevelt:

"Walk softly and carry a big stick."

"Do what you can with what you have where you are."

"Far better it is to dare mighty things, to win glorious triumph, even though checkered by failure, than to take rank with those poor spirits who neither enjoy much or suffer much, because they live in the gray twilight that knows neither victory nor defeat."

Winston Churchill:

"Never give in, never, never, never—in nothing great or small, large or petty, never give in except to conviction

of honor and good sense."

"You have enemies? Good, that means that you have stood up for something in your life."

"We British have not journeyed across the centuries, across the oceans, across the mountains, and across the prairies because we are made of sugar candy."

F. Scott Fitzgerald:

"Living well is the best revenge."

Albert Einstein:

"The definition of insanity is doing the same thing over and over and expecting different results."

"It has become appallingly obvious that our technology has exceeded our humanity."

"I fear the day that technology will surpass our human interaction. The world will have a generation of idiots."

Admiral Hyman Rickover:

"Great men talk about ideas, mediocre men talk about things, and small men talk about people."

John F. Kennedy:

"Anybody who expects fairness in life is seriously misinformed."

Margret Thatcher:

"My policies are based not on some economic theory, but on things I and millions like me were brought up with: an honest day's work for an honest day's pay; live within your means; put by a nest egg for a rainy day; pay your bills on time; and support the police."

For fun!

Plato (400 BC):

"Love is a serious mental disease."

Marcus Aurelius:

"The art of living is more like wrestling than dancing."

Voltaire:

"Anything too stupid to be spoken is sung."

John Adams:

"In my many years I have come to the conclusion that one useless man is a shame, two is a law firm, and three or more is a Congress."

Benjamin Franklin:

"Guests, like fish, begin to smell in three days."

"Wine is constant proof that God loves us and loves to see us happy."

Thomas Paine:

"To argue with a person who has renounced the use of reason is like administrating medicine to the dead."

Winston Churchill:

"Americans always do the right thing after they have exhausted all the alternatives."

"A lie gets halfway around the world before the truth even gets its pants on."

"If you're going through hell, keep going."

"My most brilliant achievement was to be able to persuade my wife to marry me."

Oscar Wilde:

"Some people create happiness wherever they go. Some people create happiness whenever they go."

Mark Twain:

"If you don't read the paper you are uninformed. If you do read the paper you are misinformed."

"Suppose you are an idiot. And suppose you are a member of Congress. But then I repeat myself."

"The only difference between a tax man and a taxidermist is that the taxidermist leaves the skin."

"Always do right. It will please some of the people and astonish the rest."

"There is no distinctly native American criminal class-save Congress."

"When I was a boy of fourteen my father was so ignorant I could hardly stand to have the old man around. But when I got to be twenty-one, I was astonished at how much he had learned in seven years."

"Man is the only animal that blushes. Or needs to."

"If you pick up a starving dog and make him prosperous, he will not bite you. This is the principle difference between a man and a dog."

"In the first place God made idiots. That was for practice. Then He made school boards."

"Golf is a good walk spoiled."

"The only way to keep your health is to eat what you do not want, drink what you don't like, and do what you'd druther not."

George Bernard Shaw:

"A government that robs Peter to pay Paul can always count on the support of Paul."

Will Rogers:

"I don't make jokes. I just watch the government and report the facts."

Jack Benny: *"My wife and I have been married for 47 years and never had a fight so serious that we considered divorce. Murder yes, but not divorce."*

John Wayne:

"Life is tough Pilgrim. It's even tougher when you' re stupid."

"A man' s got to do what a man's got to do."

Johnny Cash:

"The world is rough and if a man's gonna make it he's gotta be tough."

Ringo Starr:

"Everything the government touches turns to crap."

Bill Cosby:

"A word to the wise ain't necessary—it's the stupid ones that need advice."

Conservatives vs. liberals

Ecclesiastics 10:2:

"The heart of the wise inclines to the right, the heart of the fool to the left."

Ronald Reagan:

"The trouble with our liberal friends is not that they are ignorant; it's just that they know so much that is not true."

Morality

Solon (670 BC):

"If you do the right thing you will be slandered."

"Count no man happy until he be dead."

Confucius (550 BC):

"To see right and not do it is cowardice."

Plato (400 BC):

"The measure of a man is what he does with power."

Dante:

"The darkest places in hell are reserved for those who maintain their neutrality in times of moral crisis."

Rob Roy:

"Honor is what no man can give you and no man can take away. Honor is a gift you give yourself."

Thomas Jefferson:

"One man with courage is a majority."

Sigmund Freud:

"The precondition of civilization is the ability to defer the gratification of instinct."

Mark Twain:

"When in doubt, tell the truth."

Ghandi:

"Seven dangers to human virtue:

Wealth without work

Pleasure without conscience

Knowledge without character

Business without ethics

Science without humanity

Religion without Sacrifice"

Politics without Principle"

Dr. Martin Luther King (St. Louis Congregation speech): *"Do you know that Negroes are 10% of the population of St. Louis and are responsible for 58% of the crimes? We have to face that. And we have to do something about our moral standards. We can't keep blaming the white man. There are things we must do ourselves."*

Government

Aesop (600 BC):

"We hang petty thieves and appoint great ones to public office."

Ronald Reagan:

"The government is like a baby's alimentary canal, with a happy appetite at one end and no responsibility at the other."

"I have wondered at times what the Ten Commandments would have looked like had Moses run them through the US Congress."

"The nearest thing to eternal life we will ever see on Earth is a government program."

"It has been said that politics is the second oldest profession. I have learned that it bears a striking resemblance to the first."

God

Socrates (420 BC):

"I am a mere mortal and cannot possibly know what God wants. All I can do is live a good life, treat my fellow man as I would like to be treated, and trust that God will be pleased."

Marcus Aurelius:

"Live a good life. If there are gods and they are just, then they will not care how devout you have been, but will welcome you based on the virtues that you have lived by. If there are gods, but unjust, then you should not want to worship them. If there are no gods, then you will be gone, but will have lived a noble life that will live on in the memories of your loved ones."

Voltaire:

"If God did not exist it would be necessary to invent Him."

Philosophy 13

Socrates (420 BC):

"Wonder is the beginning of wisdom."

"Death may be the greatest of all human blessings."

Sun Tzu (500 BC):

"Opportunities multiply as they are seized."

Seneca:

"Without hardship man can neither be happy nor virtuous."

Voltaire:

"Nothing can be more contrary to religion and the clergy than reason and common sense."

"Nature has always had more force than education."

George Washington:

"Labor to keep alive that little spark of celestial called conscience."

John Adams:

"Facts are stubborn things and whatever may be our wishes, our inclinations, or the dictates of our passion; they can not alter the state of facts and evidence."

Benjamin Franklin:

"If you would not be forgotten as soon as you are dead, either write something worth reading or do something worth writing."

"Life's tragedy is that we get old too soon and wise too late."

"Wise men don't need advice. Fools won't take it."

Albert Einstein:

"All religions, art, and sciences are fruits of the same tree."

War and Competition

Plato (400 BC):

"Only the dead have seen the end of war."

Sun Tzu (500 BC):

"He who knows the enemy and himself will never in a hundred battles be at risk."

"Know thyself, know thy enemy. A thousand battles, a thousand victories."

"Pretend inferiority and encourage his arrogance."

"Strategy without tactics is the slowest route to victory. Tactics without strategy is the noise before defeat"

George Washington:

"To be prepared for war is one of the most effective means of preserving peace."

Thomas Jefferson:

"The power of making war often prevents it and in our case would give efficacy to our desire for peace."

Napoleon Bonaparte:

"Never interrupt your enemy when he is making a mistake."

Ronald Reagan:

"Man has never had a weapon that he has not used"
"Here is my strategy on the Cold War: we win, they lose"
"Of the four wars in my lifetime, none came because the US was too strong."

Chapter Twenty-Three

Thirteen-Year-Old Bounty Hunter

One might wonder why I would write about something that happened when I was a kid, now that I am doing my "Postscript" which discusses my extreme experiences after retirement and after I wrote my original book. Here are two reasons why I am sharing this now. First, the last five years have seen a relentless attack on the Second Amendment based on emotional hysteria and misinformation. Second, it occurred to me that the experience that I will share now had a major positive impact on me for the rest of my life, which very few kids today will experience and which is at risk of being lost forever, if those attacking the Second Amendment are successful.

Those people who attack the Second Amendment try to magnify and leverage the tragedy of gun violence by making it seem like a huge number of innocent Americans are killed by legal gun owners. While every death by gun violence is tragic, one needs to keep reality in perspective and weigh the value of freedom against taking away that freedom to avoid those tragedies. My favorite quote is from Illinois Governor Pat Quinn, who wants to take guns away from lawful gun owners, "because if we can save just one life, we save the world." Let's check out the logic of that comment!

According to the 2012 FBI Murder Report (most recent available), 323 Americans were killed by rifles of all kinds including "assault rifles" in 2012, which is a number most Americans would be shocked to know was so low compared to the hysteria and attention in the media. Dividing that 323 by 320 million Americans, the odds of getting killed by a rifle are 0.0000001, just about the same odds of getting hit by lightning. Fifty-three percent more Americans are killed by hammers (496) than by rifles. Using Quinn's logic, shouldn't we outlaw hammers? Five hundred and twenty-four percent more Americans were killed by knives (1694) than by rifles. Using Quinn's logic, shouldn't we outlaw kitchen knives? In 2011, 9,878 Americans were killed by drunk drivers, thirty times more than were killed by rifles in 2012. Using Quinn's logic, shouldn't we outlaw both alcohol and cars "if it saves just one life?"

Here is the hypocrisy of Quinn and those people who want to take away our Second Amendment rights. Of course, Quinn and his ilk don't want to make hammers, knives, alcohol, and cars illegal, even if they kill far more Americans than rifles. But those people don't use rifles and don't value the right to own one. That is their choice, but they have no right to force their will on those of us who do value guns and our freedom.

As I was doing this Postscript, I realized that I didn't spend much time in my first book talking about one of the key life changing events that happened when I was about thirteen years old. Then I recently found an old description of that event, which I had written a while ago, and it reminded me of that long ago exciting experience. Back then, in 1964, it didn't seem that dramatic, it was just part of growing up on a farm. Thinking about it today in our "politically correct" environment, I realize that very few boys could even imagine the experience I'm about to describe, and they are poorer for it. Filling in that gap is what motivated me to share it now, in addition to the attacks on the second Amendment I just mentioned.

Thirteen-Year-Old Bounty Hunter

This is a story that used to be very common in America, yet today is almost non-existent. It is an example of how in just one or two generations, traditional American values and experiences have essentially dried up and blown away in the wind. That can't be good for America.

It is the story of a thirteen year old kid—I could have been as young as ten, but I will be conservative since I don't trust my memory about my age at the time—from the "burbs" who was lucky enough to have a family who lived on the farm where life was still similar to the hard working rural past of America. On the farm, the realities of life were present every day and even the children understood what life was all about. Hard work, danger, and responsibility existed for everyone including the kids. One learned more about life in one year living on a farm than many people learn in a lifetime in the city.

At an early age, usually starting at ten or younger, farm kids were assigned chores to do. By the time they were thirteen or so, they helped drive tractors and trucks (as I did) to help keep the farm productive, and they saw the realities of life all around them as livestock procreated, were raised, and then harvested before their eyes. You quickly learned the realities of life as cattle, hogs, and horses might harm you if you didn't pay attention, or you could easily get killed on dangerous farm equipment if you didn't pay attention. So rural kids learned reality at an early age.

This story started at summer camp when I was about seven years old, where I learned how to use a rifle safely and effectively. Part of growing up on the farm was learning early about responsibility in life, and handling a rifle safely is all about responsibility. When I was about thirteen years old, I received my first .22 rifle as a birthday present, and I was looking forward to taking it to the farm to test my skill. Of course today, the vast majority of American kids are not only forbidden to touch a rifle, they can get suspended from school for simply drawing a picture with a crayon of a cowboy with a gun. Sheer insanity! By the way, that .22 rifle was a semi-automatic rifle with a 15 round tubular magazine which was quite common back in 1964 for farm kids. Today, that gun would be called an "assault rifle," and anyone owning one is called a Neanderthal by the politically correct crowd!

Well, we went to the family farm and on a bright and beautiful day I decided to walk from my Grandfather's farmhouse toward the river bottom land and explore it with my new rifle. The river bottom followed a small river through the farmland and was heavily wooded and loaded with poisonous water moccasins and copperheads, so it had a touch of danger which added to the excitement. Can you imagine a thirteen-year-old kid being allowed to walk alone in that setting today with a rifle? Back then and there, it was a normal "rite of passage" toward manhood.

Leaving the road, I walked down into the dense cover of the river bottom. The canopy of trees and leaves were so thick that they hid the bright sun and created a shadowy world of danger, especially for a lone, suburban thirteen-year-old kid. Nervous about the presence of the poisonous snakes that I knew were around, I intently watched where I put my feet with every step. After a while I was deep in the bottomland and not even sure where I was, although I knew that I could follow the river to get back home. But it was still scary, exciting, and riveting.

Suddenly, I heard loud crashing noises in the woods about a hundred yards away. The brush was so thick that I could not see what was making the racket, so despite my nervousness, I headed that way to check it out and satisfy my curiosity.

Peeling my way through the brush while keeping my eye out for snakes, I suddenly saw a huge red wolf aggressively jumping up and down while snapping and swinging at something I couldn't see. There was no doubt in my mind that this wolf would attack me, kill me, and eat me if he saw me, so I raised my rifle, jacked in a shell, flipped off the safety, and prepared to fire every round in my magazine to protect myself. Just then the wolf looked at me and I instantly aimed between his eyes and fired. After the first shot, I kept pulling the trigger but nothing happened so I lowered my rifle to figure out why, and I looked up to see if the wolf was about to attack me. Imagine my surprise when I saw the wolf lying on the ground clearly hit hard. Checking out my rifle, I saw that it was on "single shot" mode so I flipped it back to semi-auto, jacked in a fresh shell, and began to carefully walk toward the downed wolf (while looking out for snakes!) assuming that he was just wounded or "playing possum" to lure me in.

I was shocked when I got to that massive "red wolf" and discovered it was really a beautiful red fox with a bullet hole right between his eyes! My fear had turned that red fox into the "massive red wolf" that I shot. And the reason it was jumping up and down was to playfully swat at a butterfly which was still buzzing around. I suddenly felt sad on the one hand in having killed such a beautiful fox out of fear, but on the other hand I was proud that I had made a perfect shot when I thought my life was at stake. Not bad for a thirteen-year-old kid! No doubt that exciting experience was what led to my fifty years of hunting all across North America from the Arctic Circle to the desert, from the Rocky Mountains to the prairies, and from the woods of Wisconsin to the swamps of Savannah. I never liked killing animals, but I loved the hunt, the wilderness, the excitement, and the challenge of making that critical shot when it was "for all the marbles."

After letting the experience sink in, I decided to head back and tell Grandpa what happened. Carefully watching for snakes, I followed the river back to the road and walked back to our farmhouse. I could tell Grandpa didn't quite believe my story the way I told it. That shouldn't have been a surprise since I was just a kid from the burbs. But I was pleased when he asked me to take him back in the bottomland and show him my red fox. I was really worried that I wouldn't be able to find it, so imagine my pleasure when I did. But what was really cool was my Grandfather's reaction to the size of the fox. "He's a "biggun," he said! And then he saw the bullet hole right between his eyes just as I had said. Priceless!

Grandpa then explained that farmers hated foxes because they killed and ate farmer's chickens and other small livestock, taking meals off their table and income that was needed to support the farm. In fact, the county (or state I don't remember which) paid a five-dollar bounty if one turned in both ears of each fox they shot or trapped. Grandpa wanted to take me into town (population 600) right away and collect the bounty, so we cut off my fox's ears and headed back to the farm to get the pickup truck and go into town. You could tell my grandfather took great pride in telling the story in town, and I got a real kick out of getting the five dollars. That was big bucks back in 1964!

I have no doubt folks who have never hunted, never lived on a farm, and have always lived in the "modern" and shielded world of today, would find this story cruel, inhumane, and unnecessarily violent. Never mind that most folks kill animals every day so that they can eat their steak, their chicken, and their pork chops. They just don't know it, because they kill these animals indirectly through other people and buy that meat in pretty packages, which might let one think the meat grew on trees! The folks on the farm know where the meat comes from because they raise it and provide it, but ninety-eight percent of Americans today can think that they don't harm animals, and some may even cast shame on those folks who still live in the real world and provide the meat that others enjoy. I feel sorry for those folks. They have no idea what the real world is all about.

As I said previously, this experience really started me on my fifty-year journey with guns that put hundreds of meals on my table, protected our live-stock, protected our crops, provided great excitement in the beautiful wilderness all around North America, and saved my life several times while in the wilderness. The tragedy is that while these experiences. which were so common for most of America's history and built the tough "can do" American attitude, are rapidly disappearing for the next generation of Americans.

Chapter Twenty-four

The Greatest Nation in the History of the World Is in Trouble

After personally and passionately being involved in the 2012 elections as a minor elected politician, Freedom Writer, and member of the Tea Party, I thought I would share with you what I wrote to the Republican Party after the disaster of the election. Our country is in trouble, and we all had better wake up. Everybody is blaming someone else and nobody is accepting blame for our election disaster. I hope the following makes sense and wakes folks up:

Don't Blame Romney for our Loss, Look in the Mirror

A majority of Americans across the county just made irrational choices that may lead to a national disaster and could permanently damage the greatest nation in the history of the world. A majority of Americans just reelected a president who has managed the worst "recovery" since the Great Depression, left us with $16 trillion in debt, left 23 million Americans looking for a real job, and made us the laughing stock of Iran, Russia, China, and North Korea. How can this be?

Many conservatives and Republicans will jump to the simplistic and incorrect decision that Romney was the reason for our loss. That misguided conclusion will simply lead to more losses in the future. That is called the "circular firing squad." If we want to turn things around, we must look in the mirror and deal with the tough realities that can and must be addressed if we want to preserve American greatness.

The following is a summary of what is wrong and how to fix it from a member of the Republican Party and the Tea Party who is a semi-retired global business executive who has seen the real world. There are no easy answers and pain will be involved. But the stakes are the preservation of the greatest nation in the history of the world or being responsible for its decline and fall.

What caused the defeat of the Republican Party in the 2012 election?

1) The decline of American culture and values. A growing number of Americans don't support or understand the very values that made this country great like hard work, family values, personal responsibility, meritocracy, and free market capitalism. We are becoming an "entitlement nation." Forty-seven percent of Americans don't pay federal income taxes and don't have "skin in the game." We may have crossed the down side of the fifty percent line on values and that counts in elections.

2) A horribly biased and dishonest news media that supports Democrats and distorts Republican positions (seventy-

five percent of Americans have no confidence in the news media).

3) The parasitic loop of corrupt politicians and unions rewarding each other with other people's money.

4) An antiquated "good old boy" Republican Party that is more concerned about personal gain, promoting each other, and doing things the "good old fashioned way" that is comfortable, rather than fighting for core American values and using modern "best practices" to get the job done.

5) Cowardice and the "Casper Milk Toast" perspective of avoiding confrontation and avoiding tackling tough but critical issues openly and honestly with appropriate passion, in order to not "hurt anybody's feelings."

6) The inability to deal with facts and data and to promote issues that simply cannot mathematically succeed.

7) The inability to prioritize and focus on critical issues and to instead focus limited resources and credibility on less strategically important issues that simply can't win, damage the brand, and give the "enemy" ammo to shoot us with.

8) The apathy, ignorance, and laziness of too many Americans who have enjoyed the American dream and understand it, but are unwilling to invest the time and energy to defend it is quite simply epidemic.

9) A liberally biased education system run by extreme left wing teachers unions is brainwashing our kids, attacking American values, and delivering poorly educated kids that will not be able to compete in the "real world."

10) We are naively allowing China to massively cheat against American companies and steal millions of American jobs. America became the wealthiest nation in the world by becoming the manufacturing "Arsenal of Freedom." China cheats by manipulating their currency by 35-40%, stealing billions of dollars of American technology, breaking all civilized

rules regarding worker safety and environmental protection, and engages in other horrible practices that are illegal and immoral in America. And we and our politicians allow them to do this.

How to win back American values—We can do this!

Use the most powerful resource in the world to start reinforcing American values: Our money! Stop giving your money to those forces that are destroying American values such as Hollywood, the media, and liberal corporations that fund destructive liberal causes (i.e. Progressive, AARP, etc.). Turn off the spigot! They will respond and change their behavior. It would be wonderful to see a national conservative effort that targets the worst offenders. Most liberal businessmen care more about money than their liberal cause and they will back off if they feel the pain.

1) Turn off the liberally biased media and tell them why you did it. Quit buying products that sponsor the most liberally biased media programs and tell them why you did it. They will change their behavior! Conservatives create the money and have the money in America. Let's use that money to save America! The media and their sponsors will change or go out of business. The "freak show" media (television, movies, and games) is constantly attacking traditional American values and promoting decadence and immoral behavior. They are poisoning our children and our society. Turn them off and make them pay!

2) We must focus on holding destructive unions and corrupt politicians responsible. Fight them everywhere we can with everything we have. I have promised not to buy a GM car or any other car manufactured by the UAW for ten years because GM and the Obama regime broke the law and gave 90% of GM bond holder's money to the UAW in return for votes.

Can you imagine what would happen if all conservatives and Republicans refused to buy GM or UAW produced automobiles? They would go out of business! Or, change their behavior! Rallying all Republicans and conservatives around these issues is a must.

3) The Republican Party has to join the 21st century! They must use the same "best practices" that business uses like strategic planning, sophisticated communications, and start paying attention to input from everyone that supports American values, not just their narrow group of "good old boys."

4) It is time for all conservatives to show some spine and speak up. I can't tell you how many conservatives and Republican voters that I spoke to in my precinct that would not put a Republican candidate's sign in their yard because they were afraid. I can't tell you how many times a conservative or Republican said they were afraid to discuss "political" issues in social settings because they were afraid of "hurting feelings." Or the number of conservatives or Republicans that didn't want to aggressively address liberal lies and call them what they are, because they didn't want to hurt anybody's feelings. Grow up and stand up!

I had the privilege of speaking at length with Tony Snow, the *Fox News* host and Press Secretary for Bush. I asked him why the Bush Administration didn't counter attack the horrible lies spread by Democrats and the media against President Bush. He said he agreed with me but he lost the argument in the Bush Administration. I then read Karl Rove's book in which he said his "biggest mistake" was not counter-attacking the Democrats and media when they lied about President Bush. He thought that the press would be more professional and admitted he made a mistake. Fool me once, shame on you. Fool me twice, shame on me. Let's not repeat that mistake!

5) Let's use hard facts and data to develop our strategy and target our limited resources, not raw emotion. Clearly the facts say that national security, our massive debt, and jobs are the most critical issues that face our country. We lost the female vote (more than 50% of the total vote!) because we let the Democrats and the media focus a huge percent of the national discussion on abortion, an issue that we simply can't win now and is not part of the "triage" that is required to save America. Let's save the patient (America) first on those issues that can destroy our country (national defense, debt, and no jobs) and then once we have resurrected American values, we can work on "social" issues like abortion.

6) Our nation is in serious trouble and yet 75% of Americans did not get off their butts to vote in the primary! I can't tell you how many Republicans and conservatives told me that they were "just too busy" to vote, watch the news to stay informed, or participate in the electoral process. That is shameful and gross negligence. We have the privilege of living in the greatest and most prosperous nation in the history of the world, and all that is asked of us is that we stay informed and participate in our Democracy. Pericles said that, "Any Athenian that does not participate in the political process should not be allowed to live in Athens." Precisely. There should be shame and scorn heaped upon those that do not do their duty.

7) Every citizen must get involved in our failed education system. Step one is to inform Americans that we spend twice per student than we did in 1960 (on an inflation adjusted basis) yet our kids have gone from #1 in the world in reading, math, and science back then to 23rd, 25th, and 31st respectively in the world today. The US spends more per student than any nation in the world except Luxemburg; yet our students' results are a disaster. The answer is simple. Money is not the answer: hard work, discipline, and spending time in school and studying are.

American students spend 30% less time in school than the rest of the world because teachers unions want it that way. If we don't get back to hard work, intense competition, and basics, our kids and our country will fail.

8) Stop Chinese cheating! Competition is good, cheating is bad. Make China follow the same rules that American companies must follow or impose penalty duties until they do. Americans must quit being naïve and stop rewarding immoral and illegal Chinese behavior just to save a few bucks. American CEO's have to show some spine, morality, and patriotism.

America is at the crossroads. The good news is that if we can just get back to our core American values, we can launch the Great American Renaissance and even exceed our past greatness! On the other hand, if we continue on our present irrational and immoral course, we will see the decline and fall of American greatness and our children will never enjoy the great life we have been privileged to lead. And our ancestors that made this great nation will shun us for all eternity.

That is what I wrote to the Republican Party. In retrospect, I feel that I did make one serious mistake in that correspondence in regards to abortion. The Kermit Gosnell trial which outlined the true horrors of abortion was a wake-up call for me and convinced me that abortion is a subject worth fighting over in elections even if doing so hurts our chances of winning. Since Roe V. Wade, 53 million abortions have been performed killing 53 million human beings. We are killing roughly 1.3 million babies a year through abortion and one out of three women in America have had an abortion. Gosnell reminded us of how horrible that slaughter is as he "snipped the necks" of a hundred babies that survived abortion, as some of them were moving and whimpering, to kill them. One of those babies was "big enough to walk me to a taxi" as a witness reported

Gosnell saying to her.

I will defend the right of abortion to save the life of a mother and that is the choice I would make if my wife's life were in danger. Every deer hunter knows that is what nature does in a harsh winter when a pregnant doe cannot get enough to eat to support herself and her baby. Her body shuts down sustenance to the baby and reabsorbs the baby so that the doe may live and have another baby next season. But killing babies for convenience or because someone was lazy or irresponsible is entirely another subject.

The reason abortion is such a tough subject is that it intersects three key and legitimate fundamental rights; the right of life, a woman's right over her own body, and freedom of religion. I can understand a woman's demand for rights over her own body and therefore could legally support (but not morally agree with) legal abortion until the baby is capable of life outside the womb which occurs at about twenty weeks. But once the baby can survive outside the womb, it becomes a human being with the right of life, and abortion should be illegal except to preserve the life of the mother. In regards to freedom of religion, anybody who believes abortion is against their religion should have the right to not be associated with abortion in any way. That should apply to doctors, nurses, and pharmacists who don't want to be associated with performing abortions and anybody (or any company or organization) that doesn't want to fund abortions in any way.

Putting aside legitimate legal issues I will say this; anybody who celebrates the 53 million abortions after Roe v. Wade better pray that there is no God. Because if there is a God, I don't think He would look kindly on people that support killing unborn babies just for convenience. I would suggest that those people pack lots of sun tan lotion in their coffins because if there is a God, they are going to roast in Hell for

Eternity. The only problem is I am not sure who they will pray to if they don't believe in God!

Moving to another interesting subject, the following is what I wrote to friends after a marvelous trip to Prague and passionate discussions with brave people that survived the horror of communism under the Soviet Union:

A Lesson in Freedom from Prague

If the following doesn't "rock your boat" regarding the danger our nation faces, nothing will. Seeing and hearing first-hand how a country lost its freedom due to naiveté and apathy sounds a warning bell that should not be ignored! I felt that I had to share this with people that I believe still understand freedom. It may take a few minutes to read, but freedom is worth it.

In October, I had the privilege of spending a few weeks in Prague, Budapest, and gorgeous parts of Eastern Germany. Prague is a contrast of beauty and pain. It is a city of marvelous and beautiful buildings built during the Renaissance hundreds of years ago that are still beautiful today. On the other hand, the citizens have been slaves for decades under the Nazis and the USSR until the "Velvet Revolution" in 1989. What most people don't know is that Prague and Czechoslovakia was one of the most educated, prosperous, and advanced manufacturing areas of Europe prior to WWII. Yet they lost their freedom and prosperity, first to the Nazi's and then again to the Soviets. What was it like to experience that? What was it like to find freedom in the US? And what are the observations of those who lived through that and how do they view what is going on now in their country and in America? Stay tuned!

I had someone who experienced the Russian invasion of Prague describe to me what it was like when the Soviets invaded the Czech Republic in 1968. They were there and experienced it first-hand. This is what they said to me: "It was a cool and damp August morning in 1968 and we woke to hear this foreboding rumble in the streets of Prague. We didn't know what it was, but we knew it was bad. We looked out our windows and the streets were filled with Russian tanks. The radio just continued to play soft music and there was no news (the "state" controlled the media). We got up to go to work as usual and walked with care around these Russian tanks wondering if our lives would get even worse." You see the Czech Republic under Dubcek was demanding freedom from the Soviet Union and the horror of communism in what was called the "Prague Spring." But the Soviets invaded, imprisoned Dubcek and imposed their will. And the West did nothing.

This person who experienced the invasion told me that virtually everyone hated communism. Only fifteen percent voted for the Communist Party yet the communists got control. I asked them why the people didn't revolt and throw the bums out. Their response scared the heck out of me:

1) First, the people gave up their guns. "After WWII, the people were so tired of war that they voluntary turned in their guns in hopes of peace and safety. When they realized that they wanted to fight for their freedom, they were totally unarmed. They gave up their freedom."

2) Second, the state had total control of businesses, jobs, homes, and everything important to life. If a person was seen as unfriendly to the "state," their career and livelihood were doomed.

3) Even though the vast majority of people hated the "state," a very large number of people were willing to sell out their friends, acquaintances, and even family to the state to profit from a better job, better house, or better education. People could not discuss plans for freedom and their options because the state pitted the citizens against each other. So

the people became docile sheep.

4) The state focused its effort on brainwashing the kids. They knew that they could not erase the concept of freedom from adults that have been free, so they put those people in jail, killed them, or deported them. Kids had no knowledge of God or freedom. Did it work? In Prague, attendance at church went from over ninety percent before WWII to less than two percent under the communism (per my guide in Prague).

5) The state totally controlled the media. Radio, papers, and movies were controlled by the state and the people had no idea what the truth was. The only source for truth was "Radio Free Europe," but you would go to jail if you were caught listening to it. The people had no idea what was happening in the world or even in their own country. So when the Soviets invaded, all the folks heard was "soft music" over the radio.

This person who lived through it, then discussed what it was like to live under communism. Everybody was poor and everybody was unhappy. You could not change jobs without approval from the state. They used the quote that my guide in Prague used when discussing what it was like to work for the state. "They pretended to pay us and we pretended to work." Our guide in Prague told us that for a population of 1.3 million, there were only three department stores. But it didn't matter because there was nothing in them and the folks didn't have any money anyway. But this person told me that even though most folks didn't have any money, greed and envy were prevalent. For state officials and those that "ratted" on their family, friends and neighbors; they got better homes, cars, and food. Just as George Orwell said in Animal Farm: in communism "some animals are more equal than others."

I have been associated with people who have escaped from communist Prague, Budapest, and China to come to the US and their stories were eerily consistent. They risked everything including their lives to escape. They were all ecstatic on seeing freedom first hand in America. Even though each of them started at the bottom with manual labor jobs, they dramatically improved their quality of life and were able to buy things that they could never buy in their former communist homes. They worked their way up and now live comfortable lives that they could not even imagine in their former countries. Even though they were not wealthy when they first got here, they spent a good part of their income on traveling to see the great new country that they now lived in. They were not concerned about showy houses or cars; they bought the basics that they needed to live and used the rest to see their new country. They were overcome with the beauty of America. Many of them excelled in America and moved to executive positions or started very successful businesses. That is the good news!

Now most of them are scared to death for America and afraid that America is following their former countries down the slippery slope of state control and a loss of freedom. They all say that the people of America are not the people they saw when they arrived here in the 60s and 70s. Even back then they saw some things about America that concerned them.

But now they all see a growing "entitlement" mentality across America. And they say with sadness that they view today's young people as lazy, spoiled, naïve, and completely ignorant about the treasure of freedom and America. Universally they are all stunned that after four years of the Obama "disaster," a majority of Americans reelected a terrible president who attacks the very American values that they risked their lives to enjoy. Like many former citizens of communist countries that escaped to America that I know, several of these people are avid gun owners and spend time at the range. This time, they are prepared to fight for freedom!

I hope that America can learn from these folks who escaped communism to find freedom in America before it is too late! As Ronald Reagan said, "Freedom is never more than one generation from extinction."

If this motivates you to learn more, read Iron Curtain by Anne Applebaum. The Wall Street Journal named it one of 2012's top ten non-fiction books. It graphically describes what happened in Prague, Budapest, Poland, and East Germany under the Soviet Union and how the people were enslaved by the "state." It totally supports the stories that I heard from people who escaped the horror of communism with infinite detail.

That is the end of my "Prague Experience"!

But let me add to those two previous appeals I wrote to people to "wake up and smell the coffee" before it is too late with a dose "tough love." Some people may view the following as "Un-American." But I present it with the goal of helping to wake up America while there is still time. So, here are the hard scientific facts: Every great nation in the 5,000 year history of the civilized world has failed. And while democracy is over 2,500 years old as it was introduced by Solon in ancient Greece, America is the oldest surviving democracy on Earth after the previous hundreds of democracies have failed. Yet America is only 237 years old! Why have all the great nations in history failed? The answer is simple and sad. Greatness leads to prosperity, prosperity leads to decadence, decadence leads to sloth and entitlement, and collapse is sure to follow, 100% of the time! Just read Edward Gibbon's, "Decline and Fall of the Roman Empire" and Paul Kennedy's, "The Rise and Fall of the Great Powers" and you will see the same pattern continuously repeat itself across the ages 100% of the time.

The hard truth centers on the scientific engine of the universe, "survival of the fittest." Just like 100% of the great nations in history have eventually failed, 95% of the species that have lived on Earth have become extinct. Those species and those great nations could not adapt. And nature and evolution have no sympathy. They became extinct. America is currently in the death spiral of sloth. It is not too late, but if we don't change course very soon, we know the ending.

How did America become the most powerful and prosperous nation in the history of Earth? Once again, the answer is actually in science and math! Anybody trained in business knows the great 80/20 rule. Eighty percent of sales come from twenty percent of customers. Eighty percent of great innovative ideas come from twenty percent of employees. The bottom line is that in any stable organization (or country), the top twenty percent make the difference. America was unique in that it reversed the 80/20 rule. How? For the first 100 to 150 years of America's development, the best and brightest of Europe and Asia left their homes and came to America. These people were the biggest risk takers who risked their lives and fortunes to come to the American frontier in search of freedom. No promises, no guarantees, no entitlements, no hand-outs. Just hard work, self-motivation, personal responsibility, tenaciousness, ingenuity, etc.—the best attributes of man-kind! Contrary to the rest of the world and history, America had a reverse 80/20 rule. Eighty percent of Americans were outstanding and everyone raced to the top based on a meritocracy. And that created greatness.

Unfortunately, prosperity in America has created decadence and the "Nanny State." America is now approaching the traditional 80/20 rule of the world and history. We now have a race to mediocrity and the lowest common denominator. American kids have gone from number one in the world in every category in education to number 23, 25, or 31 depending on the subject. We have gone from the financier of the world to the debtor of the world. And we are turning into a moral cesspool. In America in 1965 the divorce rate was five percent, only five percent of children were raised without a father, and abortion was almost nonexistent. Today, divorce stands at over fifty percent, forty-one percent of children are raised without a father, there have been 53 million abortions since Roe V. Wade , and one third of American women have had an abortion. We have created a new culture of "entitlement" which is crippling American output, strength, and prosperity.

Let me add another problem. As we prospered as a nation and the "Nanny State" grew, we have created a huge group of people who are either perfectly fine with the idea of living off of other people (welfare, food stamps, Obama phones, etc.) or we have created a new "elite" group of people that feel that they are special and the rules of history don't apply to them. We all know these people. Many of them have enjoyed the wealth and greatness of America created by their parents (trust fund brats!) or their spouses. They have never competed in the "real world," nor have they ever created a job or created wealth for other people, but they criticize the people who do create the jobs and the wealth which drive American prosperity. They have enjoyed the fruits of that wealth and don't have a clue how it was created.

These people drive me nuts! They are childishly naïve, arrogantly ignorant (they refuse to listen to people who do live in the "real world" and who do create jobs and wealth), and they are narcissistically apathetic. They will openly tell you that they don't vote "because it is so frustrating" and that discussing politics is "just too uncomfortable." They are not embarrassed that they don't listen to the news because they would rather watch "Dancing with the Stars!" Aren't we glad that our Founding Fathers, our Civil War ancestors, and our fathers who fought in WWII didn't act so arrogantly and childishly! Growing up in a proud immigrant neighborhood with a grandfather who fought the Germans in WWI and a father who fought the Japanese in WWII, and working on the farm with a family that had ten generations of ancestors who fought for America signing the Declaration of Independence, fighting with Andy Jackson, fighting with Sherman, and serving with General McArthur in Japan, anybody who said anything that stupid would have been scorned and maybe tarred and feathered!

We can turn this around, but first we have to acknowledge the problem and who is causing this decline and then make up our minds to get back to greatness. And those of us who understand what is at stake must stand up and fight to bring America back to greatness, for the sake of our children and grandchildren!

If we can get back to our great traditional American values, we can launch the "Great American Renaissance," creating enormous wealth and prosperity by tapping our enormous energy resources of oil, gas, coal, and nuclear power. By stopping Chinese cheating and focusing on recreating the "US Manufacturing Arsenal of Freedom," we can create so many jobs we will be begging the best and brightest from the world to join us here in America. If we can establish a business friendly government that reduces our massive and wasteful government overregulation and punitive taxes, businessmen will unleash the trillions of dollars sitting on the sidelines or kept in other countries to create jobs here in America. We can be the new "Greatest Generation" that revitalized America!

But if we stay on our current destructive course and allow our childish naiveté, arrogant ignorance, and narcissistic apathy to rule, we will go down in history as the "Worst Generation in

History" that destroyed the greatest, most powerful, and most prosperous nation in the history of the world. Our ancestors will revile us for eternity if we allow that. Worse than that, we will be destroying our children's futures. We are at a critical crossroads and each of us has a vital choice to make. Choose wisely!

Epilogue

Conclusion

This book has been a labor of love. As I was going through the process of deciding if I wanted to retire or not, I did my own "bucket list" to see if I had enough things to do to keep me busy during retirement. I came up with about thirty things including getting my captain's license, master diver certificate, taking a long Mediterranean cruise, learning how to play the guitar, serving on the board of directors of some charities that I believe in, and of course a lot of sailing. At the top of the list of things that I wanted to do however, was to write this book.

I figured that it would take me at least one year writing at the leisurely pace of a few hours a week. Wrong. Once I started, I became addicted. I worked at least sixty hours a week, sometimes starting as early as 4:00 a.m. or working as late as 2:00 a.m. (poor Ev!). Once I started, I believed that I had an obligation to write this book—that it was my duty.

When I began, I realized that I have been granted the special privilege of living through an extreme range of experiences and being exposed to a life that very few people get to experience in the same scope. Those extreme experiences have given me knowledge, and I hope wisdom. And with privilege comes responsibility. The responsibility is to share what I have learned.

Obviously there are a lot of people who are born to immigrant parents; or have experienced life on the farm; or have gone from rags to riches; or have hunted in extreme locations; or have achieved world-class business awards; or have had exciting sailing and diving experiences; or have traveled the world; or have worked with criminals, the poor, and disabled; or have experienced riots; or have worked with the Pentagon and White House. But I doubt that there are many people who have had the collective impact of having done all those things. The collective impact of those experiences is where I feel that I have been so lucky. The breadth of those extreme experiences has given me a perspective that I feel obligated to share with those who have not been as lucky.

I also feel obligated to share my experiences because many of them are disappearing in our world today. Being part of a proud and legal immigrant family devoted to learning English, being good citizens, feeling immensely proud of our country while at the same time being part of a "founding family" was a great joy. Today, if you express pride in your country or demand that immigrants come here legally and learn English to succeed, you are labeled a racist.

So few people in our country have or will experience the magic and incredible lessons to be learned from the farm or the wilderness that grounded mankind for thousands of years. Today, most people live in a technology cocoon that is making us weak and (in my view) vulnerable to the dangerous world that will always lurk just below the surface. Our kids will simply not experience the positive moral environment and values of John Wayne and *Father Knows Best* as did my generation and those before me. Instead they are deluged by our media with immorality 24/7, and as a result are being cheated of the opportunity to form solid core values.

I was also fortunate to have been exposed to extreme danger, injury, very hard work, hardship, risk, and failure. Yes, even failure helped me because it motivated me to do better or it pushed me to find something else that I could excel in. And that has been a natural process for all of mankind's history. Today, we shield our kids from hard work and failure. Today, every kid is a pretend winner which, of course, can never be true and it means that nobody is a winner and excellence is a lost virtue. And today's kids lose as a result.

I chose the book's title because I fear that I may symbolically be the last man to live the real American dream—that dream of the American melting pot and an immigrant family raising its kids to accomplish great things through education, hard work, and being good citizens. I am afraid that being a man as symbolized by John Wayne and all we learned and treasured as kids growing up is rapidly disappearing and being replaced by overly sensitive and politically correct metro sexual males. If that is the future for men, then I am very glad that I lived when I did and I will not be part of that program!

In closing, I know that in the grand scheme of things that I am not important. One of the things I kept on my desk as group president was a 300-million-year-old fossil. It gave me perspective and reminded me that in less than 150 years from now, I will long-since be dust and nobody will even know that I existed. But I truly hope that the values that I was taught and the breadth of experiences that I was so fortunate to have experienced, do not fade away from future generations. This book is a tiny effort to try to keep those values alive so that others may experience that same great joy generations from now.

ABOUT THE AUTHOR

Randall C. Rossi retired as the group president of an international company that was named a world-class company by British Standards Organization, named one of the Top Ten Plants in the USA by *Industry Week* magazine, and named a finalist for the prestigious Shingo Award while on his watch. He has traveled extensively for decades all over the US, Europe, and Asia for business and pleasure exposing him to a wide range of cultures.

For fun he has hunted from the Arctic Circle to the Rocky Mountains and the swamps of Savannah for fifty years and has sailed and dived in blue waters all around the world.

He is now dedicated to sharing his business experience through consulting, charity work, and his love of sailing and traveling with his wife Evelyn.

MIDWEST BOOK REVIEWS
The Last Man To Live The Real American Dream
Randy Rossi
Nightengale Press

'The American Dream' comes in as many variations as there are Americans who aspire to live their own definitions of 'the good life.' Randall C. Rossi is the son of an Italian immigrant father and a mother who was one of the 'Daughters of the American Revolution.' His memoir takes the reader along a true 'rags to riches' story that began on a farm and led him to associate with members of the White House and the Pentagon. From a night shift laborer at a foundry to becoming the Group President of an international corporation with hundreds of employees and millions of dollars in annual sales, Randy Rossi experienced, embodies, and represents why America has become a beacon for men and women around the world seeking to improve their lives and the prospects for their children for personal fulfillment and success.

Much of the economic landscape has changed and evolved with the passing of time and the introduction of new technologies, customs, and events both domestic and international, but the message of "The Last Man To Live The Real American Dream" remains constant—American Dreams live on and it is possible for anyone to achieve their own aspirations with hard work, a little luck, and a whole lot of perseverance.

Highly recommended reading that is as informed and informative as it is inspiring and inspirational.

This title is available on Amazon.com, BN.com, and as a eBook for the iPad, Kindle, Nook, Kobo and more...

CPSIA information can be obtained
at www.ICGtesting.com
Printed in the USA
BVOW06s2249041117
499548BV00011BA/433/P